ZIG ZAG ZEN

Buddhism AND Psychedelics

EDITED BY **Allan Badiner** • ART EDITOR **Alex Grey**
PREFACE BY **Huston Smith** • FOREWORD BY **Stephen Batchelor**

SYNERGETICPRESS
expanding human knowledge

SANTA FE & LONDON

Published by Synergetic Press
1 Bluebird Court, Santa Fe, NM 87508
24 Old Gloucester St. London, WC1N 3AL England

Library of Congress Cataloging-in-Publication Data

Zig Zag Zen : Buddhism and psychedelics. -- New Edition.
     pages cm
     Includes bibliographical references.

     ISBN 978-0-907791-61-4 (hardcover) -- ISBN 0-907791-61-1 (hardcover) -- ISBN 978-0-907791-62-1 (pbk.) -- ISBN 0-907791-62-X (pbk.) 1. Drugs--Religious aspects--Buddhism. 2. Hallucinogenic drugs and religious experience. I. Badiner, Allan. II. Grey, Alex.

BQ4570.D78Z55 2015   2014049993
294.3'442--dc23

Cover and book design by Ann Lowe
In-house editor: Linda Sperling
Printed by Friesens in Canada
This book was printed on FSC certified 70# Sterling Ultra Matte
Typeface: Garage Gothic and Adobe Garamond Pro

CONTENTS

Section Three: LESSONS

ACKNOWLEDGEMENTS ✆ Allan Badiner

IN GRATITUDE, I offer this book to all Buddhas and Bodhisattvas throughout space and time. May it shed some measure of light on the relationship between the mystical wisdom of the Buddha and the wisdom of mystical plants.

Kindest thanks to Synergetic Press, and specifically Deborah Parrish Snyder and Johnny Dolphin, as well as Linda Sperling, Ann Lowe, Debbie McFarland, Mitch Mignano, Stephanie Joelle Smolarski, and Gregg Weiss. I remain indebted to Nion McEvoy for publishing the original *Zig Zag Zen* at Chronicle Press, and the great team there, notably Alan Rapp and Sara Schneider.

Many of the essays found in this book were previously published in the fall of 1996 issue of *Tricycle: the Buddhist Review* and much appreciation and thanks go to the founding editor Helen Tworkov. The possibility of this book began with her daring to be dedicated to a truthful inquiry into this controversial confluence of subjects.

The contributors of essays, the artists and the interviewees, are my real heroes and heroines—it is they who gave kindly and generously of themselves without reward, for which I will be endlessly in their debt. So many people contributed in a multitude of ways to the creation of this book, and while space does not allow for the full thanks they are entitled to, certain individuals must be acknowledged for their help and support, and they include Stephen Batchelor, Rick Doblin, Omar Fayed, Mark Epstein, Mitchell Albert, Dan Goleman, Sharon Salzberg, Gary Snyder, Brother David Steindl-Rast, Jack Kornfield, and Robert Thurman.

Deep thanks must go to my agent Suresh Ariaratnam.

Thich Nhat Hanh and Sister Chan Khong always deserve my greatest gratitude for many years of inspiration, mindfulness training, and for our pilgrimages together to India, China, Japan, and Vietnam.

Alex Grey has my undying gratefulness for bringing such beauty, refinement, and visual intelligence to this endeavor.

India, my loving daughter, inspired me throughout the process and I'm lucky to be her father. It is for her, and future generations, that I have undertaken this project.

Finally, I wish to dedicate this book to the memory of four great beings without whose friendship and guidance *Zig Zag Zen* may not have been a reality: Rick Fields, Terence McKenna, Venerable Dr. Havanpola Ratanasara, and Sasha Shulgin. May this effort be worthy of their memory.

–Big Sur, 2014

ACKNOWLEDGEMENTS ✺ Alex Grey

THANKS TO MY DEAR FRIEND Allan Badiner for bringing me on board the *Zig Zag Zen* project. A deep bow of gratitude to all the brave artists and authors willing to bring Dharma and psychedelics together in their work and much appreciation for their participating in *Zig Zag Zen*.

–Brooklyn 2014

FOREWORD ◉ Stephen Batchelor

IT IS UNDENIABLE that a significant proportion of those drawn to Buddhism and other Eastern traditions in the 1960s (including the present writer) were influenced in their choice of religious orientation by experiences induced by psychoactive substances such as cannabis and LSD. Despite the fact that experimentation with such drugs was illegal, potentially dangerous and unmonitored, the startling shift in consciousness it occasionally provoked was considered to be worth the risks involved. Now, thirty years later, many of these Buddhists are priests, meditation teachers, therapists, college professors, and writers: respected members of the very society against which they rebelled in their youth. Yet although they often eschew the use of psychedelics themselves and warn others of the dangers of abuse, few would deny the role of these substances in opening their eyes to a life of spiritual and religious meaning.

The connection between drug use and spirituality is not, however, limited to the experience of a few aging hippies. The ritualized use of drugs is still practiced among sadhus and shamans of traditional cultures from India to Peru. The current use of drugs such as MDMA (Molly)—originally popular at clubs and raves, but now in numerous shared settings—is likewise associated with heightened states of individual consciousness as well as with the forging of a deep ecstatic bond between participants. Language and symbols borrowed from Asian and indigenous American sacred traditions permeate the literature, lyrics, and imagery of underground dance culture, as much as—or even more than—they did in the festivals and happenings of the 1960s.

It is all too easy either to dismiss claims of spiritual significance for drugs as thinly veiled justifications for hedonistic indulgence, or to invoke the tragic consequences of heedless excess as grounds for denying the validity of any drug-induced experience at all. In so doing, one fails to recognize the spiritual aspirations of people who are seeking expression and fulfillment in this way. One likewise ignores the harsh fact that Western societies have lost the ability to address the religious feelings of a considerable segment of their youth.

In swinging between liberal tolerance one moment and outraged repression the next, modern societies seem chronically incapable of reaching consistent attitudes about drugs. Consider, for example, the double standard applied to the achievement of physical, as opposed to cultural, excellence. While a sportsman will have his Olympic medals revoked for using drugs that enhance his performance, a musician would not be stripped of her Grammy awards if it turned out that her songs were composed and played under the influence of an illegal substance. Why are regulations imposed on the behavior of one but not the other? Why should the athlete be punished, but the artist not?

When the broad culture sends out such contradictory messages about drugs, to who can people turn for informed and sympathetic guidance? If drug use can be linked to spiritual issues, then surely such guidance would be forthcoming from religious leaders. Yet the spokesmen and women of the mainstream denominations seem to have little to say on the subject beyond pious encouragement to abstinence. Traditional schools of Buddhism are no exception. The five lay precepts, which are considered the foundation of ethical behavior, list the taking of intoxicating drugs along with killing, sexual misconduct, theft, and lying as something every good Buddhist is expected to relinquish. Although certain ecstatic Zen masters and Tantric yogins may be deemed sufficiently awakened to be exempt from strict adherence to this precept, there is no discussion about the role that drug use might play in propelling someone onto the path in the first place.

As Buddhism comes of age in the West, it needs both to honor its traditions and respond to the actual conditions of the world in which people live today. Simply reiterating answers to moral issues that have worked well in the past may serve only to alienate those who otherwise would find great value in the Dharma. Before Buddhists can even begin to have a serious discussion about the use and abuse of drugs in contemporary society, there needs to be an acceptance of at least the possibility that certain currently illegal drugs can produce life- and performance-enhancing effects. Such a shift in attitude may require considerably greater openness, understanding, and tolerance from those in the Buddhist community entrusted with offering moral and spiritual guidance.

Although we live in a world in which the widespread consumption of legal, illegal, and prescribed drugs keeps growing, we seem incapable of conducting an intelligent and compassionate debate around their use and abuse. We might be reaching a point where the contradiction between what society doesn't permit and what people actually do in terms of ingesting psychoactive substances becomes intolerable. This contradiction undermines the credibility of those in positions of political and religious authority and fractures the moral consensus needed to hold together an increasingly pluralistic society. Unless the hysteria and repressive blindness around drug use begin to diminish, a sane and constructive response to an issue that threatens to spiral dangerously out of control will elude us.

It is in this context that the voices collected in *Zig Zag Zen* may offer a much needed wake-up call. The contributors to this volume find themselves in the privileged role of being intermediaries between one culture and another. Because of their position at this moral and spiritual crossroads, they are free to offer a perspective that need not be tied to the dogmatic certainties of either Buddhist or Western traditions. I very much hope that their collective wisdom will not only illuminate the relation between the use of psychedelics and the Buddhist path but, more importantly, help our society as a whole see its way more clearly through the deep confusion that surrounds its attitude to drugs.

–Aquitaine, December 2000 (revised 2015)

ROTHKO CHAPEL INTERIOR Mark Rothko, 1971

ZIG. Buddhism stemmed from a vision, a vision that was literally world-transforming, for when the Buddha came to his senses (as we rightly say) after his enlightenment under the Bo tree, the world that greeted him was very different from the one that he had left. During that night that was to portend so much for the historical future—the Buddhist *Sangha* is the oldest humanly devised institution that is still intact—the Buddha's meditation had deepened until, as the morning star glittered in the transparent sky, his mind pierced the bubble of the universe and shattered it to naught; only, wonder of wonders, to find it restored with the effulgence of true being. "Wonder of wonders," he is reported to have exclaimed, speaking now from what his Third Eye had disclosed to him, "all things intrinsically are Buddha-nature. There is a Buddha in every grain of sand . . ."

ZAG. Twenty-five hundred years later people are still having their Third Eyes opened, only now often through microscopic ingestions of a small class of entheogenic plants and chemicals. This difference may not be quite as different as it sounds, for medical anthropologists have discovered that brain changes that result from taking entheogens are very much like those that are produced by physical exhaustion from prolonged fasting and other ordeals of the sort the Buddha undertook before he assumed his seat under the Bodhi Tree. This being the case, it may be one of the great paradoxes of history that one of its greatest religions was launched (chemically speaking) by a state of mind that is virtually indistinguishable from ones that are produced by fudging the fifth of the Five Precepts in the Eightfold Path that the Buddha prescribed as leading to enlightenment, the one that proscribes the taking of intoxicants.

ZEN. Be that as it may, there is a saying that Zen is slippery and slick, like picking up an egg with a pair of silver chopsticks, and the saying certainly holds when it comes to the presiding issue of this book, the relation between Zen and entheogens. Aspects of this issue extend back to the times when Zen took shape. There has been a long-standing debate as to whether enlightenment arrives suddenly or gradually, and the issue split Zen into its two major schools, with Rinzai Zen championing the former view, and Soto Zen the later. *Satori*—a thumping foretaste of *Nirvana*—is important in Rinzai, whereas Soto settles for passing glimpses of it called *kenshos*. Both schools require rigorous training, but in Rinzai the rigor reaches samurai proportions, with sleep deprivation a major factor. This fits in with the anthropologists' discovery that ordeals bring on chemical brain states that accompany major epiphanies.

THE BOOK IN HAND. A major virtue of this particular collection of essays and art is that it rigorously abstains from drawing conclusions regarding the never-never land it leads the reader into. Readers will not find here any attempt to turn the slippery Zen egg into putty that chopsticks could handle with ease. Instead, the book lays before the reader the major issues that must be taken into account in any serious reflection on this problem. Entheogens have entered Buddhism to stay; there can be no turning back from the point that has been reached. Nor can the issue any longer be swept under the rug. The facts that bear on the matter are contained in these pages, as are the leading theories that try to make sense of the facts. Compelling visionary art and vivid accounts of personal encounters lace the facts and theories together in ways that make for a gripping experience. This book will be a landmark for years to come.

INTRODUCTION ☙ Allan Badiner

THE TURN OF THE TWENTY-FIRST CENTURY was near. For the moment, there was stillness in our discussion circle at Plum Village as someone had just finished speaking. In moments when it was really quiet, I often looked up to the beautiful parade of bright bulbous clouds so characteristic of Plum Village, Thich Nhat Hanh's retreat center in Southwestern France. This time, I reflected on what might be useful to share about drugs, the subject of our Dharma discussion that morning.

Each person had a different story to tell, different substances, different circumstances, different experiences, and different lessons drawn. It was clear that no one was going to have a final word on this subject, nor was there even such a thing as the final word. For some, it was a story about giving in to temptation and suffering a lack of clarity, or worse, lasting confusion and addiction. For others, it was a brief glimpse into a rarefied world of intense sense impressions accompanied by fanciful but useless imagery. For a few others still, it was the very threshold of their journey into the truth of Buddha's teachings, with unforgettable, if fleeting, insights. Each person's facet of the truth of drugs and Dharma was riveting and revealing of so much.

It became obvious to me that a more inclusive story needed to be told about Buddhism and psychedelics. After all, the best known apostles of each were the same characters: Alan Watts, Allen Ginsberg, Richard Alpert (Ram Dass), and Jack Kerouac. Equally clear to me was that the "truth" on this subject, just as in all the subjects of our Dharma discussions, would emerge only from hearing a wide spectrum of experiences, investigations, observations, and cherished opinions.

Unlike a casual group conversation, Dharma discussion follows a series of primary Buddhist practices: a sustained period of meditation, and a Dharma talk by an accomplished teacher. Meditation concentrates and calms the mind, while Dharma discourses, such as the legendary ones given by Thich Nhat Hanh, never fail to stir the heart and touch the deepest current of truth within. Buddhism in action is nothing if not psychedelic, or mind-opening. So as we went around the circle and shared our stories that morning, there was an almost palpable psychedelic quality to the experience.

Ultimately, Buddhism and psychedelics share a concern with the same problem: the attainment of liberation for the mind. While psychedelics lurk in the personal histories of most first-generation Buddhist teachers in Europe and America, today we find many teachers advising against pursuing a path they once traveled. Few Buddhists make the claim that psychedelic use is a path itself—some maintain that it is a legitimate gateway, and others feel Buddhism and psychedelics don't mix at all. But just as Buddhism itself must be held to the test of personal experience and to the wholesomeness or unwholesomeness of the results, so also must the question of how, or if, psychedelics can be part of a Dharma practice.

The place of critical examination and analysis, and the freedom to make these discoveries for oneself is an essential foundation of Buddhism and is found as far back as the *Kalama Sutra*: "Do not go upon what has been acquired by repeated hearing; nor upon tradition; nor upon rumor; nor upon what is in a scripture; nor upon surmise; nor upon an axiom; nor upon specious reasoning; nor upon a bias towards a notion that has been pondered over; nor upon another's seeming ability; nor upon the consideration that this monk is our teacher," warned the Buddha to the Kalamas. "Only when you yourselves know—these things are good; these things are not blamable; these things are praised by the wise; undertaken and observed, these things lead to benefit and happiness—should you abide in them."

Just as social prohibitions on what ideas to let into your consciousness are antithetical to the Middle Path, so also must be such restrictions on what plants to let in. Tibetan Buddhists, for one, have developed over the centuries a wide field of psychopharmacology and have an endless number of psychiatric botanical medicines—none of which have ever been previously identified or scientifically tested in the West.

Both the terms "psychedelic" and "entheogen" are used to describe the substances referred to in this book. While many Buddhists, being essentially agnostic, might have a problem with the "theo" in entheogen, most would agree that it is the entheogenic use of psychedelics, or using plant materials to trigger primary spiritual experience, that is of interest here. The problems caused by cocaine, heroin, methamphetamine, and other consciousness-constricting drugs are indisputable and nowhere defended in this book. The notion that all "drugs" are fundamentally alike is at the root of the confusion in our drug laws and the social debate about them. Drugs differ. Uses and occasions differ. Policies and practices also ought to differ appropriately. Drug use will always be with us, and responsible recreational drug users should be treated more or less the same way recreational drinkers are. Abuse of dangerous drugs is less of a legal issue than a medical one.

In the past, awareness about the deepest "occult" or "hidden" parts of our spirit selves was considered the private preserve of shamans, priests, or spiritual masters who had earned their way to it. Religious experience was mediated by these authorized few, and this is a tradition still with us in the form, if not attitude, of many religions. The democratization of psychedelics, however, and of Buddhism to a similar extent, has been very much about the breakdown of this restricted access to the divine. In Buddhism, as in psychedelics, the individual takes responsibility for their relationship to the source of their being, and for access to the highest states of spirit mind.

An awareness of the relatedness between separate objects and opposites is one of the key insights that psychedelic travelers often bring home from their chemical "pilgrimages." Perhaps the popularization of both Zen and psychedelics has shifted the cultural mind from a dominantly conceptual and linear view of reality to a mode of awareness that is more ecological and holistic. While we will always continue to think in linear ways, awareness is growing that this mode of consciousness is relative, a human construct, and not a reflection of "objective reality."

This way of seeing is not something people necessarily need psychedelics to experience. It is, in fact, one of the central premises underlying Zen. This emerging worldview brings us closer to a perspective that is perhaps equally comfortable being called "dharmic" or "psychedelic." Views on psychedelics and psychoactive plants in mainstream Buddhism are continuing to evolve. His Holiness the Dalai Lama has recently expressed support for the use of medical cannabis. American Buddhist teacher Robert Thurman told a crowd at Burning Man in 2014, "while we all have within the chemicals that allow us to experience insight, clarity and bliss, at a time of global crisis on so many levels, the careful use of entheogens to accelerate our progress may be a skillful means, and compatible with the practice of Dharma."

"Over the centuries humans from across the globe have employed the respectful use of psychoactive substances in seeking insight into the nature of mind and consciousness," says Tara Brach, clinical psychologist, Vipassana teacher, and author of *Radical Acceptance*. "The effects of Buddhist meditation and psychedelic drugs have a number of parallels, including increasing the value of the present moment, deepening levels of awareness and increasing compassion and loving-kindness."

Putting aside the well-founded arguments for and against psychedelic use, there is an essentially Buddhist response to the long entrenched, ongoing, and devastating war on drugs: great compassion. Draconian drug laws still ensnare millions of otherwise law-abiding people in an ever growing spiral of wasteful and counterproductive strategies whose foundation is punishment. It has resulted in an incarceration rate so unimaginable that almost one in four of every person behind bars in the entire world is locked up in the United States. At this very moment, American jails and prisons hold tens of thousands of people—vastly disproportionate numbers of them black—whose only crime is possession of the cannabis plant. Prisons become classrooms for more advanced crime, as dangerous drugs are readily available to everyone from school children on up, criminals outspend and outsmart police, and no one feels safer.

The newest casualties in the failed war on drugs are our personal liberties. A society that actively banishes personal exploration with all psychedelic plants will need to closely monitor its citizens. All our communications, transactions, and expressions are under increasing surveillance by a growing and expensive bureaucracy of control and repression. None of this is conducive to the peaceful and free contemplation of strategies for our personal liberation and fulfillment. In reality, this ceases to be a war on drugs, but rather becomes a war on consciousness, war on free exercise of that most precious of gifts bestowed on a human being.

Finally, we are now seeing signs that the drug war is ramping down. Several agencies of the US Government are working with the Multidisciplinary Association of Psychedelic Studies (MAPS) in exploring psychedelics such as Psilocybin and MDMA for use with veterans suffering from Post-Traumatic Stress Disorder.

Two significant studies are currently underway focusing on the use of psychoactive mushrooms in long term meditators. Vanja Palmers, senior Dharma heir of Kobun Chino Roshi, is a respected Soto Zen priest living in Switzerland.

He recently received permission from the Swiss government to do an experiment using low doses of psilocybin during a *sesshin* or intensive meditation retreat. The study will look at any changes that the meditators report both immediately after the experiment as well as six months later.

A more formal scientific study of psilocybin in long-term meditators is being conducted by Roland R. Griffiths, PhD, in the departments of Psychiatry and Neuroscience at Johns Hopkins University School of Medicine. Griffiths already conducted a similar study with beginning meditators. He will investigate similarities and differences between deep spiritual experiences occasioned by spiritual practice and deep spiritual experiences occasioned by hallucinogenic drugs. The goal is to provide new insight into both the nature of mind and the role of various brain areas in supporting different states of consciousness.

The enhanced capacity for extraordinary cognitive experience made possible by the use of plant psychedelics may be as basic a part of our humanness as is our spirituality or our sexuality. The question is how quickly we develop into a mature community that is able to address these issues.

While psychedelic use is all about altered states, Buddhism is all about altered traits, and one does not necessarily lead to the other. One Theravadin monk likened the mind on psychedelics to an image of a tree whose branches are overladen with low-hanging, very much ripened, heavy fruit. The danger is that the heavy fruit—too full and rich to be digested by the tree all at once—will weigh down the branches and cause them to snap.

On the other hand, Alan Watts, one of the first prominent Westerners to follow the Buddhist path, considered both Buddhism and psychedelics to be part of a comprehensive philosophical quest. He was not interested in Buddhism to be studied and defined in such a way that one must avoid "mixing up" one's thinking about Buddhism with other interests, such as in quantum theory, Gestalt psychology, aesthetics, or most certainly, psychedelics.

Freeing us from the binds of language, American visionary artist Alex Grey has brought a graphical and colorful component to this inquiry by sharing with us the creative imaginings and yearnings of many artists from around the world. Both in text, and in images, the vision bringing forth this book (and the Fall 1996 issue of *Tricycle* magazine on the same subject) is that Dharma discussion of years ago, and a sheer delight in truthful self-discovery.

Zig Zag Zen is a celebration of where Buddhism and psychedelics have informed each other, as well as penetrating criticism of where such a confluence may have led us astray. In the tradition of inquiry set in motion by the Buddha, we let a thousand flowers blossom—even if some of them are psychedelic. Only in the open-minded and courageous effort to see the truth in every voice do we recognize the deepest reflection of what is relatively real.

INTERSECTION

THE PLANT MEDICINE SUTRA ❦ Robert Schrei

THUS I HAVE HEARD. That night the bodhisattva awoke and found herself surrounded by vines, branches, flowers, roots, sap, essence of the plant world, and the wildness of nature, all supplicating her for a teaching that would illumine their minds. The bodhisattva spoke: No, it is you, not I, who needs to speak; it is you, it is your voice that is needed to awaken the self-centered human species to the vast web of life and love and awareness that is the intimate birthright of us all. Your sap, your juices, your fibers, your chemistry. We ask that all of you speak through and to our species, blood and bone, in a language that is unmistakable, unfettered by the intellect we have come to value so highly. Speak to us of our interconnectedness, teach us how to hold each other in love, teach us how to experience our own primal essence, true nature, teach us how to know the essence of each sentient being, trees, grasses, rocks, mountains, stars, clouds, animals, insects, spirits, other realms of existence. We have lost our connection and wander here and there without center, unaware of the web that you sustain. It is from you that I learned from countless rebirths of the altruism of the natural world. Teach us how to enter the stream, the stream of vows, the stream of wishes, the stream of the hearts and minds of our ancestors. It is you who came forth and affirmed my nature when on that perilous night, I touched the Earth and called you to witness . . . Yes! Yes! You are worthy and it was your grace and blessings raining down from the spreading, unfolding branches of the bodhi tree that sustained me on my journey; it was you, as the early morning star that affirmed my nature and the nature of all sentient life, all beings, just as they are, whole and complete, lacking nothing, soaked with wisdom and compassion. We bow before you and ask for your teachings.

A NEW LOOK AT THE PSYCHEDELIC
TIBETAN BOOK OF THE DEAD ✏ Ralph Metzner

IN OUR 1964 BOOK *The Psychedelic Experience*, Timothy Leary, Richard Alpert and I, following a suggestion from Aldous Huxley, had adapted the *Tibetan Book of the Dead* as a paradigm for a spiritually-oriented psychedelic experience. With appropriate preparation and orientation, so we proposed, psychedelic travelers could be guided, or guide themselves, to release their ego-attachments and illusory self-images, the way a Tibetan Buddhist lama would guide a person who was actually dying to relinquish their attachments while noting the physical signs of bodily death.

In the years since that publication, my co-authors and I have received numerous letters expressing the grateful appreciation of readers who used it to prepare themselves for spiritually transcendent psychedelic experiences— even when they were not actually dying, or anywhere near the end of their life. In the course of experiencing their attachments and identifications with the bodily ego, they could let go their fears of letting go and move into expanded and liberated states of consciousness. The experience, like any state of consciousness, was temporary and the fear of death could return—but the memory of the experience remained as an inspiration.

Indeed, experiencing the transcendence of your physical identification, with the certain knowledge that your essence, your spiritual core, your soul, persists beyond the boundary of bodily death is without doubt the most precious gift that psychedelic experiences can provide. This was the gift vouchsafed in the mystery religions of ancient civilizations, where initiates went through an experience of death and rebirth, in which they were provided an experiential preparation for death and a vision of the reality of the spiritual worlds beyond.

We do not know the details of what was involved in these ceremonies, since initiates were sworn to secrecy. However, in the case of the Eleusinian Mysteries, which were for two thousand years the fountainhead of Western spirituality, the scholarly and pharmacological researches related by R. Gordon Wasson, Albert Hofmann and Carl Ruck in their book *The Road to Eleusis*, have demonstrated with high probability that the ingestion of an LSD-like ergot derivative was involved.

The relevance of spiritually-oriented and guided psychedelic experiences in alleviating death anxiety and helping prepare people for the ultimate transition has found modern expression and application in medical-psychiatric research. Stanislav Grof and Joan Halifax, in their book *The Human Encounter with Death*, described the work they did in the 1970s, using DPT with patients suffering from terminal cancer. More recently, psychiatrist Charles Grob, working at UCLA, has done studies using psilocybin (the active ingredient in the visionary mushroom of ancient Mexico) with people who were diagnosed with terminal cancer. It is a significant advance and positive expansion of the accepted medico-scientific worldview that a medicine can be approved that has not been shown to effect a cure of an illness—but rather to alleviate the normal near-universal human anxiety about the end-of-life. The following is a report on one person from that study.

A woman with end-stage cancer who participated in this study, related (in a filmed interview) how all her fears about death, her guilt and worries about surviving family members, congealed into a kind of mass that pressed on her chest, squeezing her life-force—and then, as the psilocybin medicine came on, simply dissolved. At that exact moment she had the insight that all her fears and worries were about a future that had not yet happened. She realized that she could choose instead to focus her attention on the life she still had, with its love of family, the beauty and pleasure afforded by her garden and even a renewed devotion to improving her well-being through yoga.

Studies such as these have led visionary physicians and scientists of consciousness to consider the far-reaching possibilities of future care for the dying, involving selective use of entheogenic medicines. While the growth of the hospice movement, involving palliative in-home pain-management, is an encouraging sign, the mainstream medical establishment still tends to regard death as a condition to be aggressively delayed and prevented—perhaps because as long as a patient is alive there is insurance money to be made with life-prolonging medications and operations.

From my fifty years of exploration and research on consciousness expanding substances and methods, my conviction has grown that the two most beneficent potential areas of application of psychedelic technologies are in the treatment of addictions and in the psycho-spiritual preparation for the final transition. Considering the widespread fearful misunderstanding of the journey to that "undiscovered country, from which no traveler returns," as well as the increasing likelihood of massive human population reduction in our time of global collapse, the significance of such developments can hardly be overestimated.

With an expanded spiritual worldview that recognizes the continuity of life after death and the possibilities of communication with the spirits of the dead, one can envision centers, in beautiful natural environments, in which meditative practices with guided psychedelic amplification could be offered for those in the final stages of life. Just such centers for preparation for the dying were envisioned by Aldous Huxley (1894-1963), in his last utopian novel *Island*. Huxley, who had done so much to first bring psychedelics to the attention of the larger culture, described how this utopian community used what they called a *moksha*-medicine. *Moksha* is a Sanskrit term meaning "liberation." In Huxley's vision the psychedelic *moksha*-medicine was used in the utopian community during transition rituals for adolescents, for adults in transition crises, and for preparation for the dying. Huxley had characterized the psychedelic medicines at best providing a kind of "gratuitous grace"—a spiritual blessing that could never be prescribed, demanded or bought.

The aged philosopher put his vision into practice when he was himself dying from cancer of the throat, on the same day that President John F. Kennedy was assassinated—November 22, 1963. He and his wife Laura had prearranged with physician friends that he could choose to take LSD when the end time was at hand. Laura Huxley, has related in her autobiographical *This Timeless Moment* how at a certain point, suffering from debilitating discomfort, Aldous seemed to know his time was coming and he asked her to give him an injection of 100 micrograms of LSD. A second dose of 100 mcg was given a short while later. While the Dallas murder drama was unfolding on a TV set in another room, she described how his breathing, which had been labored, became easy, his expression, which had been agitated, became serene and peaceful. Her soothing voice guided him into a deeper and deeper meditative state, urging him to release all struggle and attachment into ultimate peace. In my book, *The Life Cycle of the Human Soul*, I quoted the letter which Laura Huxley wrote to the family describing his final, psychedelically facilitated passing. It was her express wish that this letter be made public—as a kind of final legacy concerning the *moksha*-medicine.

Tibetan Buddhist Teachings on Death and the Afterlife

The original *Bardo Thödol*, or *Tibetan Book of the Dead*, is attributed to the legendary eighth century Indian Buddhist adept Padmasambhava, who brought Buddhism to Tibet. It is widely known that the *Bardo Thödol* describes three bardos (the word means "phases" or "stages") occurring between death and rebirth. These are the infamous bardos that have become Western mass culture memes as afterdeath experiences. It is not so well known that the Tibetan Buddhist teachings actually concern a total of six bardos: the other three—the bardos of waking life, of dreaming and of meditating—are phases of consciousness in ordinary life between birth and death.

In the so-called "Root Verses" appended to the original text of the *Bardo Thödol*, there is a summary one-verse teaching describing the essential practice while in each of these six possible stages of consciousness. The text by the great fifth century Indian philosopher Naropa, called *The Yogas of the Six Bardos*, describes the yogic practices by means of which one can attain enlightenment or liberation from each of the six bardo states. The *Bardo Thödol* (literally, *The Book of Liberation through Understanding the Bardo States*) concerns itself primarily with providing guidance for the dying person on how to find their way through the three afterdeath bardo states, giving detailed and explicit instructions on how people can be helped to make the most favorable kind of rebirth possible.

According to Tibetan Buddhism, both proficient yogic practitioners as well as ordinary people with no particular yogic aptitude or experience, can be helped to find their way through the confusing and terrifying afterlife states. Liberation from the samsaric round of conditioned existence can occur in, or from, any of the bardo states, if we understand and remember the teachings, recognize the bardo state we are in, and choose the most enlightened conscious option available to us. It is for this reason that Buddhist teachers refer to it not only as a book of preparation for dying, but really a profound guidebook for both living and dying.

In practical terms, the teachings of the *Bardo Thödol*, are that immediately at death, in the bardo of the moment of dying, the dying person is urged (by the attendant lamas reading from the ancient texts) to maintain one-pointed concentration on the "clear light," which is also referred to as "the Uncreated."

In the Root Verses the essential teaching related to each of the bardo states is summarized. Here is (my version of) the "Root Verse" for the bardo of dying, which emphasizes paying attention to releasing one's attachments to the physical body and world.

> Now as the bardo of dying dawns upon me,
> I will abandon desires and cravings for worldly objects.
> Entering without distraction into the clarity of the teachings,
> I will merge my awareness into the space of the Uncreated.
> The time has come to let go this body of flesh and blood—
> It is merely a temporary and illusory shell.

If the deceased, like most ordinary people, is not able to pass on to the unobstructed "pure land" realms during the bardo of dying and gets caught up in fear and confusion, due to insufficient concentration and preparation, he or she will wander through the "intermediate realms" of the second bardo realm.

In this realm or phase, called the bardo of the experiencing of reality, the dominant features are dramatically contrasting visionary encounters with peaceful, angelic beings and ferocious, demonic ones. These "peaceful and wrathful deities" are described with elaborate detail in the fantastic iconography of Tibetan Buddhism. The deceased is repeatedly reminded, by the attendant lama-priests reading from the *Bardo Thödol*, not to be overwhelmed by either the heavenly or the hellish visions, but to remember that they are all projections of one's own mind. "These beautiful and ugly visions," he is told, "are the reflections and projections of your mind and life, as seen in the mirror held up by the death god Yama. If you stay centered in the middle path between the extremes of dualistic judgment, you will still be able to pass through to the pure light realms of the higher dimensions." There are also encounters with mysterious "knowledge-holding deities"—whose flame-surrounded bodies burn off the false images obstructing and distorting true knowledge.

Here is the encapsulated teaching from the Root Verses concerning this second afterdeath phase, which the Evans-Wentz translation calls the bardo of experiencing reality. Since it deals essentially with the heaven-and-hell visions that one may encounter in this phase, I am calling it the bardo of visions.

Now as I enter into the bardo of visions,
I will abandon all awe and terror that may arise.
Recognizing whatever appears as my own thought-forms,
As apparitions and visions in this intermediate state.
This is a crucial turning point on the path.
I will not fear the peaceful and terrifying visions in my mind.

Again, due to lack of training and/or preparation on the part of most ordinary people, the bardo-traveling soul, after repeatedly lapsing into unconsciousness, then finds itself in the third phase, the bardo of seeking rebirth, in which he or she wanders about seeking to orient itself again to ordinary existence and find a family to be born into. Thus the life between lives, the second bardo, ends with the process of choosing another human incarnation.

What the *Tibetan Book of the Dead* calls the bardo of rebirth is the phase that involves the choosing and preparing for one's next incarnation. This phase includes the soul's selection of a new set of parents, the conception event and the entire prenatal journey up to the new birth. Although the Buddhist texts do not explicitly use our current terminology of prenatal epoch or prenatal experience, we can find in the teachings of the afterdeath states striking parallels with findings now emerging out of the work of prenatal and past-life regression therapists as well as highly developed intuitives.

In this third phase, called the bardo of seeking a new life, the traveler in the intermediate realms is repeatedly admonished to remember where he is, and that his thoughts and intentions will profoundly affect the kind of experience he or she will have in a new life. He is told that he is not in his ordinary body, but a "mental body," or "bardo body," or "desire body"—a body that can't be killed, but that can fly, pass through walls, and has all kinds of non-ordinary capacities. In other words, he or she is experiencing what in esoteric traditions is referred to as the etheric double and the intermediate planes, descending step by step to the time-space material level of existence.

The deceased is then reminded of the six possible worlds of samsara (existence) into which one might find him or herself drifting, carried along by the karmic propensities of their previous existence. Here the teachings of the *Bardo Thödol* converge with the teachings represented in the well-known "Wheel of

Samsara" with its six possible realms or states of consciousness in which we may find ourselves after death, but also during life. Francesca Freemantle, a student of Trungpa Rinpoche, writes in her book on the *Tibetan Book of the Dead,*

"Many Western Buddhists have difficulties with the concept of rebirth in the six realms, or even with rebirth at all. No one can prove to us what lies beyond death. However, we can investigate our minds here and now and discover all the worlds contained within. We can find out what life as a human being really means at this very moment. . . . Trungpa Rinpoche always spoke of the six realms as states of mind, and emphasized the importance of understanding them in this way while we have the opportunity in this life" (Freemantle, F. *Luminous Emptiness*, pp. 143-44).

I discuss the six realms and the Wheel of Births and Deaths in more detail in my book *Worlds Within and Worlds Beyond,* but will mention here only briefly the chief characteristics and qualities of these realms—and how we (human beings) may find ourselves in these realms, because of unconscious karmic tendencies. These six "worlds" can best be thought of as states of consciousness in which we may find ourselves in dreams and hallucinogenic experiences. And, as we know, these "worlds" may be manifested in outer reality—for some of us, at some times. For example, one may be in the hell of an actual prison being tortured by diabolical human beings, or one may be in a purely internal hell of profound despair and depression, while outwardly in normal conditions. We may be in states of heavenly ecstasy induced by beautiful scenes in nature, or in a quiet mood of contemplation in ordinary external circumstances, like a street corner.

The hell realm is marked by claustrophobic and catastrophic feelings of pain, suffering and victimization. The *preta* realm of "hungry ghosts" is a world of perpetually frustrated craving, symbolized by the distended stomachs but thin mouths of the spirits in this realm. The animal realm is a world focused on survival instincts—food, sex, sleep, self-preservation, with lack of aspiration for higher values. The *asura* realm is a world of struggle, competition and violence, into which we come through discontent and grasping envy. The world of *devas* or gods is a realm of pleasure and aesthetic delight of the senses. In the Buddhist view this realm or state is not a goal to be sought but merely a pleasant though transient state resulting from good karma but not contributive to growth or new learning. The human realm is described by Trungpa as "the epitome of communication and relationship," in which there is curiosity for knowledge and aspiration for spiritual values. It has some of the qualities of all the other realms, but is less fixated and bound than those.

In the *Bardo Thödol* the bardo traveler is admonished and reminded to avoid being caught or driven into any of the realms, but if and when rebirth becomes unavoidable to aim our intention either for the deva realm or the human realm. The human world is considered the best of the six to be born into—because it offers the "precious opportunity" of liberation and enlightenment. When we are in any of the other five realms of experience our existence is more or less totally conditioned by our past karmic actions and determined by external circumstances.

The remaining instructions in the bardo of rebirth phase of the after-death journey deal with instructions on how to first delay being born at all, and then to choose the best kind of human birth. The guidance for the soul embarking on its journey into a new incarnation are couched as instructions on how to "close the womb-door"—the point here being to delay the rebirth as long as possible, so that one can avoid being sucked into unfavorable births by one's unconscious karmic propensities (*samskaras*). The first method of closing the womb-door is to remember that you are in this bardo of rebirth and focus on positive intentions: "holding in mind one single resolution, persist in joining up the chain of good karma; . . . this is a time when earnestness and pure love are necessary."

The second, third, fourth and fifth methods of closing the womb-door all involve different ways of responding to visions of men and women copulating. The bardo traveler is urged not to join in the sexual activity, although he or she may be tempted to do so. It's as if the Buddhist masters are saying "Do not rush into incarnation. Staying with conscious intention at the very beginning is more likely to lead to a more conscious human lifetime." I suggest that the visions of couples copulating are the soul's vision of its own conception. This existential choice-point, where the soul chooses which couple to have as parents, and the future parents choose to have a child, can be reached in prenatal regression divinations and is here arrived at from the other side, at the end of the afterlife period, when the decision to reincarnate has been made.

Although I do not believe that conscious remembering of one's own conception is a very common part of recreational psychedelic experiences, there is an extensive literature of adults and children reporting dreams and hypnotic regression states in which they vividly remember the events and circumstances of their own conception. In my book *The Life Cycle of the Human Soul*, I describe psychedelically amplified intentional divination journeys, in which the parental imprints at conception could be identified and integrated, as well as memories of the soul from before conception.

The *Bardo Thödol* says that if the voyager feels attraction to the female and aversion to the male, he will be reborn as a male; and if attraction to the male and aversion to the female, she will be born as female. As we now know from medical research, the gender of the child is determined in the earliest phases of embryonic development, and can involve all kinds of variations of genital anatomy. As Sigmund Freud famously observed, "anatomy is destiny." Some scientists now believe the origin of the inclination to homosexuality may be in embryonic development. These scientific findings could be seen as consistent with a view that sees homosexuality, as well as gender and its anatomical variations, as soul choices made to provide certain learning conditions for that soul in its earthly-human existence.

If, even after using the various methods of preventing or postponing rebirth by meditating with conscious intention on one's chosen deity, one is still drawn down into a womb for birth, the bardo-traveling soul is given instructions for "choosing of the womb-door." First there are "premonitory visions of the place of rebirth"—the continents in four directions are described, where one might be born. "All the places of birth will be known to you, one after another. Choose accordingly." The soul in the bardo of rebirth is advised to use their foresight to choose a human birth in an area in which religion and ethics prevail.

To summarize, the instructions of the *Bardo Thödol* for the most favorable kind of rebirth, are: to delay the return from the light and wisdom-filled heaven worlds as long as possible, and when the time finally does come, which you will know by seeing acts of copulation and conception between men and women, to choose a birth family where the likelihood of coming into contact with the dharma teachings are greatest. The ending of the interlife period is the beginning of the bardo of rebirth: the decision is made to reincarnate, in a blending of karmic tendencies and conscious choice, and conception takes place in a fleshly human womb. This rebirth phase then ends with the actual physical birth, nine months later, when we start cycling through the three bardos of waking life, dreaming and meditating. In conclusion, below is my version of the Root-Verse for the bardo of rebirth:

> Now, as the bardo of rebirth dawns upon me,
> I will hold one-pointedly to a single wish—
> Continuously directing intention with a positive outlook.
> Delaying the return to Earth-Life as long as possible.
> I will concentrate on pure energy and love,
> And cast off jealousy while meditating on the Guru Father-Mother.

MYSTICISM: Contemplative and Chemical @ Roger Walsh

MYSTICAL EXPERIENCES are usually conceived of as coinciding with altered states of consciousness. As a result, a consideration of mystical states should begin with a discussion of consciousness itself. Yet the nature of consciousness is one of the most fundamental and difficult of all philosophical questions.

The answers to this question have ranged across an enormous spectrum throughout cultures and eras. At one extreme, they include the idea that consciousness is a mere by-product of matter; this is the philosophy of materialism. At the other extreme is the idea that consciousness is the fundamental substrate of reality; this is the philosophy of absolute idealism as proposed, for example, by Yogachara Buddhism. For Nietzsche, consciousness was a suffering-producing disease of life, while for the Vedantic religion of India, it is being and bliss. Small wonder, then, that two contemporary researchers, Douglas R. Hofstadter and Daniel Dennett, claim "So far there is no good theory of consciousness. There is not even agreement about what a theory of consciousness would be like. Some have gone so far as to deny that there is any real thing for the term 'consciousness' to name" (Hofstadter and Dennett, 1982).

Yet whatever consciousness is, the desire to alter it is clearly common and widespread. In a cross-cultural survey, anthropologist Erika Bourguignon found that 90 percent of the several hundred societies she surveyed possessed institutionalized means to alter states of consciousness. She concluded that "this represents a striking finding and suggests that we are, indeed, dealing with a matter of major importance, not merely a list of anthropological esoterica" (Bourguignon, 1973). Moreover, she found that in traditional societies, these altered states were viewed as sacred, almost without exception. In his book *The Natural Mind*, Andrew Weil, a leading researcher on psychoactive substances, concluded that "the desire to alter consciousness periodically is an innate normal drive analogous to hunger or sexual desire" (Weil, 1972).

If this is so, it raises the obvious question of the nature of an "optimal" state of consciousness. This is the question I would like to discuss here, along with a related issue of whether psychedelics can ever induce these optimal states.

In the West it is commonly assumed that our usual waking state is optimal. Yet many religious and contemplative traditions make claims about consciousness that run counter to Western assumptions, among them that:

1. Our usual state of consciousness is severely suboptimal or deficient;
2. Multiple states of consciousness—including true "higher states"—exist;
3. These states can be attained through training;
4. Verbal communication about them may be necessarily limited.

The teachings of mystical traditions inform us that our usual state of consciousness is not only suboptimal, but dreamlike and illusory. They assert that whether we know it or not, without mental training, we are prisoners of our own minds, unwittingly trapped by a continuous inner dialogue that creates an all-consuming distortion of perception. These traditions suggest that we live in a collective dream variously known as *maya*, "illusion," or what psychologist Charles Tart calls "consensus trance."

Obviously, if these various philosophies regard our usual state as suboptimal, they must regard some other state(s) as superior. Numerous traditions converge on the idea that the *unio mystica*, described by mystics and saints, constitutes the supreme states of consciousness—and in fact is the highest achievement of human existence. In these states the mystic transcends the usual boundaries of ego and feels at one with the universe. Usually the state of mystical union arrives after years or even decades of intense spiritual and mental discipline. This training aims to overcome the fact that, as Sigmund Freud said, "man is not even master in his own house . . . in his own mind." This is why, as the great Hindu sage Ramana Maharshi expressed it, "all scriptures without any exception proclaim that for attaining salvation mind should be subdued" (Maharshi, 1955).

Yet with the advent of psychedelics in the West came a remarkable claim. Noncontemplatives who took these substances reported a vast range of experiences—some high, some low; some ecstatic, some demonic—but also some that seemed remarkably similar to those described by mystics across the centuries. This set off a debate that still rages about the nature of "chemical mysticism."

Proponents, such as writers and scholars of religion Aldous Huxley, Walter Houston Clark, and Huston Smith, offered arguments supporting the equivalence

GREEN BUDDHA Ed Paschke, 2000

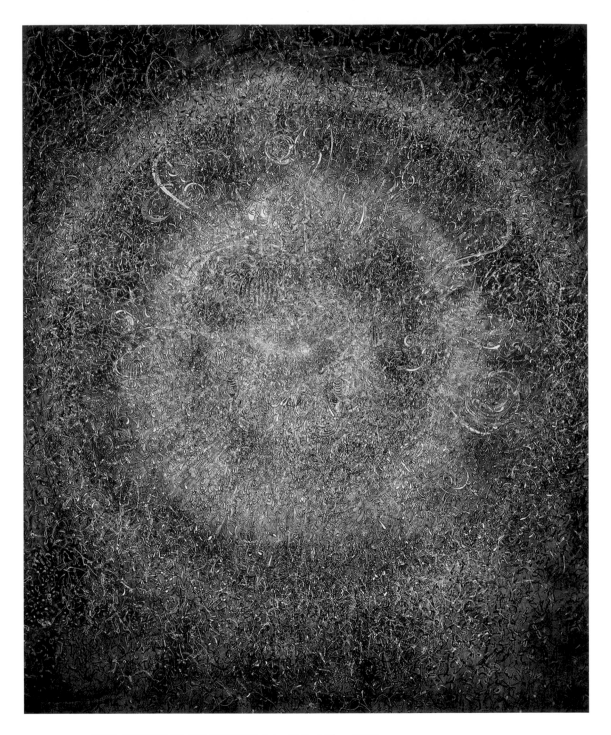

DARK RHYTHMS OF THE UNIVERSE John F. B. Miles, 1981

THE TRAIL Dean Chamberlain, 2000

CONSUMMATION Ethel Le Rossignol, c. 1920

MOMENT OF FLIGHT Bernard Maisner, 1987

GRAIN OF SAND Mati Klarwein, 1962-1968

THE ROOM WHEN NO ONE IS THERE John F. B. Miles, 1979

MIND PHYSICS: THE BURNING OF SAMSARA Paul Laffoley, 1967

of chemical and natural mystical experiences. They based their arguments on the experiential similarities between natural and chemical states and on experiments such as that of Walter Pahnke, who in 1962 administered psilocybin to students at the Harvard Divinity School before a Good Friday church service. The majority of the group reported a variety of experiences including difficult psychological struggles that sounded indistinguishable from reports of classical mystical experiences. Twenty-five years later, almost all the subjects who were given psilocybin still affirmed that they "considered their original experience to have had genuinely mystical elements and to have made a uniquely valuable contribution to their spiritual lives" (Pahnke Study, 1991).

Others, including scholars of religion R. C. Zaehner and Arthur Koestler, argued vehemently against the idea that a few milligrams or even micrograms of some chemical could possibly induce experiences that contemplatives labor for decades to achieve. In a piece entitled "Do Drugs Have Religious Import?" (the most frequently reprinted article in the history of the *American Journal of Philosophy*), Huston Smith considered the arguments against the equivalence of chemical and natural mysticism. He concluded that these arguments were unconvincing (Smith, 1964).

The arguments, and Smith's responses to them, can be summarized as follows:

1. *Some drug experiences are clearly anything but mystical and beneficial.* Agreed! But this does not prove that no drug experiences are mystical or beneficial.
2. *The experiences induced by drugs are actually different from those of genuine mystics.* They are obviously different in causation, but, as the Harvard Good Friday study showed, they may be experientially indistinguishable.
3. *Mystical rapture is ostensibly a divine gift that can never be brought under mere human control.* This argument is, of course, unlikely to convince atheists, nontheists such as Buddhists, or those Christians who believe more in the power of good works than of grace.
4. *Drug-induced experiences are too quick and easy to be considered identical to contemplative experiences.* However, if the states are experientially indistinguishable, then the fact that they rise from different causes and

with different degrees of ease may be irrelevant. The philosopher W. T. Stace has called this "the principle of causal indifference."

5. *The aftereffects of drug-induced experiences are different, less beneficial, and less long-lasting than those of contemplatives.* Smith put this point eloquently, noting that if "drugs appear to induce religious experiences, it is less evident that they can produce religious lives." Nonetheless, the fact that aftereffects may be different does not necessarily mean that the experiences are.

Despite these well-argued points, the debate continues over whether psychedelically induced mystical experiences are "really genuine." The psychiatrist Stanislav Grof, who probably did more research on psychedelics than anyone else before authorized research was curtailed in the mid-1960s, wrote that "after thirty years of discussion, the question whether LSD and other psychedelics can induce genuine spiritual experience is still open" (Grof, 1980).

One reason the debate continues is that there is no adequate theory of mystical states that could resolve it. For the purposes of this discussion, the term "mystical experience" will refer to an altered state of consciousness characterized by:

1. Ineffability: the experience is of such power and is so different from ordinary experience that it seems to at least partly defy description;
2. A heightened sense of understanding;
3. Altered perception of space and time;
4. Appreciation of the holistic, integrated nature of the universe and one's unity with it;
5. Intense positive affect, including a sense of the perfection of the universe.

Such experiences have many names. In the West they have been described as "cosmic consciousness" by Richard Bucke (Bucke, 2001) in his classic work of the same name, and "peak experiences" by the psychologist Abraham Maslow. In the East, common terms include *samadhi* in yoga and *satori* in Zen.

We lack a theory that accounts for the induction of identical states by such different means as LSD and meditation, as well as for their different aftereffects. It may now be possible to advance such a theory in the light of current understanding.

Psychologist Charles Tart's model of consciousness is helpful here. Tart suggests that any state of consciousness is the result of the interaction of multiple psychological and neural processes such as perception, attention, emotions, and identity. If the functioning of any one process is changed enough, the entire state of consciousness may shift. It therefore seems possible to reach a specific altered state in more than one way by altering different processes. For example, one may attain states of calm by reducing muscle tension, visualizing restful scenery, or focusing attention on the breath. In each case, the brain-mind process employed is different, though the resulting state is similar.

A similar phenomenon could occur with mystical states. Thus different techniques might affect different brain-mind processes, yet still produce the same mystical state of consciousness. For example, a contemplative might finally taste the bliss of mystical unity after years of cultivating such qualities as concentration, love, and compassion. Yet a psychedelic substance also might affect chemical and neural processes so powerfully as to temporarily induce a similar state.

Tart's theory of consciousness could explain the supposition that chemical and natural mysticism may be biochemically and experientially identical.

But what of the fact that the long-term effects of the two can differ? These differences may also be compatible with Tart's theory.

Both psychological and social factors may be involved. The psychedelic user might have a dramatic experience, perhaps the most dramatic of his or her life. But a single experience, no matter how powerful, may not be enough to permanently overcome psychological habits conditioned over decades. The contemplative, on the other hand, may spend decades deliberately working to retrain habits along more spiritual lines. Thus when the breakthrough finally occurs, it visits a mind already prepared. In addition, the contemplative has acquired a belief system that provides an explanation for the experience, a discipline that can cultivate it, a tradition and social group that support it, and an ethic that can guide its expression. One is reminded of Louis Pasteur's statement that "chance favors the prepared mind." The contemplative's mind may be prepared, but there is no guarantee that the drug user's is.

This is not to say that the contemplative will always be spiritually transformed and the drug user never will be. Some psychedelic users may be psychologically and spiritually mature enough to be transformed by their experience. Likewise some mystics may not be, or at least may have areas of personality, behavior, and neurosis that remain relatively untransformed.

In summary, these ideas suggest a qualified equivalence between contemplative and chemical mysticism; that some drugs can indeed induce genuine mystical experiences in some people on some occasions. However, they seem more likely to do so and more likely to produce enduring benefits in prepared minds.

Yet we may be able to push our investigation a stage further, for it is becoming increasingly apparent that there is not a single type, but rather multiple types, of mystical experiences. In *The Spirit of Shamanism* I attempted to show that careful mapping of mystical experiences may enable us to identify states that are in reality quite different from each other yet have not been distinguished in the past. For example, the states induced by yoga, shamanism, and Buddhist meditation have sometimes been described as identical. Yet careful comparison of the experiences shows that they may be quite distinct.

The general principle seems to be that different contemplative techniques are more likely to induce certain types of mystical experiences than others. For example, some shamans may feel a sense of unity with the universe, with all of creation (which may be described as "nature mysticism"), whereas Buddhist *vipassana* meditators aim for an experience of nirvana, in which all objects and phenomena of any kind disappear.

I suspect that careful studies would show that specific psychedelics are more likely to facilitate certain mystical states than others. LSD and analogous substances, for example, may induce experiences of nature mysticism or nonduality more often than nirvanic experiences. Likewise, other substances, for example empathogens such as MDMA (Ecstasy), which are reputed to have a strong "heart" effect and induce feelings of love, may be likely to foster other kinds of mystical experiences. Clearly a further level of sensitivity and discernment may be possible in research on mystical experiences, however they are induced.

For those people who are graced with the mystical experience—whether induced spontaneously, contemplatively, or chemically—the crucial question is what to do with it. It can be allowed to fade; it can be ignored or even dismissed, or perhaps clung to as a psychological or spiritual trophy. Or it can be consciously used as a source of inspiration and guidance to direct one's life along more beneficial directions.

One such direction—indeed the one recommended by the great mystics—is to undertake the necessary contemplative training of life and mind so as to be able to reenter and extend the mystical state. The aim is to extend a single peak experience to a recurring plateau experience, to change an altered state into an altered trait, or, as Huston Smith so eloquently put it, to transform flashes of illumination into abiding light (Smith, 1964).

Even this personal experience of abiding light is not the endpoint of the journey. For beyond personal realization lies the stage of sharing that realization with the world, of using one's wisdom and illumination to teach, serve, help, and heal. The mythologist Joseph Campbell described this as the "hero's return." The world's religions offer many descriptions of this opening of the spirit; in Zen it is called "entering the marketplace with help-bestowing hands," and in Christianity it is known as the "fruitfulness of the soul." Thus the task is first to open to the experience of illumination, then to bring that light back to the world for the benefit of all.

DISSOLVING THE ROOTS OF SUFFERING ⊚ Dokushô Villalba
Translated by Stuart McNicholls

FROM THE POINT OF VIEW of Buddha's teaching, all the causes of suffering can be reduced to one: ignorance. There are various ways of defining this ignorance. Claudio Naranjo, inventor of the Enneagram, identifies it with the "ontic void," or loss of a clear awareness of the nature of one's own Being. The Japanese term for this is *mumyo*: obscurity, lack of clarity, in the sense of an absence of clear awareness. Another way of presenting this state of ignorance is to consider it as an error of perception, an error in the cognitive process through which the human mind attempts to understand reality—an incomplete or incorrect representation of the reality of Being itself. The result of this error is an illusory, distorted mental image of reality, and maladjusted behavior. The manifestation of all this is none other than pain and suffering, the wretched state of everyday existence in which the basic longing for happiness is not fulfilled. From this point of view, we could define happiness as a perfect emotional, mental, spiritual, physical, social, and environmental adaptation of the human being to its true reality.

Scope of Action and Internal Dynamics of Zen Meditation

The Buddhist Dharma is a healing path to transcend existential or essential suffering. Each of the traditional forms of meditation that the Buddhist Dharma has adopted specializes in the development of one or more levels of being. Tantric Buddhist tradition cultivates development of the psychic, subtle, and causal levels. The Dzogchen and Zen traditions focus directly on the causal and non-dual levels; Zen meditation operates by means of an inner technique that tends to favor the irruption and consolidation of transpersonal levels of being. Zen tradition characteristically "aims directly for the root, without pausing at the branches or the leaves." It aims directly to attain the causal level of Supreme and Perfect Wisdom (*anokutara samyaku sambodhi*, in Japanese).

Regarding Entheogens

Entheogens (literally, "that which gives rise to inner divinity") are substances or preparations, natural or synthetic, that allow users to free themselves momentarily from the perception of reality created by the logico-rational mind, putting them in touch with experiences originating at other levels of the Chain of Being. In the natural domain we find ayahuasca, peyote, cannabis, psilocybin mushrooms, *yopo*, the *Amanita muscaria* mushroom, *Salvia divinorum*, San Pedro cactus, *iboga*, and so on, to name only the most well-known. The active constituents of many of these have by now been synthesized in laboratories.

Entheogens have been used as spiritual tools since the origins of humanity; theories that situate them in the very genesis of religions and spiritual traditions are gaining increasing credence. As tools they have specific powers, but the outcome of their use depends on the attitude and purpose with which they are employed.

The Therapeutic Power of Entheogens

The beneficial potential that such substances, employed conscientiously by scrupulous professionals, offer in the field of psychotherapy is undeniable. As for the debate among Western Buddhists on the use of psychedelics, it is my view that no practicing Buddhist can object to the psychotherapeutical use of entheogens, a use whose ultimate aim is to cure a human being of some kind of painful trauma generated at a given moment of his or her development. One of the maxims in the Buddhist Dharma reads: "That all beings be freed from suffering and from the causes of suffering." I can find no morally valid reason why psychotherapists should not use these substances in the pursuit of the healing of human beings' suffering and pain, especially when their rational use neither leads to any physical or mental damage, nor provokes addiction.

The Spiritual Potential of Entheogens

Many Native Americans have been able to overcome addiction to alcohol and its underlying causes through use of peyote within a ritual and traditional spiritual context. In the shamanic traditions that use entheogens, their therapeutic potential and their potential for spiritual awakening are not separated. The shaman is at the same time a healer and a spiritual guide. Most often the healing arises precisely thanks to an experience of spiritual awakening—in which the so-called transpersonal or transcendental levels (psychic, subtle, causal, or non-dual) emerge. Entheogens offer the potential to favor the emergence of these spiritual realms, which are inherent to human nature.

By dissolving the firm hold of the logico-rational mind over the perception of reality, entheogens propitiate, on the one hand, the appearance and observation of contents arising from pre-personal levels (their regressive aspect) and, on the other, the appearance and observation of contents arising from transpersonal levels (their transcendental aspect). Thus it is the responsibility of the therapist or guide to help the individual to integrate these contents appropriately, promoting the healing of traumas and access to higher states of consciousness.

The question that many people pose is the following: Can a serious Buddhist, a committed meditator, occasionally or systematically use entheogenic substances as tools of self-exploration to support his or her pursuit of spiritual awakening?

My answer is yes and yes, yes and no, no and yes, and no and no. That is, it depends on why, how, when, with what, with whom, what for, how much. It depends on the external and internal circumstances of any person in any given moment, what has come to be known as the "set and setting." Above all it depends, according to my own experience, on the capacity of the explorer to focus/defocus her or his attention.

Buddhist practice is a training of attention that attempts to avoid the extremes of rigid fixation and dispersion. Training in meditation is an excellent preparation for confronting the expanded states of consciousness which entheogens generate and, conversely, the intensity and forthrightness of these expanded states can provide a great impetus to apply the achievements attained during meditation in an emphatic way.

Buddhist teachings describe five states of awareness that are contemplated according to the level of attention:

1. The ordinary state, in which attention is centered on "me" and "mine."
2. The state of unconscious sleep with dreams. The attention works unconsciously, moving in and out of focus from one content to another, following the unconscious karmic tendencies.
3. The state of unconscious sleep without dreams, during which consciousness rests in its original nature (*dharmata*), without being aware of itself.
4. The state of conscious sleep with dreams, or "lucid dreaming." Attention is not centered on "me" and "mine" but rather acts as a mirror that

reflects without choosing or rejecting. This is a state characteristic of deep meditation.

5. The state of conscious sleep without dreams. This state is characteristic of very advanced meditators, whose carefully trained attention allows them to remain in the unborn and undeceased nature of the Consciousness in which nothing is born and nothing dies.

These states correspond to the different states of bardo described in Tibetan Buddhism. In general, an untrained mind that enters the universe of entheogens tends to fluctuate between states two and three and, rarely, also state four. A well-trained mind can easily recognize that the states generated by entheogens are very similar to the states of deep meditation or lucid dreaming. If the mind is really well trained, the explorer will be able to leave behind the state of lucid dreaming and enter that of conscious sleep without dreams. Entheogens tend to promote in each individual the internal attitudes and karmic tendencies of her or his own mind.

Regarding the Fifth Precept, "Do not intoxicate body or mind"

It is my view that in the Buddhist Dharma there is no moral or dogmatic principle that absolutely encourages or prohibits the use of entheogens. The decision one way or the other depends exclusively on the consciousness and individual determination of each person, be they Dharma master or a simple practitioner. It is true that in Buddhism there are the Sixteen Precepts (*sila*, in Sanskrit; *kai* in Japanese). The articulation, understanding, and practice of these teachings differ from one Buddhist tradition to another. In the Soto Zen tradition, one receives the precepts in the course of the ordination ceremony (*jukai*). The first three correspond to "taking refuge" in the Buddha, Dharma, and Sangha. Next are the Three Pure Precepts (avoid evil, do good, benefit all living beings). The next ten are known as the Ten Main Precepts. Among the latter, the fifth precept reads: "Do not intoxicate the body or the mind." A superficial reading can lead us to the premature conclusion that the use of entheogens is prohibited for serious Buddhists.

Nevertheless, we should study the matter further and clarify the meaning of terms such as "toxic," "inebriation," "inebriating," or "intoxication of the body and of the mind."

A simple glass of good red wine is toxic or a good meal can be considered toxic, giving rise to toxins within the body and causing a state of mental somnolence. The air we breathe has become toxic. Aspirin is toxic. Natural remedies can also be toxic. We must not forget the expression first employed by Paracelsus, one of the fathers of Western medicine: "The only difference between a poison and a remedy is the dosage." But entheogens, taken in appropriate doses, are not poisons that contaminate the body and stultify consciousness, but rather medicines which dissolve certain poisons of consciousness. The dosage is important, as well as the state of mental attention of each individual.

In the "Commentaries of Bodhidharma on the Precepts of the Only One Mind," transmitted by Eihei Dogen as the quintessence of the Precepts of Buddha in his work *Kyojukaimon* (or *The Gate of Transmission of the Precepts*) we find the following commentary about this fifth precept: "The Dharma is intrinsically pure. When the blindness of ignorance does not arise, the precept of nonintoxication is practiced."

This is the essence of the fifth precept: the greatest toxin of all is ignorance. When consciousness is freed of ignorance, the precept of nonintoxication is practiced. The correct use of entheogens allows access to higher states of consciousness, characterized by greater lucidity, greater understanding, and important and quantifiable changes in conduct. That is, they facilitate the dissolution of ignorance, understood as limited perception of reality centered on "me" and "mine."

I am not proposing an entheogenic free-for-all, any time, any place. At all times entheogens must be used with wisdom (*prajna*) and with skillful means (*upaya*), in the appropriate context (setting), with an appropriate purpose (*bodaishin*), and in an appropriate internal state (set).

Summing Up

Entheogens, used in the appropriate context, by qualified individuals, with a suitable purpose, in appropriate dosages and with the correct inner state, manifest great potential for alleviating the different types of suffering generated in the different existential levels of human beings. Given that the ultimate goals of psychotherapy relate to the Buddhist intention that "all beings be freed from suffering and from the causes of suffering," I do not feel there to be any contradiction between the use of entheogens in psychotherapy and the teaching and practice of Zen Buddhism.

The use of entheogens, like the practice of meditation itself, requires a global vision and an ethical basis with an ultimate objective of the happiness of all living beings. The entheogens can be used erroneously as mere inebriators or narcotics, in the same way that religion, be it Buddhist or any other—politics, culture, or baseball—can be erroneously used as an "opiate of the people."

Entheogens facilitate the emergence of higher states of consciousness, states which must afterwards be integrated into the totality of the person who experiences them and into her or his daily life. I feel that the simple use of entheogens is not sufficient to integrate these states into the totality of the personality and daily life, just as a simple example experience of *satori* or insight does not suffice to generate a real transformation of the personality if it is not accompanied by integration and the knowledge derived from daily experience.

As a practical matter, I do not advocate the use of entheogens in my Zen community, or in the context of practice; my research into their use is personal and private. But I feel that the prohibition of entheogens is an infringement of the freedom of conscience and of religious freedom. Entheogens are helping me, among other things, to clarify the purpose of my existence, to discover and integrate the darker sides of my shadow, and to free my creativity. Through the use of entheogens, I have experienced with an uncommon intensity the state of lucid sleep and of sleep without dreams in which the Clear Light of Being shines beyond time and space, beyond birth and death.

A HIGH HISTORY OF BUDDHISM IN AMERICA ☉ Rick Fields

THE WAR ON AT LEAST ONE variety of drugs—the psychedelics—has been won, at least for a while. In place of the alchemicals that reigned supreme for a momentarily eternal moment, young would-be mind explorers now toke their way through a fractalized marketplace of pot, coke, weak acid, heroin, cocaine, ludes, Ecstasy, speed, crack. Set and setting? The set is the fresh curious wary jumpy insecure brain of a bright young kid—fourteen, twelve, ten, the age keeps dropping—and the setting is the schoolyard, the street corner, the stall in the boys' or girls' room before homeroom. Or maybe (at best?) it's a tribal merge at a thumping, flashing rave or a concert. Always a buzzing swarm. But still hardly the contemplative gardens or paisley candlelit retreats of the first psychedelic illuminati. The heady halcyon days and nights of psychedelia, which once led so many to Buddhist practice, have been inefficiently eliminated, reduced to retrofashion. The young now turn on in a world in which the sacred has been trivialized into the recreational. No wonder so many are relieved to see Buddhism as a recovery program: in the morning a half-hour of meditation in a halfway house.

That practice can be helpful, even lifesaving, to the strung-out is of course good news. But there is another sort of good news—for some unreformed heads at least. There is something of a psychedelic revival going on these days—and more than a few Buddhists are taking part in it. The sacramentals are partly the old familiar (LSD), the new (Ecstasy and other designer drugs), and the ancient (entheogens—sacred plants that bring forth the divine from within—such as the mushrooms, peyote, and the Amazonian ayahuasca). Interestingly, it is the last category, the ancient plants used by the oldest indigenous peoples on the earth, which seems to hold the most promise for the future.

There are a number of reasons for this psychedelic revival. For one thing, psychedelics have proven to have a certain staying power. Stamped down countless times, abandoned for various reasons, they nevertheless somehow manage to pop up like mushrooms from one generation to the next. Timing is also part of it. A dynamic back-and-forth relationship between psychedelics and Eastern spirituality has existed in the West since the nineteenth century.

In the [nineteen] fifties, Buddhist and Hindu texts inspired aristocratic British exiles like the writers Gerald Heard and Aldous Huxley to seek an experiential illumination through psychedelics. In the sixties the same psychedelic experience inspired American academicians like Timothy Leary and Richard Alpert (Ram Dass) to investigate Eastern texts and practices.

During the eighties the use of MDMA (Ecstasy) became fashionable, both among psychotherapists and in the new youth culture in the rave and dance club scene. Ecstasy is not a hallucinogen or entheogen, but has best been described as an empathogen: it seems to relax the stranglehold of the individual ego and open the way to an unusually high level of intimacy and communication (hence its popularity with marriage counselors). The general calmness, serenity, and spaciousness of the experience have led, in some circles, to its being called the "Buddha-drug." If psychedelics correspond (for some at least) with Tibetan or Tantric Buddhism, then Ecstasy could be seen as the Mahayana or bodhisattva drug of choice. In fact, at least one rumor told of a serious circle of practitioners who used Ecstasy as a support for their *metta* (loving-kindness) practice.

During the seventies and eighties, psychedelic drug use seems to have been largely discounted in Buddhist communities—as it was in the larger culture—though it was not entirely absent from either arena. It simply went underground. Buddhist groups quite understandably were anxious to stay on the right side of the law and seemed as anxious as most organizations to separate themselves from the sixties drug and antiwar countercultures. Individual students were growing older, taking on the responsibilities of families and careers. For most students, psychedelics were remembered as a boat that had gotten them to the other shore of real practice but was now a distraction to be abandoned.

But just as in the larger culture, a small number of students continued to experiment with psychedelics when they were off-duty—in the "post-meditation state." Most of these, perhaps, fell into the fashion of using psychedelics for largely recreational reasons. A loosely floating post-hippie tribe of Buddhist Deadheads, the Dead Buddhists of America, kept something of the old spirit alive. When Jerry Garcia died in 1995, the editor of their 'zine, the *Conch Us Times*, led a meditation of Chenrezi, bodhisattva of compassion. In the middle of the meditation, he instructed everyone to see Jerry as the bodhisattva, "merging with the lights of Buddha-mind in the journey through the bardos."

Now, in the new century, we may be seeing a generation who has steeped themselves in practice become inspired to take another, more mature—and more penetrating—look at psychedelics.

During the soporific fifties, access to both psychedelics and Buddhism was limited to a small but influential elite. A British psychiatrist working in Canada, Dr. Humphry Osmond, enlisted Aldous Huxley as a subject for his experiments with mescaline in Los Angeles one afternoon in the middle of May 1953. Huxley was well prepared. He and his fellow expatriate, the writer Gerald Heard, had studied Vedanta and practiced disciplined meditation for some years, and Huxley had ransacked the world's mystical writings for his anthology *The Perennial Philosophy*. Sitting in his garden with Dr. Osmond, he experienced the grace and transfiguration he had read about. Remembering a koan from one of D.T. Suzuki's essays, "What is the Dharma-Body of the Buddha?" he found the answer: "The hedge at the bottom of the garden." What had previously seemed "only a vaguely pregnant piece of nonsense" was now as clear as day. "Of course, the Dharma-Body of the Buddha was the hedge at the bottom of the garden," he reported in *The Doors of Perception*. "At the same time, and no less obviously, it was these flowers, it was anything that I—or rather the blessed not-I, released for a moment from my throttling embrace—cared to look at." Of course Huxley still had his famous wits about him. "I am not so foolish as to equate what happens under the influence of mescaline . . . with the realization of the end and ultimate purpose of human life: Enlightenment," he reassured his reader. "All I am suggesting is that the mescaline experience is what Catholic theologians call 'a gratuitous grace,' not necessary to salvation but potentially helpful and to be accepted thankfully, if made available." When Maria, Huxley's wife of more than thirty years, lay dying of cancer, he read to her the reminders from the *Tibetan Book of the Dead*, reducing them to their simplest form and repeating them close to her ear: "Let go, let go. Go forward into the light. Let yourself be carried into the light." He continued after she had stopped breathing, "tears streaming down his face, with his quiet voice not breaking," his son Matthew remembered.

A few years earlier, in July 1953, the ex-banker ethnomycologist Gordon Wasson and his wife, Valentina, had reached the Mazatec village of Huautla de Jiménez, where they discovered the magic psilocybin mushrooms (*teonanácatl*, the "flesh of the gods") and managed to take part in an all-night *velada*. Wasson's evenhanded and respectful article on his adventures was published by *Life* in 1957. The article was read by a Berkeley psychologist, Frank Barron, who had tried some of the mushrooms, and passed on his enthusiasm to another academic psychologist and old friend, Timothy Leary. Before taking up his new job at Harvard's Center for the Study of Personality, Leary spent the summer in Cuernavaca, Mexico. Naturally, he tried the mushrooms. "The journey lasted a little over four hours," he wrote. "Like almost everyone who had the veil drawn, I came back a changed man" (Leary, 1983).

Leary was now more interested in transcendence then personality assessment. As head of the Harvard Psychedelic Drug Research Project, he ran a session for MIT professor Huston Smith, who made the experience available as a laboratory experiment for his seminars in mysticism. Next, in a now-famous double-blind experiment performed in 1962 on Good Friday in a chapel of the Boston University Cathedral, divinity students were given either psilocybin or a placebo. To no one's surprise, only those who had taken the psychedelic sacrament reported what appeared to be bona fide mystical experiences. *Time* published a favorable report, with reassuring quotes from Professor Walter Clark of Andover-Smith and other leading theologians. "We expected that every priest, minister, rabbi, theologian, philosopher, scholar, and just plain God-seeking man, woman, and child in the country would follow up the implications of the study," wrote Leary. Instead, "a tide of disapproval greeted the good news." What followed was much worse. As use spread and the less expensive and much more powerful LSD became the drug of choice, all heaven and hell broke loose. Huxley, while guest lecturing at MIT in the sixties, advised discretion, keeping the drugs inside a small, charmed circle—a kind of aristocratic mystery school. Leary put forth a plan for training and certifying guides. But it was all too much, too fast, and too late. A generation gap had been blown open. The old were appalled, the young enthralled. "Some students quit school and pilgrimaged eastward to study yoga on the Ganges," Leary wrote in *Flashbacks*, "not necessarily a bad development from our point of view but understandably upsetting to parents, who did not send their kids to Harvard to become buddhas."

Leary and Alpert left Harvard in 1963. Now they were but one wave, albeit a very visible and noisy one, in a counterculture transformation that was sweeping across America and about to crest in San Francisco. The center of activity was of course the Haight-Ashbury district, which was just a short stroll from a Soto Zen mission, Sokoji, and its American offshoot the San Francisco Zen Center. But the spiritual atmosphere was more than Zen—it was eclectic, visionary, polytheistic, ecstatic, and defiantly devotional. The newspaper of the new vision, the *San Francisco Oracle*, exploded in a vast rainbow that encompassed everything in one great Whitmanesque blaze of light and camaraderie. North American Indians, Shiva, Kali, Buddha, tarot, astrology, Saint Francis, Zen, and tantra all combined to sell fifty thousand copies on streets that were suddenly teeming with people. When the *Oracle* printed the *Heart Sutra*, it presented a double spread of the Zen Center version complete with Chinese characters, but also with a naked goddess, drawn in the best Avalon ballroom psychedelic. While the Beats had dressed in existential black and blue, this new generation wore plumage—beads and feathers worthy of the most flaming tropical birds. If the previous generation had been gloomy atheists attracted to Zen by iconoclastic directives—"If you meet the Buddha, kill him!"—these new kids were, as Gary Snyder told Dom Aelred Graham in a 1967 interview in Kyoto, "unabashedly religious. They love to talk about God or Christ or Vishnu or Shiva."

Snyder himself had gotten a firsthand look at the counterculture when he returned from Japan for a short visit in 1966. He was just in time for the first Be-In at Golden Gate Park, where he was joined by a number of friends from the early Beat days. Allen Ginsberg was there, as were Lawrence Ferlinghetti and Michael McClure. Kerouac was conspicuous by his brooding absence. He wanted nothing to do with it all. (When Leary had offered him LSD back in Ginsberg's apartment in New York he had objected: "Walking on water wasn't built in a day.") These new hippies horrified him. When a bunch of kids showed up at his mother's house in Northampton, Long Island, with jackets that said "Dharma Bums" across the back, he slammed the door in their faces.

But now, at the Be-In, with the sun shining through a deep blue sky and thousands of people at ease in all their finery on the meadow, Snyder read his poems and Ginsberg chanted the *Heart Sutra* to clear the meadows of lurking demons. Even Shunryu Suzuki Roshi of the burgeoning San Francisco Zen Center appeared briefly, holding a single flower.

Also present on the stage that afternoon were Timothy Leary and Richard Alpert, the two ex-Harvard psychology professors, who in three short years had become prophetic psychedelic pied pipers. Whatever else LSD became in time, at that moment it was the messenger that led a fair number of people into the dazzling land of their own mind. What had begun as the private discovery of a few intellectuals and experimenters had spread in a flash, and for a split second of history it was as if everyone's veil had been rent and all the archetypes of the unconscious now sprang forth.

There were those who claimed that psychedelics had changed the rules of the game, and that the mystic visions once enjoyed only by saints could now be had by anyone. In any case, it was obvious to the university researchers at Harvard, who had searched the scientific literature in vain, that the scriptures of Buddhism (and Hinduism) contained descriptions that matched what they had seen and felt. So Timothy Leary recast the verses of the *Tao Te Ching* in a book called *Psychedelic Prayers*, and in 1962 Timothy Leary, Ralph Metzner, and Richard Alpert adapted the *Bardo Thödol*, the *Tibetan Book of the Dead*, retranslated from Evans-Wentz's "Anglo-Buddhist to American Psychedelic" in *The Psychedelic Experience: A Manual Based on the Tibetan Book of the Dead*. Because the book was apparently meant to acquaint a dying person with the liberation of the Clear Light of Reality and then guide him or her through the peaceful and wrathful deities of the bardo, it was fairly easy to recast it as a guide in which physical death was reconfigured as the death of the ego during a psychedelic trip. *The Psychedelic Experience*, published in 1964, went through sixteen editions and was translated into seven languages.

One of the manuscript's most interested readers was Aldous Huxley, who called Leary from Los Angeles, where Huxley was dying of cancer. When Leary flew out to see him, Huxley asked him to guide him through the bardos. Leary suggested that it would be better if Huxley's second wife, Laura, guided the sessions. "No, I don't want to put any more emotional pressure on her," Huxley replied. "I plan to die during that trip, after all." In the end, Laura did give him the sacrament (LSD) and read him the instructions from the *Tibetan Book of the Dead*. And so, in 1963, Aldous Huxley passed peacefully into the Clear Light of Reality.

Before long, a number of the psychedelic luminaries made their way to India. In 1966, Ralph Metzner introduced Timothy Leary to the German-born Lama Anagarika Govinda, who lived in Evans-Wentz's old cottage in the

Himalayan village of Nanital. "The lama had been most impressed to learn that *The Psychedelic Experience* contained a dedication to him," Leary wrote in *Flashbacks* (Leary, 1983). Govinda had requested an LSD session, which Metzner provided. For the first time, after thirty years of meditation, the lama had experienced the *Bardo Thödol* in its living, sweating reality. According to Leary, Govinda told him that "many of the guardians of the old philosophic traditions had realized that the evolution of the human race had depended upon a restoration of unity between the outer science advanced by the West and the inner yoga advanced by the East." The teachings of Theosophy, Gurdjieff, Ramakrishna, Krishnamurti, and Evans-Wentz's translation of the *Tibetan Book of the Dead* had all been part of this plan. "You," the lama told Leary, "are the predictable result of a strategy that has been unfolding for over fifty years. You have done exactly what the philosophers wanted done." Presumably referring to Gerald Heard and Huxley, he said, "You were prepared discreetly by several Englishmen who were themselves agents of this process. You have been an unwitting tool of the great transformation of our age."

Ginsberg arrived in India that same year. Lately his psychedelic visions had become frightening, and he was wondering if he ought to continue. In Kalimpong he visited Dudjom Rinpoche, the great yogi-scholar who was head of the Nyingma (Ancient Ones) lineage. "I have these terrible visions, what should I do?" he asked. Dudjom Rinpoche sucked air through his mouth, a traditional Tibetan sign of sympathy, and said, "If you see anything horrible, don't cling to it; if you see anything beautiful, don't cling to it."

Leary's partner, Richard Alpert (now known as Ram Dass), reached India in 1967, "hoping to find someone who might understand more about these substances than we did in the West." When he met his guru, Neem Karoli Baba, Ram Dass gave him a hefty dose of nine hundred micrograms. "My reaction was one of shock mixed with the fascination of a social scientist, eager to see what would happen," Ram Dass wrote. "He allowed me to stay for an hour—and nothing happened. Nothing whatsoever. He just laughed at me."

Another time the old man swallowed a mind-boggling twelve hundred micrograms. "And then he asked, 'Have you got anything stronger?' I didn't. Then he said, 'These medicines were used in Kulu Valley long ago. But yogis have lost that knowledge. They were used with fasting. Nobody knows how to take them now. To take them with no effect, your mind must be firmly fixed on God. Others would be afraid to take. Many saints would not take this.' And he left it at that" (Dass, 1979).

Of course, the voyage was not always necessary. In his 1967 essay "Passage to More than India," Gary Snyder wrote, "Those who do not have time or money to go to India or Japan, but who think a great deal about the wisdom traditions, have remarkable results when they take LSD. The *Bhagavad Gita*, the Hindu Mythologies, *The Serpent Power*, the *Lankavatara Sutra*, the *Upanishads*, the *Hevajra Tantra*, the *Mahanirvana Tantra*—to name a few texts—become, they say, finally clear to them. They often feel that they must radically reorganize their lives to harmonize with such insights." At times, as Snyder noted, the psychedelic experience led straight to meditation. "In several American cities," he wrote, "traditional meditation halls of both Rinzai and Soto are flourishing. Many of the newcomers turned to traditional meditation after initial acid experience. The two types of experience seem to inform each other."

It was impossible for any roshi to ignore the question of LSD and its relationship to Buddhism. Koun Yamada Roshi, Yatsutani Roshi's chief disciple in Japan, was said to have tried it only to report, "This isn't form is the same as emptiness; this is emptiness is the same as form." If Suzuki Roshi said (as Gary Snyder told Dom Aelred Graham) that "people who have started to come to the zendo from LSD experiences have shown an ability to get into good zazen very rapidly," he also said in New York (as Harold Talbott, Graham's secretary, told Snyder) "that the LSD experience was entirely distinct from Zen." In any case, it seemed that in practice, Suzuki Roshi mostly ignored it. When Mary Farkas of the First Zen Institute asked him what he thought of the "Zen-drug tie-up we kept hearing so much of," she gathered from his reply "that students who had been on drugs gradually gave them up and that highly structured and supervised activities left little opportunity and lessened inclination."

But not everyone was so tolerant. In New York a student walked into the zendo on acid, sat on his zafu until he felt enlightened enough to get up off his cushion in the middle of zazen, then knelt in front of the teacher, Eido Roshi, rang the bell, and walked off nonchalantly into the small rock garden in back of the zendo. Eido Roshi followed, and the two stood locked eyeball to eyeball, until the teacher asked, "Yes, but is it real?" and the student, who seemed to have held his own till then, fled. After that, there was a rule that no one could sit zazen who used LSD in or out of the zendo.

Others in the Zen world were equally concerned. In Japan, D. T. Suzuki wrote an essay as part of a symposium on "Buddhism and Drugs" for *The Eastern Buddhist,* in which he warned that the popularity of LSD "has reached a point where university professors organize groups of mystical drug takers with the intention of forming an intentional society of those who seek 'internal freedom.' . . . All this sounds dreamy indeed," he wrote, "yet they are so serious in their intention, that Zen people cannot simply ignore their movements."

If Dr. Suzuki sounded the alarm, the Americans were more moderate in their reactions. Ray Jordan, a former student of Nyogen Senzaki's and then an assistant professor of psychology, had written in *Psychologia* that "LSD might be a useful aid both to the realization of *prajna* [wisdom], and to the development of meditational practice," but a *sesshin* with Yasutani Roshi had since convinced him that he had been mistaken. The *sesshin* had "included a moment which the roshi identified as *kensho*," and Jordan was now able to testify that "even the deepest and most powerful realizations associated with LSD were weak and dim compared to the reality and clarity of *sesshin* events." Jordan admitted that "in a small number of cases psychedelic experiences may have revealed to persons the everyday presentness of the Pure Buddha Land [but] from that point on the psychedelics are of no value whatsoever in so far as the Way is concerned. Without relying on anything one must walk step by step, moment by moment in the daily reality of the Pure Land."

Alan Watts was more sympathetic. He pointed out, to begin with, that everyone must speak for himself since so much depended on the "mental state of the person taking the chemical and circumstances under which the experiment is conducted." In Watts's case, these had been benign, and LSD had given him "an experience both like and unlike what I understood as the flavor of Zen." His mind had slowed, there were subtle changes in sense perception, and most importantly, "the thinker" had become confounded so that it realized "that all so-called opposites go together in somewhat the same way as the two sides of a single coin." This in turn had led to an experience of what the Japanese Buddhists call *ji ji-mu-ge,* the principle of universal interpretation.

But if one were not trained in yoga or Zen, warned Watts, this insight might lead one to believe either that "you are the helpless victim of everything that happens to you," or that, like God, you are "personally responsible for everything that happened." To go beyond this impasse, one needed either "an attitude of profound faith or letting-go to you-know-not-what." In that case, "the rest of the experience is total delight . . . what, in Buddhist terms, would be called an experience of world as *dharmadhatu*, of all things and events, however splendid or deplorable from relative points of view, as aspects of symphonic harmony, which, in its totality, is gorgeous beyond belief."

And yet, the most interesting part of the experience for Watts was not this ecstatic and sublime state, but the moment of return to the ordinary state of mind. There "in the twinkling of an eye" lay the realization "that so-called everyday or ordinary consciousness is the supreme form of awakening, of Buddha's *anuttara-samyak-sambodhi*." But this realization, remembered clearly enough, soon faded. "It is thus," concluded Watts, "that many of us who have experimented with psychedelic chemicals have left them behind, like the raft which you used to cross a river, and have found growing interest and even pleasure in the simplest practice of zazen, which we perform like idiots, without any special purpose."

It was left to Robert Aitken to describe the new psychedelic-influenced generation in detail. The early members of Koko-an Zendo, Aitken remembers, were former Theosophists. The turning point had come in 1963 or 1964 "when utter strangers would come into the dojo, bow at the entrance, seat themselves and sit like stones through the first period, and then at *kinhin* [walking meditation] time they would get up and fall down."

Aitken couldn't figure it out—until he later discovered that word had gone out that the Koko-an Zendo was a good place for tripping.

In 1967 the Aitkens bought a house on the island of Maui in anticipation of Robert's retirement from the East-West Center at the University of Hawaii. The long-haired young had begun to flock to Maui by then, and many of them had rented rooms in the Aitkens' house. Those from "the yogic end of the counterculture," he wrote in *The Eastern Buddhist*, "had a consuming interest in illuminative religion, a sense of wholeness and essence, a love of nature, a devotion to poverty and asceticism, a sensitivity to one another, and a desire to 'get it on,' that is, to practice rather than simply to talk."

Many of these were interested in zazen, and the Aitkens decided to establish a branch of Koko-an on Maui. In its first stages, Maui Zendo served "as a kind of mission to the psychedelic Bohemia." "Virtually all the young people who knock on our front door have tried LSD, mescaline, or psilocybin," he wrote—a situation that he thought true for the San Francisco Zen Center as well as other groups across the country.

The Maui Zendo soon became known as "a place where you could get your head together" and a regular zazen schedule was begun. But the turnover was enormous. "The thing that created this marvelous spirit also destroyed it," Aitken says now, "and that was the dope." The regular use of marijuana, Aitken had observed, "destroyed the sense of proportion," while LSD, as he had written in his essay, seemed to "shatter much of the personality structure, and the impulse of the moment assumed paramount importance."

It was, finally, the "human problem of distraction" that Aitken found most crucial. "The new gypsies," he found, "blow like leaves in the wind, now in Mendocino, now at San Francisco, then all the way to Maui, then back to the mainland, always with a convincing reason that may be no more than a faint interior or exterior impulse." Zazen was a natural corrective to this, and the Maui Zendo began to develop more and more in the direction of a training center.

If the sixties marked the high point of the Zen generation, the seventies belonged to the Tibetans. The proximate cause, of course, was the Tibetan diaspora. But the hallucinogenic aspect of the psychedelic experience itself was certainly a contributing factor. The visual pyrotechnics of psychedelia made a close fit with the colorful flamboyance of the radiant gods and goddesses and fiery deities of Tibetan art. The putative correspondence was further strengthened by seeming similarities between the visionary experience of the most popular Tibetan text of the sixties, the *Bardo Thödol* or *Tibetan Book of the Dead*, and the psychedelic experience. These elements of psychedelia had their part to play in the increasing popularity of Tibetan Buddhism. But as most would-be practitioners soon discovered, the first wave of lamas were more interested in students who were willing and able to engage in a series of demanding practices. The point was not to have visions, but to *visualize*.

Another point of divergence was that many people had hoped that meditation and yoga would provide the "permanent high" lacking in psychedelics.

But as more people actually threw themselves into the practice, it turned out that practice was not really about getting high at all. In Buddhism, at least, the instructions seemed to be to not cling to any experience, high or low. A fragment from a Gary Snyder poem springs to mind: "Experience, that drug. . . ."

With the advent of actual practice came Buddhist critique of the psychedelic experience. Some teachers slotted drugs into the mind-intoxicant category of the precepts. This was not really convincing for many, however, because whatever psychedelics might be, anyone who had taken them knew that "intoxicating" was a limited, reductionist description, at best. And more often than not, the Asian teachers making such pronouncements had no actual experience of psychedelics.

The few teachers who did have such experience, however, were in a uniquely privileged position to compare the two experiences. The most sympathetic of these was Trungpa Rinpoche, who had tested and tasted the splendors of Western civilization in England. He was one of the few Buddhist teachers one could talk to about such things, which many of his students—myself included—asked him about. Officially, of course, all illegal drugs were prohibited. But privately Trungpa Rinpoche had, as he told me (and here I paraphrase loosely from memory), a lot of sympathy for students who had taken LSD. He even volunteered that we might take it together sometime in the future—an opportunity or challenge that I never got to take him up on, to my regret and relief. The suggestion was both exhilarating and scary. His style and skill, after all, lay in cutting through trips of spiritual materialism rather than guiding them.

This is hardly surprising. More than most spiritual paths, Buddhism tends not to be very impressed by "experiences," be they spiritual or psychedelic. And Trungpa Rinpoche, for all his outwardly wild nonconventional behavior, was a Tibetan mastiff when it came to practice: your ass was on the line, which meant on the cushion. Still, at least in the "early days" of the seventies, his *sangha* was wilder and more open than many. The point, it seemed, was not to avoid samsara but to get into it directly, as long as you returned to the cushion next morning, hung over or fried. As he said in one of his few public statements about it, LSD was a kind of "super-samsara," and inasmuch as it heightened certain samsaric tendencies it could be a useful method.

About marijuana he was less tolerant. The main problem, he once told me, was that marijuana tended to "mimic meditation." This take led to a dramatic confrontation with a group of his earliest students. In the early seventies a tribe of hippies, known as the Pygmies, became students and were the first to colonize the undeveloped land that has since become known as Rocky Mountain Dharma Center. They cobbled together an odd assortment of living quarters—yurts, one-rooms, A-frames, a six-sided cabin. "At night the main entertainment tended to be kicking back, pouring a beer, smoking a joint," reported Barbara Stewart about that time in *The Vajradhatu Sun* (August/September 1991) "but a meeting ensued, a powerful and violent clash that would eventually mean the beginning of the end of the Pygmies' private commune. . . . Smoking marijuana, Rinpoche said, was lying to themselves, indulging in self-deception. They should burn both, marijuana and self-deception.

The Pygmies were taken aback, angry and confused. But only one person— call him Mike—fought back. Jim Lowry remembers this scene: 'Mike hit Rinpoche and Rinpoche hit Mike. It was violent, it was a huge eruption. Rinpoche threw a flowerpot—he missed Mike. Maggie screamed, 'Stop!' Rinpoche built a fire in the fireplace. 'Destroy self-deception,' he was saying. . . . It was tense but calm. . . . Everyone went and got dope and threw it in the fire. We were kind of chanting: 'Destroy self-deception, destroy self-deception'. . . . The first *dathun* [month-long group meditation] was a turning point, confirming the obvious, that this land was to be a meditation center and not an Eden-like Pygmy crafts commune."

Such was the powerful antidrug drift. As always, however, there were countercurrents. During the seventies and up to the present, a small number of committed Buddhist practitioners have used the sacrament in the context of formal practice. This was necessarily a secret use, harking back to the earliest tantric circles in India, where unlawful and taboo substances such as meat and wine were transformed into sacraments. This group was naturally self-selecting, composed mostly of practitioners experienced in both modalities, who found that, handled properly, psychedelics can be a useful skillful means. If the practitioner has the balance and moves to surf the psychedelic waves, the argument went, then the experience can be useful in one's *sadhana* [formal practice]. Myron J. Stolaroff, active in psychedelic research since 1960, is one of these Buddhist practitioners. "For myself," he wrote in *Gnosis* in 1993, "I found training in Tibetan Buddhist meditation a potent adjunct to psychedelic exploration. In learning to hold my mind empty, I became aware that other levels of reality would more readily manifest. It was only in absolute stillness . . . that many subtle but extremely valuable nuances of reality appeared. While I achieved this to some extent in ordinary practice, I found this effect to be greatly amplified while under the influence of a psychedelic substance. This in turn intensified my daily practice."

Such a claim will be outrageous to many—probably most—Buddhist practitioners. After all, the use of any intoxicants is proscribed by the precepts. And while Shaivite Hindu sadhus smoke ganja, and Christians drink wine, and Sufis (some at least) have been known to smoke hashish, Buddhists seem to have been a decidedly sober if not straight, square group. It's true that green tea, a powerful stimulant, is connected with Bodhidharma, and is used by Zen monks as a stimulant to ward off sleep during meditation. And alcohol also has a small but enduring place in Buddhist practice—Zen masters have exhibited a fondness for sake—and liquor is used ceremonially in tantric feasts, while *chang*, a potent Tibetan barley-beer, is consumed by monks and lay practitioners in tantric ceremonies (as well as for fun) throughout the Himalayas.

But what about psychedelics? Is it really the case that Buddhism, the one "major world religion" without a personal creator God, is lacking in a mind-altering or mind-opening sacrament? And even if it lacks such a sacrament today, has it always been so? Certain images in Buddhist texts suggest that this has not always been the case. The most glaring example is the existence of *amrita*, a drink or substance that is said to confer deathlessness or liberation. If this *amrita* is not an actual mind-altering substance or plant—what we would so crudely call a "drug"—is it "merely" a symbol? But even if it's a symbol, that still leaves the question: a symbol of what?

This question leads back to one of the greatest explorer-researcher-theorists of psychedelic lore: amateur ethnomycologist Gordon Wasson, who introduced the world to the magic psilocybin mushrooms of indigenous Mexico. When Wasson extended his exploration to other cultures, most notably India, he found compelling evidence that the mysterious soma of the Vedic hymns was, in fact, an infusion made from the psychedelic mushroom *Amanita muscaria*, or fly agaric, the sacramental basis for a shamanistic ur-religion, which he traced back to the late Ice Age in Siberia. Wasson had an antipathy to hippies and "Timothy Leary and his ilk," and so was uncomfortable with the term "psychedelic." He, Carl A. P. Ruck, and others, suggested the word *entheogen*, "god generated within," for the sacred plants that he felt lay behind the mysteries of the ancients.

Wasson's line of research exemplifies an ethnobotanical school of psychedelic research that was contemporaneous with—and obscured by—the sensationalistic and hysterical LSD furor of the sixties. But during the eighties this lineage of ethnobotany continued to be enriched by gifted academic botanists, such as Shultes at Harvard, and gifted amateurs like Wasson. The most interesting of these post-Wassonites, for our purpose at least, is one Scott Hajicek-Dobberstein, who published a fascinating paper, "Soma Siddhas and Alchemical Enlightenment: Psychedelic Mushrooms in Buddhist Tradition," in the *Journal of Ethnopharmacology*. Hajicek-Dobberstein argues that the Vedic soma cult—or something very similar to it—survived among the tantric Buddhist siddhas who lived in India from the eighth to the tenth century CE, and whose biographies are recounted in a twelfth-century Tibetan text, *The Legends of the Eighty-four Mahasiddhas.*

The most compelling evidence is found in the story of the siddha Karnaripa. His guru, Nagarjuna, instructed him to demonstrate his austerity by collecting only as much food for alms as he could balance on the head of a needle. Karnaripa returned with a large pancake balanced on the tip of a needle—a symbol, suggests Hajicek-Dobberstein, of the *Amanita muscaria*. More symbols are suggested, but the most convincing evidence is an exchange in which Nagarjuna says, "We need to eat the alchemical medicine." Karnaripa does so, and then spreads his spittle on a dead tree—which bursts in blossom—and then urinates in a pot. This behavior is taken as a sign of realization by Karnaripa's teacher. For Hajicek-Dobberstein, it is a "marker" of the presence of *amanita-soma* because drinking the urine of a shaman who has consumed *amanita* intensifies the potency of the mushroom and is a well-known practice among Siberians.

The possible use of *amanita* (or other mushrooms or plants) by siddhas also offers a possible solution to two thorny Tibetan etymological puzzles. The Tibetan name for cannabis, *So.Ma.Ra.Dza*, from the Sanskrit soma-raja, or "king of soma" can now be read as a linguistic trace of a long-forgotten tradition. The second puzzle involves the Tibetan translation of *amrita* (deathless) as *bDud. rTsi*. The word *rTsi* is "drink, juice," but *bDud* means "demon." How did the deathless drink of *amrita* become "demon juice" in Tibetan? In an unpublished paper, another amateur ethnobotanist, one K. Tendzin Dorje, retells the story of Vajrapani, who recovers the *amrita* that had been stolen by the demon Rahu. "Demon juice" may therefore refer to the *amrita* stolen by the demon Rahu. (I am indebted to Dr. Richard Kohn for this suggestion.)

Such speculative ethnobotanical Tibetan scholarship does not occur in a vacuum. It reflects the ethnobotanical bent of the current psychedelic revival. In place of the "chemical" intensities of acid, contemporary psychedelic explorers prefer the "organic" psychedelics or, to use Wasson's preferred word, "entheogens." These include the psilocybin mushrooms first discovered by Wasson, the peyote used by the Huichols of Mexico and the Native American Church, and the ayahuasca used by Amazonian shamans and ayahuasca circles and churches. All of these plants have coexisted for millennia with human beings, who have developed intricate rituals and beautiful ceremonies to use sacred plants safely and wisely.

The all-night Native American Church ceremony, for example, combines the discipline and mindfulness of a Zen ritual, the spontaneous song prayer of the Tantric *doha* tradition, and the compassion of the bodhisattva. I remember one night in a tepee in northern Montana, the clear mind of peyote glowing in the fire before the crescent-moon sand altar, the thump-thump-thump of water drum and gourd rattles keeping time with the ancient peyote songs—and it was clear as the dawning light that something close to this went on way back, possibly to the dawn of our human consciousness.

And why not into the future as well? We have much to learn from indigenous shamans. Both the Native American Church and the Brazilian ayahuasca churches have successfully grafted an ancient entheogenic practice onto Christianity. There is nothing to prevent this from happening with Buddhism as well. Indeed, Buddhism has demonstrated a genius for adapting—or mutating, in Professor Robert Thurman's phrase—to a wide range of cultures. In Tibet, this included a shamanistic culture. Whether or not the ancient siddhas used mushrooms or other alchemical substances, there is no reason why an ecologically informed American Buddhism cannot likewise draw from shamanistic earth-wisdom. Sacred plant sacraments could be offered as *amrita* in the context of a tantric feast, for the development of compassion and wisdom in our ravaged world. At least for the tantric lineages of Buddhism there is no limit to the skillful means available to a bodhisattva, which includes many teachings on transforming poison into nectar. As unlikely as it may seem, this devil juice may be just the antidote for the out-of-control materialism that is ravaging our planet.

One thing at least seems certain. Whatever the ancient or recent past history of psychedelic entheogens and Buddhism may be, the story is hardly over. As Hajicek-Dobberstein says, "Some contemporary non-orthodox Buddhist 'alchemists' find precedents in Mahasiddhas Nagarjuna and Aryadeva, who agreed, 'We need to eat the alchemical medicine'. . . Orthodox scholars may object but they can no longer 'Just Say No'" (1995).

PSYCHEDELIC EXPERIENCE AND SPIRITUAL PRACTICE:
A Discussion with Jack Kornfield ✇ Robert Forte

ROBERT FORTE: Is there a Buddhist point of view on psychedelics?

JACK KORNFIELD: No. Psychedelics are found rarely, if at all, in the Buddhist tradition, and generally would be lumped in the precepts under "intoxicants." In Zen, Vajrayana, and the Theravada traditions, there is very little mention of them and there is no traditional point of view about their use. It is important to understand that. What points of view we have come from the understanding of Buddhist masters and teachers based on contemporary experience.

The precept in Theravada Buddhism for dealing with intoxicants is one of the five basic training precepts for living a wise life: not to kill, not to steal, not to speak falsely, not to engage in sexual conduct that causes suffering, and lastly, to refrain from using intoxicants to the point of heedlessness, or loss of awareness. An alternate translation says not to use any intoxicant that removes the sense of attention or awareness. Then it is left up to the individual, as are all the precepts, to use these guidelines to become more genuinely conscious.

FORTE: Are the precepts understood similarly in the East and the West?

KORNFIELD: They are much more fundamental to practice in Asia. There you traditionally begin with *sila*, or compassionate action. This commitment to not cause harm is the foundation upon which all spiritual life is built. It is universally understood that you can't meditate properly after a day of lying and stealing! To free the heart from entanglement in greed, fear, hatred, and delusion, a non-violent relationship with the world must be developed. Out of this ground of compassionate conduct grows the whole range of other meditative and spiritual practices.

FORTE: How would that function?

KORNFIELD: By living a compassionate and harmonious life, you have already begun to quiet the mind and open the heart. Then the second domain is to train your heart through meditations, visualizations, and yogic practices that tame the wild monkey mind. It is the power of these practices that dissolve the barriers of the mind, the identification with our small sense of self. They unify our body, heart, and mind through concentration, and open us up to the vast inner realms.

The third domain is the arising of wisdom, or *prajna*. Based on a foundation of compassionate living and meditative training, consciousness becomes clear and open. Wisdom arises as we see the whole nature of how consciousness creates the world, and discover freedom and the great heart of a Buddha in the midst of it all. With this foundation of wise conduct and inner training, you have a context for the deepest wisdom and it's naturally integrated in your life. What has happened in the West seems to be a reversal of that.

FORTE: A reversal? What do you mean?

KORNFIELD: Many people who took LSD, mushrooms, and other psychedelics, often along with readings from the *Tibetan Book of the Dead,* or some Zen texts, had the gates of wisdom opened to a certain extent. They began to see that their limited consciousness was only one plane and that there were a thousand new things to discover about the mind. They saw many new realms, got new perspectives on birth and death, and discovered the nature of mind and consciousness as a field of creation, rather than the mechanical result of having a body, and even opened beyond the illusion of separation to the truth of the oneness of things.

But in order to maintain this vision they had to keep taking the psychedelics over and over. Even though there were some transformations from these experiences, they tended to fade for a lot of people. Following that some people said, "If we can't maintain the highs of consciousness that come through the psychedelics, let's see if there is some other way." And so they undertook various kinds of spiritual disciplines. They did kundalini yoga and *bastrika* breathing, or they did serious hatha yoga as a *sadhana*, raja yoga, mantra and concentration exercises, visualizations, or Buddhist practices as a way to get back to those profound and compelling states that had come through psychedelics.

FORTE: Would you say this thirst for experience is considered to be the cause of suffering in terms of the Buddha's second noble truth, i.e., that we suffer because of our desire or thirst for sensual or mental experience?

KORNFIELD: Psychedelics awakened in people not just a thirst, but a sense of the possibilities for exploring the mind and body — that they could live in a different way. Then they began to develop those sensitivities and those visions without repeatedly taking psychedelics by undertaking some spiritual discipline, yoga, or meditation. Finally, many people began to see that even their meditative practices wouldn't stabilize when the rest of their life wasn't included. They found it was necessary to take care with their actions in a way that was nonharming and compassionate. So we have gone on to discover that the root of fundamental change must be grounded in our ethical behavior and compassion, followed by a systematic inner training. Those are the supports for long lasting and integrated access to these transformative experiences.

FORTE: How important was LSD for importation of Eastern spiritual practices into the US during the sixties?

KORNFIELD: They were certainly powerful for me. I took LSD and other psychedelics at Dartmouth after I started studying Eastern religion. They came hand-in-hand as they did for many people. It is also true for the majority of Western Buddhist teachers, that they used psychedelics at the start of their spiritual practice. A number still do on occasion. But of the many hundreds of people I know who took psychedelics, only a few had radically transformative experiences, many others were greatly inspired, and a few were damaged. It is like winning the lottery. A lot of people play, and not so many people win big, but the potential is there.

FORTE: There is a story that when the Dalai Lama was asked if you could use drugs to attain enlightenment, he said, "I sure hope so." And when Zen master Seung Sahn was asked what he thought about using drugs to help in the quest for self-knowledge he said: "Yes, there are special medicines, which, if taken with the proper attitude, can facilitate self-realization." Then he added: "But if you have the proper attitude, you can take anything—take a walk, or a bath."

KORNFIELD: I have the utmost respect for the power of psychedelics. They have inspired and awakened possibilities in many people in really important ways. They have provided transformative experiences. In taking a tempered view of them, it does not mean that I do not have a lot of respect for them, and for the work that certain courageous researchers have done with them.

My sense from my own Buddhist training and from teaching traditional practice for many years is that people underestimate the depth of change that is required to transform oneself in spiritual life. True liberation requires a great perspective—called "a long enduring mind" by one Zen master. Yes, awakening comes in a moment, but living it, stabilizing it can take months, years, and lifetimes. The propensities or conditioned habits which we have are so deeply ingrained that even enormously compelling visions do not change them very much. Therefore, the practices of liberation taught by the Buddha, and other similar traditions, draw on many dimensions of life to help empower such a deep transformation. The possibility of human liberation is the center of these teachings. Liberation of the heart from greed, hatred, delusion, and liberation from all sense of separateness and fear. This is a very compelling possibility for humans.

To come to this level of illumination, inevitably one has to face the powerful forces in the heart and mind that bind us to "the body of fear," and causes of human suffering worldwide. When you have undertaken a deep spiritual practice of whatever kind, and I will include psychedelic experiences as part of that, you begin to encounter the roots of Greed with a capital "G," the most primal kinds of grasping; and Hatred, finding Hitler and Attila the Hun in your mind; and Delusion which manifests as the darkest blindness of confusion. We must learn to work with these forces and transform them in a way that leads to genuine liberation.

A lot of people use psychedelics in mindless or misguided ways, without much understanding. The spiritual context gets lost. It's like taking a synthetic mescaline pill and forgetting the two-hundred-mile desert walk and the months of prayer and purification the Huichols use to prepare for their peyote ceremony. Some modern explorers like Stan Grof and Ram Dass have a much greater sense

TEARS OF JOY Alex Grey, 2014

TIMELESS Mati Klarwein, 1968

THINGS THAT POP IN MY HEAD Ang Tsherin Sherpa, 2009

SPIRAL Bernard Maisner, 1984

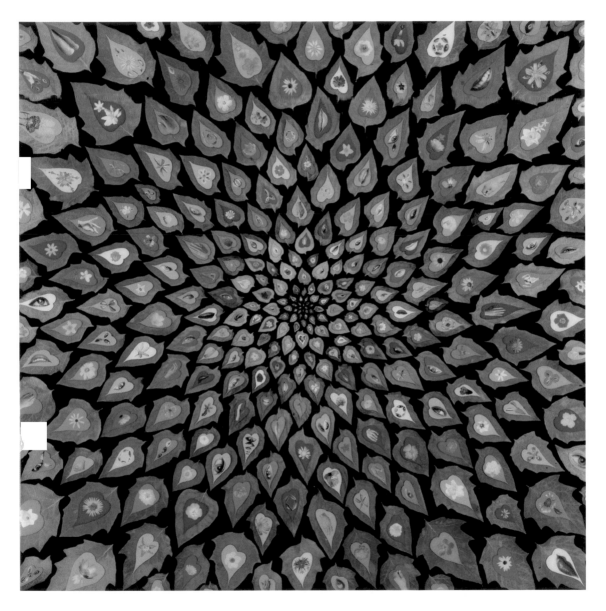

DATRONIC Fred Tomaselli, 1998

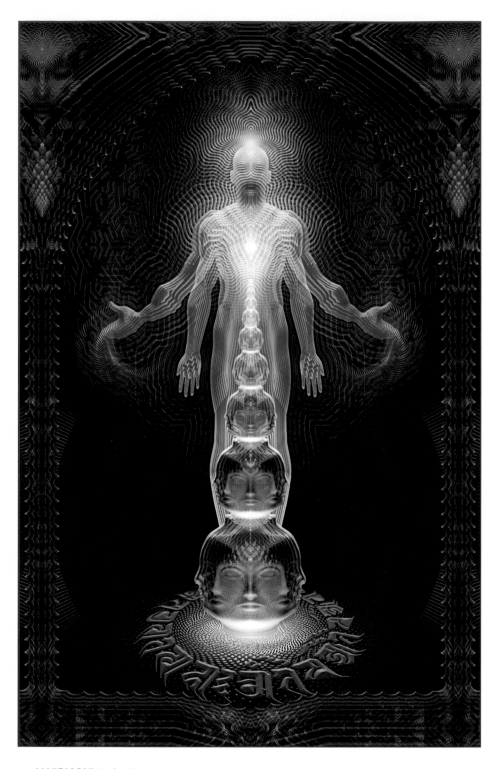

LIGHTSPEAK Luke Brown, 2013

ORDER WITH CHAOS LETTERS Allyson Grey, 2000

BLACK DIAMOND #1 Fred Tomaselli, 2000

of the power of the forces that one may confront. One needs to respect the depth of these experiences and make a conscious commitment to the full journey of spiritual change.

FORTE: Say more about the "journey."

KORNFIELD: Chogyam Trungpa Rinpoche once began a public talk in Berkeley by saying: "My advice to you is not to undertake the spiritual path. It is too difficult, too long, and is too demanding. I suggest you ask for your money back, and go home." He added, "This is not a picnic. It is really going to ask everything of you. So it is best not to begin. However," he said, "if you do begin, it is best to finish."

So if psychedelics were to be used in the spiritual journey they need a proper context, within a framework of ethics and inner training; they need a proper "launching pad," as John Lilly would call it.

FORTE: What about addiction to getting "launched?"

KORNFIELD: Even among the most conscious explorers of contemporary psychedelics, addiction and attachment has sometimes been a problem. Even more critical is the overly positive message about both the spiritual and the casual use of these drugs that has been adopted by quite a few people who could not handle them well at all. As many of us who have used psychedelics have discovered, it is not an easy practice. What matters from the point of view of this precept is to make their use nonhabitual (which probably means occasional). If one uses any substances, whether it is wine, marijuana, LSD, or mushrooms, this precept says to make that a conscious and careful part of your life. Without these precepts, anyone who even begins the journey will get lost or go off the track. You can not complete the journey until you get the basics right. This is really a very simple message.

Almost every system in the world that is assisted by substances, including the wide range of shamanism, exists in a context of purification.

FORTE: What are the purifications that might be applicable to a psychedelic experience today?

KORNFIELD: First, there is the purification of your actions, or *sila*. Following that, there are purifications of the body through yoga, breathwork, fasting, and other practices that allow your body to feel and to be open enough to touch these deeper levels and to integrate them. You can take a very powerful substance and even if you are physically a wreck, you can touch those deep places, but there will be a physical price to pay for it. There can be the burning of the kundalini from opening much too quickly. When your body is in tune and open, you can go to those places with much less of that burning and overwhelming physical disharmony that can come from it. It also allows the experience to be integrated. Without preparing the body, one can not hold those understandings.

Then there are the purifications of the heart and mind; that is, emotions and thoughts. For many this involves an emotional transformation which takes place by extending forgiveness and opening the heart, seeing the fears, angers, and memories that have been locked in and releasing them. There is the purification in the realm of thought: taking the crazed monkey mind and nonstop inner dialogue and beginning to train a stability of mind. This often involves working with mindfulness in a specific systematic way. But first you stabilize the mind. Most people find that happens with a long regular practice, using sitting meditation, mantra, visualization, or a hundred other ways. Once the mind is stabilized you can apply that clarity to discover the laws of the mind, or the laws of consciousness.

FORTE: This sounds like we are getting to the whole point of the journey, the real significant discovery. Where do you begin?

KORNFIELD: The point is to awaken to our natural inner freedom, our True Nature. To do this we must start where we are. In beginning to quiet the mind and open the heart you often encounter waves of desire, fear, anger, laziness, or restlessness. These are the preliminary hindrances to transformation. You learn how to use wise attention so that you don't become caught up or lost in them. As your body and mind become more open and purified, you take that ability to be balanced and less caught by these energies, and use this ability to enter other domains of consciousness.

Now, if you should enter a domain of pure light filled with love and ecstasy, you will have learned how to do it without getting too attached. You see it as part of the passing show. And you can go to the hell realms that arise within you with the same attitude. You become free in the realms of birth and death. You learn how to open to them without so much grasping and attachment. Here you learn not just the content of the various realms of consciousness, where psychedelics can also take you, but how to relate to it all wisely. If I were to put any sentence in this interview in capitals it would be that spiritual awakening is not about just visiting the many realms of heart, mind, and body, but learning how to relate to their content wisely, compassionately, and with real freedom.

On the subject of visions, one of my teachers, Ajahn Chah taught: "Though they have come about, do not take them seriously. Do not take anything as yourself—everything is only a vision or construction of the mind, a deception that causes you to desire, grasp, or fear. When you see such constructions, do not get involved. All unusual experiences and visions are of value to the wise person but harmful to the unwise. Keep practicing until you are not stirred by them."

FORTE: How can we understand the healing effect of psychedelic experience from the perspective of Buddhist psychology and meditation?

KORNFIELD: Healing takes place in a number of ways, but the most fundamental healing in Buddhist practice comes by bringing awareness to that which was twisted, knotted, or held in darkness in the body, feelings, or mind. Through systematic meditation practice one brings the power of compassion and mindfulness to these knots and the deepest patterns of holding open up. Without even doing a physical yoga, through sitting meditation, the deepest body release can occur. There are many patterns of mind in which we get entangled: beliefs, opinions, and views, all that leads us to hold onto our sense of self as separate. These too can be opened and healed.

Healing with psychedelics is much the same. Healing comes when you have a suitable and careful situation, and one's unconscious is opened by the psychedelics. Maybe you will relive a past trauma, or experience the pain that is held in your physical body from an accident, or an operation, or the tension from deeply stored anger or grasping comes into consciousness and begins to release. The healing effects come through the power of bringing into consciousness that which has been below the threshold of awareness. Part of the difficulty with psychedelics, and even with meditation at some points, is that it comes too quickly and people get overwhelmed. There is a danger that they will shut down immediately afterward. They will touch a place that is too fearful or too difficult. But there are healings that take place in that way on all those levels of body, feelings, and mind.

FORTE: A crucial aspect of both ancient wisdom and the new paradigm is that separateness is an illusion, a superficial level of reality, and that at a fundamental level, all things are connected. This is hard to understand on the sensory or intellectual level where experience suggests that things are separate. If psychedelics can take you to that place of essential unity, are they not a valuable tool in the development of a new paradigm that emphasizes wholeness?

KORNFIELD: Any tool or practice which can open the heart and show that we are not separate, that touches the realms of universal loving-kindness and universal compassion can be valuable. For some people, the use of psychedelics can open the mind and reveal that consciousness creates the world, that physical reality is created out of consciousness and not the opposite. It can show that reality can be filled with light and humor. It can show that there are realms of tremendous transcendent understanding, and realms of many different scales of time, eternally slow or eternally rapid. It can also open us to hell realms where there is extraordinary pain and seemingly no way out.

FORTE: It seems that something very powerful is required to show that this level of reality is not the only one, especially today in the West where we have developed such mastery over the material world.

KORNFIELD: I see psychedelics as having been enormously useful as an initial opening for people, and at certain stages it may be possible to use them again wisely, but with the constraints of *sila*. They can be easily abused if one is not careful about the set and setting. To explore some of this territory, Stan and Christina Grof and I offer annual retreats that integrate Holotropic Breathwork (much like psychedelic experience) and Buddhist meditation. Participants seem to really respond to this combination of practices.

FORTE: One of the best applications of the psychedelics in modern times may be in the work with people who are dying a little faster than the rest of us. Research with terminal patients indicates that the psychedelic experience illuminates the process of dying and lessens one's fear of it.

KORNFIELD: From what I know of this work it holds great potential, primarily for people who have not done a disciplined spiritual practice. In many ways spiritual practice is intended to prepare us to die. By going through a meditative death-rebirth process deliberately, we can dissolve the illusion of a separate self, access other realms of consciousness beyond our limited view, and learn to live more wisely because of that. If we have never learned that, perhaps psychedelics could assist us in preparing for death as it opened so many in the initial stages of spiritual practice. Whatever leads to opening the heart and mind and letting go is beneficial.

FORTE: At a meeting held at the Harvard Divinity School in 1985, psychologist Dan Brown brought up the distinction between ecstasy and enstasis in a discussion about psychedelics. Ecstasy would be the flight of the soul from the body, "the soul's ecstatic journey through the various cosmic regions," whereas yoga pursues enstasis, or the final concentration of the spirit and "escape from the cosmos" (Eliade, 1958). What do you think about this distinction with regard to psychedelic experience and meditation?

KORNFIELD: Buddhist meditation goes from enstasis to ecstasy. There exist some purely ecstatic practices in Buddhist meditation, but primarily they work not so much by turning up the volume, as by tuning the receiver. By training sacred attention you can awaken to the deepest levels of body and mind, and beyond that to the non-dual nature of reality. All the realms of consciousness become available through a powerfully tuned awareness. You can enter realms where the body fills with light, you experience tremendous rapture, and ecstasy, and are catapulted through all the realms of the heavens and hells.

FORTE: Do you think Buddhism and psychedelics will continue to intersect in the future?

KORNFIELD: I see psychedelics as one of the most promising areas of modern consciousness research. I would not be surprised if at some point there comes to be a useful marriage between some of these materials and a systematic training or practice that I have described. That marriage will have to be based on an understanding and respect for the ancient laws of karma, grounded in compassion, virtue, an open heart and a trained mind, and the laws of liberation. Given those, there might be some very fruitful combination.

BUDDHISM, SHAMANISM, AND THANGKA PAINTINGS
Claudia Müller-Ebeling and Christian Rätsch

UNLIKE BUDDHISM, shamanism is not a codified religion or belief system. It is an archaic technique to enter different states of consciousness in order to help and heal people. Techniques to enter trance may involve the use of psychoactive plants, or entheogens. This entrance to the "other world"—or, according to a shamanic worldview, to the "three worlds"—has mostly been shut down, destroyed, or demonized by established religions and political systems on a worldwide basis.

By nature, shamanism involves individuals contacting mystical realms. By means of trance, shamanism may lead talented individuals to a mystical union with the center of creation; in Western terms, to a *unio mystica*. No established religious hierarchy is interested in promoting access to the spiritual realm on an individual level. On the contrary, to have the monopoly over "communication to god" is the prevailing intrinsic motivation of such hierarchies. Every religion, even peaceful Buddhism, has made a great effort to suppress shamanism or any encounter with psychedelics. Of course, there are exceptions—which the biographies of Chogyam Trungpa Rinpoche, Ram Dass, and others demonstrate.

In their daily lives, shamans in Nepal—both men and women—are ordinary people. They work in the fields, cook and take care of their children; they are manual workers or craftsmen; they earn their living in the army or in factories; they are employees or engaged in their own small businesses. Yet these are people contacted by spirits or gods, and called on to help their communities with the power of healing. Only after his or her ability to enter trance states becomes obvious to the public does the prospective shaman learn and cultivate this natural gift. Following initiation experiences that occur mostly in early childhood, the shamans undergo an apprenticeship under the guidance of an experienced shaman. They call him or her guru or guruama. Only after successfully completing the teachings with their guru are they installed in public, to begin their duty as healers.

In Nepalese shamanism, accessing altered states by means of entheogens is still being practiced. Shamans (Nepalese: *Jhankri*) use a large variety of poisonous and mind-altering plants; some have yet to be identified by Western botanists. Some are well known, like *Papaver somniferum*, *Atropa belladonna*, or *Peganum harmala*; their use originated with shamans. Several are difficult to use and even dangerous, such as *Aconitum spp.* or *Datura spp.* Moreover, what is most spectacular and hitherto little known is the evidence that shamans use mushrooms, such as *Amanita muscaria* and different kinds of psilocybes (the latter as inhaled powders). During our research in Nepal—over an eighteen-year period—we recorded eighty-eight psychoactive plants ("traveling plants," as the shamans call them). When shamans are asked how many entheogens they know and use, they mention the idealized number of 108 plants and mushrooms, to be used as offerings, incense (*dhoopas*), remedies, or mind-altering agents.

The importance of these entheogens to shamans in Nepal has long been unrecognized by Western scholars; no previous study on Nepalese shamanism mentions the use of mind-altering plants. Physicians and psychiatrists, even ethnologists who did fieldwork among the Tamang or other tribes of Nepal, did not report the shamanic, medicinal, and recreational (and obvious) use of cannabis in the region. They especially overlooked the appreciation of cannabis by the traditional shamans.

Why is that? Factors include Western observers' lack of knowledge about local botanicals, their inability to recognize cultural uses, and their bias against psychedelics. Also, in the midst of dramatic shamanic healing sessions it is difficult to identify the plants used for smudging and smoking.

Since Mircea Eliade's well-known book *Archaic Techniques of Ecstasy*, was first published in 1951, many anthropologists believe that psychedelic shamanism is a kind of degeneration. His opinion was that a "true" shaman has a natural ability to enter the trance states without using entheogens. However, anthropological and ethnobotanical studies of the last decades, published in numerous books, show that, in terms of actual practice, Eliade may be wrong. These publications focus mainly on shamanism in Central and South America.

In general, Nepali shamans do not use entheogens for daily therapy. Only in special cases will a *jhankri* administer entheogens to a patient. They may prescribe datura—a plant sacred to Shiva—to people who are mentally confused or disturbed as a kind of homeopathic medication, using a preparation with high pharmacological action. (The concept of homeopathy is to treat an illness with something that causes the same symptoms, a practice found in many indigenous cultures.) *Jhankris* use entheogens to activate and enhance their own healing power. They also use them in precarious moments, such as when they struggle to find out why someone is seriously ill, or to restore a patient's life.

Jhankris seek a quiet place in nature where they can be alone and are able to connect with the magical properties of animals and plants. This kind of meditation in nature is called *gupha*. In these situations they may use psychoactive plants, whether ingested, smoked, or used as *dhoopas*, to regain their healing power, or *shakti*. With the help of mind-altering substances they are able to leave the path of daily routine and travel through the three worlds where they get insights and find hidden sources, remedies, or other tools for healing.

The shamans in Nepal see entheogens as plant teachers, just as the *ayahuasqueros* in Amazonia do. They "consult" them, to cross the boundaries from their individual human limitations to the realms of animals, plants, and even minerals. This may sound fantastic, but it means nothing more than to experience being actively part of the whole circle of life—the core of our existence. To heal means to bring isolated parts back into balance. Only those who have experienced the dissolving of the boundary between life and death and between different forms of life are able to heal. The psychedelic experience enables one to cross these unknown boundaries as needed. Shamans also smoke ganja (cannabis) for relaxation after exhausting *chintas* (healing sessions) which may take, in serious cases, a couple of nights in a row.

The thangka is at the heart of the encounter between Buddhism and psychedelic plants. Thangkas are paintings of tempera, gold, silver, and pigments derived from minerals such as lapis lazuli (blue), coral (red), or malachite (green). They are painted on canvas and sewn into brocade borders, so that they can easily be rolled and stored, and are traditionally exposed only on special occasions or during rituals.

Thangkas are paintings that represent the iconography of Buddhism, and are considered tools for meditation. Both the production and contemplation of a thangka help one to visualize the universal principles of life, represented in Buddhist (and Hindu) deities, bodhisattvas, and other beings. Looking deeply, we see that thangkas are one of the few remaining vestiges of shamanism in Buddhism.

However, many Buddhists do not want to acknowledge the shamanic origin of thangka painting, nor are they inclined to accept that some of their rituals and ritual objects were originally shamanic.

A widespread misconception places the origin of the iconography of shamanic Buddhism in Tibet—a conviction reflected in the many exhibitions of thangkas in museums throughout the world as well as in books. Visitors to the bookshops or the numerous thangka galleries of Kathmandu will have the same impression. Collections are described as "Tibetan Thangka Treasures" or "Thangkas from Tibet." Eighty percent of books on the culture of the Himalayas emphasize Tibetan thangkas in the context of Tibetan Buddhism. Only twenty percent are dedicated to Nepalese cultures and even less to specific ethnic groups in Nepal such as the Newari, Tamang, Kirati, or Gurung people.

Given the historical evidence, this well-established idea that thangkas are Tibetan in origin proves to be incorrect. This revision is called for by early sources on the activities of Nepalese thangka painter Anige (1245-1306). He was invited to Tibet by his sponsor Phagpa (1235-1280), with the task of generating architectural projects for the Mongol leader Kublai Khan. The renowned thangka of the Green Tara from the Cleveland Museum of Art is attributed to Anige, and there is also reference to Anige having taught Tibetans the art of thangka-painting. Many thangkas from the thirteenth century bear traces of his stylistic impact. The early thangkas differed a great deal from what is typically known as Tibetan, in style as well as content. A close look reveals Hindu or Hindu-Buddhist iconography. Anyone familiar with the typical styles of the ethnic groups such as the Newari or Tamang will see traces of these styles in the many so-called Tibetan thangkas sold in Kathmandu or featured in exhibition catalogues. Moreover, every possible ethnic style-mixture is evident, such as works of a Tibetan thangka painter, painted in Newari style, imitating Tibetan style.

There is little question that the shamans of Nepal invented the art of thangka painting. Even today, there are many shamans who paint thangkas. The oldest known thangka specimens clearly feature the typical Newari style of thangka painting. This is also the case in the well-known Green Tara dated to the last third of the thirteenth century, as well as in many other specimens mentioned in the exhibition catalogue of early Tibetan thangka-painting *Sacred Visions: Early Paintings from Central Tibet* (Kossak and Casey Singer, 1998). If one is familiar with the Newari features of thangka painting one clearly recognizes these in the many motifs that predominate in the Kathmandu valley to the present day.

Traditionally reserved for apprentice shamans, thangkas depict the worlds that shamans enter. Most thangkas are divided into three parts, presenting the topography of shamanic journeys through the three worlds. In the center, the main figure is depicted—Buddhas or bodhisattvas, or the center of a mandala. This is the middle-world, the world of all existent beings. This is also the present moment. It is from here that shamans communicate with the principles of life, represented by a pantheon of deities.

The iconography of thangka paintings is incredibly rich and complex, and further reveals their Nepalese origins. For example, in the representation of the Green Tara attributed to Anige, one sees the so-called *sirpech*—a feature we also find in the architecture of the Sundhoka palace in Bhaktapur, one of the three royal cities of the Kathmandu valley. It is a bronze arch, laced with gold, decorating the entrance to the courtyard of the palace. In the top center we see the mythical Garuda-bird, represented with a snake in his beak. Garuda is the vehicle of the Hindu god Vishnu. Garuda is also the force that the shamans of the tribes (classified by ethnically different language groups) of Nepal face and visualize to the north, in ritual—their backs being protected by Rahula, the god of the south, and his wall of flames. To their left they visualize Kali and to their right, Shiva—their main god who existed long before Hinduism. Shiva's archetypal features were later molded into the form of the god of ecstasy and asceticism.

The snake is a holy animal in Nepal. Nagaraj and Nagarani are the royal couple of cobras and water snakes, representing fertility of water and earth. Without them, no soil could be cultivated in Nepal; snakes guarantee rain and growth of crops. However, snakes can also be dangerous to humankind. Garuda is the only creature that is able to cope with their poison. The mythical bird Garuda, with the ability to walk the earth and fly to the skies, combines the three worlds: under, middle, and upper-world. He helps the shaman to travel from the underworld to the upper-world, passing through the middle-world, which is the realm of all existing beings in our world. To be able to do that, even in very dangerous circumstances, and to defeat any deadly poison, shamans need the assistance of Garuda. As depicted on the *sirpech*, both ends of the snake lead into ornamental volutes and enter on both sides into a mouth of the mythical creature Makara.

Makara owes its existence to the *garwal*—a crocodile that still lives in some rivers of northern India. The crocodile is also important in the shamanic world. The crocodile is one of four animals that support the shield of the world—seen as a tortoise—in an endless ocean, which is also, according to shamanic knowledge, the cradle of life.

In 1999, while doing our research on shamanism in Nepal, we discussed a seventeenth-century thangka now in Basel with two contemporary shamans, Indra Doj Gurung and Maile Lama. The painting represents Srimati Devi (Tibetan: Palgyi Lhamo) (Gerd-Wolfgang Essen and Tsering Tashi Thingo: *Die Götter des Himalaya*, 1989). We were surprised by the shamanic interpretation of this painting, which may appear to be a rather cruel depiction to Westerners. It shows a divine being riding on a mule across a lake filled with blood and parts of human bodies. The *jhankri* called it a healing thangka and emphasized its shamanic content.

They identified the divinity as Bhairung—not a name but an invocation, which shamans use to identify the wrathful aspects of Shiva and Parvati, thus of Bhairab and Kali, represented as one person (in Sanskrit, Ardhanarishvara). "This divinity rides through the middle-world," the shamans Indra Doj Gurung and Maile Lama told us. "This world is ruled by the destructive energies of mankind. Bhairab/Kali uses all weapons to fight these greedy and needy energies. He/she destroys what is out of balance in order to restore a peaceful world."

In thangkas, the lower part of the painting often depicts a lake or area of minerals. This is the underworld, the past, where the source of an illness is hidden. *Jhankris* say that this is the most dangerous world to travel to, but also the one they like most. "It is a fluorescent world of shiny minerals, of water and animals which look like plants." There is no ocean in the Himalayas, only rivers, streams, and lakes. But shamans describe what an underwater world looks like. In the underworld they encounter dangerous forces, demons, who have abducted parts of the soul of an ill person. Shamans do not destroy these forces since they are part of the world. They deal with them to establish a balance. For that reason they have to be good psychologists; they have to know the characteristics of the force that holds pieces of the health of their patient in hand. The better they know the demon, the better they can convince it to release the soul.

The sky with the sun, moon and stars, the birds of prey, the mythical Garuda, and deities, represent the upper world. This is depicted in the upper part of many thangkas. The upper world represents the future. It is to this world that the shamans must travel, often with the use of psychoactive plant preparations, to find solutions in life and death cases. It is often reported that a shaman will have died during his or her first experience of initiation. Appearing to the outer-world as dead, seriously ill, or mentally disturbed, they were in fact crossing the borders between life and death, present, past, and future—traveling the three worlds for the sake of others. The story behind Buddhist thangka art is primarily a shamanic one—a fact which has remained hidden, until now.

A BUDDHIST-PSYCHEDELIC HISTORY OF ESALEN INSTITUTE
Interview with Michael Murphy and George Leonard
Allan Badiner

ALLAN BADINER: In the past, we've talked about Aldous Huxley and Alan Watts being at Esalen. Some of the previously unknown tales were told, like when a young Hunter Thompson chased a nude gang of S&M motorcyclists out of the baths with barking Dobermans. Beyond the periods of a frequent sea of faces with red eyes in the lodge, what, essentially, is the psychedelic history of Esalen?

MICHAEL MURPHY: Esalen was hatched conceptually and physically in 1961. In 1962, the idea that drove me, and my partner Dick Price, was the vision that we could have a cross-cultural, cross-disciplinary place for exploration of integral transformation.

BADINER: What is integral transformation?

MURPHY: It is the result of long-term practices that may include philosophical inquiry, contemplative practice, psychotherapy, somatic education, and the martial arts. Integral means to integrate mind, body, heart, and soul, and transformative means to aim at positive change.

BADINER: What inspired the vision to create Esalen? Were psychedelics involved?

MURPHY: I'd been influenced primarily by Sri Aurobindo, who saw human nature as part of cosmic evolution and participating in the awakening of the latent divinity in all things. In framing the language about Esalen, we got considerable help from the last essays of Aldous Huxley, who was writing about human potentialities. His language was more accessible than Aurobindo's. So, our first brochure was titled "Human Potentialities," and the first seminar was led by Willis Harman and Jim Fadiman.

Fadiman was getting his PhD at Stanford, studying psychedelic drugs. Willis Harman was in charge of an institute up there with Myron Stolaroff, researching psychedelics. But when we hatched the institute, I hadn't had a psychedelic drug experience. My path had been, and still is, meditation.

BADINER: And Dick Price?

MURPHY: Dick had come in his own way to this partly through personal upheaval and partly through Eastern philosophy. Many of the philosophers of transformation like Anton Wilson—and later, an early Ronnie Laing—and Stan Grof already had a shamanistic perspective, and saw some forms of psychosis as a way forward.

BADINER: So while Esalen had significant psychedelic origins, you weren't there yet?

MURPHY: I was not impelled by any knowledge of or interest in psychedelics, but once we started, there it was. It was there, first of all, among the first famous figures who came here—like Aldous Huxley. In Mexico, he gave me Sandoz laboratory LSD and his wife Laura was my sitter. We did it in such a way that it was perfectly legal.

BADINER: Speaking of legal, what legal conditions did the ascendancy of drugs here create?

MURPHY: We had to clarify our legal status, because it became a great issue. We went to the head of the Food and Drug Administration [FDA] in Northern California twice in 1963 and 1964 because Willis Harman suggested we get straight about our responsibility. People were coming in and out of Esalen stoned and possibly selling stuff. So, we became very clear what our responsibilities were.

Under the Second Amendment of the Constitution, an innkeeper or a hotel person can't just come in and search your room. They have no right to do that. Freedom from that kind of search is a fundamental right. So, the head of the FDA twice told me, "Your responsibility is in the dining room, and on the public grounds." Now, while we didn't go around giving blood tests, we prohibited and actively stopped any trading in illegal drugs. Esalen has been in business thirty-eight years and has never been in trouble with the law about drugs because we've obeyed the law. But, there were occasions when I would come out and look at the audience, and by the expanded eye pupils, knew that half of them were stoned while they listened reverently to this or that program leader. But we abided by the law.

BADINER: Who were some of the psychedelic figures of early Esalen?

MURPHY: Gerald Heard, partly a mentor to Huxley and the furthest out in a group that included Swami Prabhavananda, Christopher Isherwood, and Igor Stravinsky. Heard was attempting to relate the expansion of human consciousness to the world's evolution. At the time, he was giving LSD to Clare Boothe Luce. I made my decision to start Esalen after listening and talking to Gerald in his Santa Monica home.

Humphry Osmond, who invented the word "psychedelic" [psyche—the psyche, delic—opening] taught seminars here. In 1964, Tim Leary came here with Dick Alpert (Ram Dass). There was a crazy night here with Dick Price, Bernie Gunther, Erica Weston, me, Ram Dass, draped in sheets, walking around on LSD. Stan Grof came here with Virginia Satir in '65. He was doing LSD experiments in Prague, and ended up living here for fourteen years. John Lilly arrived about that time. Claudio Naranjo was very important to us, as was Mike Harner, who brought Carlos Castaneda—who wrote part of his first book at Esalen. And of course, Alan Watts.

BADINER: So, as you explored this larger territory of the human potential, psychedelics was part of the package from the beginning.

MURPHY: They came with the territory. Marijuana, LSD, peyote, mescaline, morning glory seeds. Later there came ayahuasca and psilocybin mushrooms. Much later came the designer drugs, such as MDMA, 2CB, and others.

BADINER: At this stage, early in the game, is there a relationship to Buddhism? Of the people you mentioned, is there a double track going at all?

MURPHY: For some, but not all. For Alan Watts, it was Buddhism, of course. For Aldous Huxley, it was the Vedanta. To Harner and to Carlos Castaneda, it was shamanism.

We had a seminar with Willis Harman and James Fadiman. And shortly thereafter, I took my first psychedelic trip. I got into this extraordinary laughing thing that, you know, people have, and it went on for a long time. It has happened to me again and again in very intense meditation when I confront just the utter hilarity of existence. I had to leave a *sesshin* at San Francisco Zen Center once, because I couldn't control it. Along with the laughing, another significant experience stands out as being common to both modalities: a simple movement of the heart. People who were perhaps less than good looking—even homely—became utterly radiant, shining with their inner beauty. What could be more luminous?

It's a quality of attention, that with practice, I have managed to achieve without drugs. The gift of meditation is that you quiet the mind and you notice. Esalen became a place to sort out and bring forth to the world the issues relating to all of this.

BADINER: So you are not an advocate of psychedelic use?

MURPHY: My commitment that I share with George is to long-term integral transformative practice, without psychedelics, involving physical practices, psychological work, contemplative practice, and education of the whole person. My bias is apparent in my book, *The Future of the Body*. Tim Leary criticized it. He said, "My God, there's not a single chapter on psychedelics in there." And it is in a sense a shortcoming. But it does reflect my bias.

BADINER: George, you have described your psychedelic experiences in your books *Walking on the Edge of the World* and *The End of Sex.*

GEORGE LEONARD: When I started coming down to Esalen, I began exploring altered states of consciousness. That was one of the big ideas—to see this ultimate reality, this non-dual state. We were having a talk in Esalen's Big House, and I was asking Michael questions—maybe interviewing him for a big *Look* magazine piece on human potential. Michael told me about the state of being where you're in touch with everything at the same time and so forth. And I said, "How can I experience that?" And Michael said, "Well, of course, meditation." Well, that takes a long, long time. And then he said kindly, "There's a lot of people who are now doing it a shorter, faster way through plants and chemicals like LSD." And of course, I had heard of LSD. And I said, "Well, maybe I'll try it." After all, I'm a journalist, and I have to go wherever the story is.

BADINER: Where did it take you? Was it a good trip?

LEONARD: Everything was exactly the way it had been before except much, much, much more so. I did have some strange hallucinations, but mostly it was just intense realism—the quality that cannot be expressed in words. Everything was utterly real. It was Plato's chair—the absolute ideal chair where everything was perfect.

BADINER: In your journalistic explorations, did the story take you to the Buddha?

LEONARD: I went to Zen Center, Tassajara, and Green Gulch to practice on numerous occasions. I knew more about Buddhism at that time, and I was more of a Buddhist than I was a Christian. But I was not a regular practitioner. I found the psychedelic way very valuable and I realized there are other forms of reality, or "Another Reality." But also that there must be a better way to do it than slamming through the wall. There must be a better way than drugs to do it.

BADINER: What would you say to someone twenty years old who had just done a retreat at Green Gulch and was now considering taking mushrooms or ayahuasca or something similar? What advice would you offer this person?

LEONARD: Well, I'm fairly conservative on it. First of all, I'm very concerned about possible brain damage with many psychedelics. Now that we know more about the subtlety of brain chemistry and brain structure and so forth, I'd give words of caution. And then the second thing I would say is, be damn sure what you have is very pure and that you have good circumstances.

MURPHY: People ask me from time to time. I say, "First, I look at what the whole psychedelic culture has produced, and not produced. Has it brought forth a

Buddha or Ramana Maharshi? Or an Aurobindo? Or a Ramakrishna? Or any saint, or great realized mystic like St. Teresa or St. John of the Cross? It hasn't produced that yet. All I have seen through the Esalen window and meeting many of the psychedelic leaders is, at best, openings or illuminations that have led people to an ongoing path. My big fear about the drugs is when they are used in a trivial way, they reinforce the quick fix habits of our culture . . . the school of fast, easy, and cheap. And—

LEONARD: And blow your mind.

MURPHY: And blow your mind. The patience required for this other drugless transformative practice, as we conceive it, opens you to such beauty and depth. This is what I wish the world knew more about. And I say, "Thank God for these great Buddhist teachers, for these Zen Centers like Richard Baker is creating." And for the other practices we've seen here at Esalen. Psychedelics can be just another distraction.

BADINER: Has the psychedelic culture survived at Esalen?

MURPHY: To some extent. But often in the form of an attractive nuisance or a *trompe l'oeil*, when they compete with the long-term and more subtle practices. Nondrug programs at Esalen have survived because they are the fittest. What I think will happen over time is that these drugs will have their place as initiatory agents with the right set and setting. We're developing a culture of consciousness connoisseurs that range from very high connoisseurs to, you know, the people who are just getting on the path.

BADINER: Has meditation, as a practice, grown in importance at Esalen?

MURPHY: Yes. Esalen has a beautiful meditation zendo and we are planning to build a new and larger hall to balance the power of the new baths. We're asking Richard Baker Roshi to help us, because he really has an amazing aesthetic sense, and he's designed three world-class centers. The Buddhists have great aesthetics, I believe, for accessing direct contemplative practice. For Esalen, Zen particularly has emerged as a primary form of Buddhist practice because it's stripped down and relates more to the kind of awareness practices we've promoted, whether it's out of Gestalt or the many other forms of body-mind awareness practiced here.

LEONARD: I'm probably more influenced by Zen than I might think, because my wife Annie lived for six months in Mt. Baldy under Suzuki Roshi, and also a year and a half at the Lama Foundation in New Mexico. You can't escape Buddhism.

BADINER: Who are some of the other psychedelic characters that found Buddhism inescapable?

MURPHY: Alan Watts. I have never met a more generous person than Alan in terms of praising people and enjoying life and everything. My guru said no sex, so I was a virgin until I was thirty-two, but here we have Alan writing a book about mysticism and sex and saying drugs are another way in. He was ahead of the curve by about ten years. He was even ahead of the beatniks. He was not a celebrant of long-term contemplative practice, but he was a glorious human being. Alan would come down here and stay in the Big House. He led his first seminar here in January 1962. So before I got into gear to create a brochure and build a program, he was already one of the marvelous characters at the beginning, along with Abraham Maslow, Aldous Huxley, and Gerald Heard. After all the trips; the eye openers; the jaunts down the primrose path; there is, as Jack Kornfield puts it, the laundry. We all come back to our breath—to the need to quiet and concentrate the mind. Esalen has always been a place of encounter—between Buddhism, psychedelics, and all the worlds in between.

SHADOW PATHS ☉ Peter Matthiessen

In 1959, in the jungles of Peru, I would experiment with *yagé*, or *ayahuasca*, a hallucinogen of morbid effect used by shamans of the Amazon tribes to induce states that we called "supernatural," not because they transcend the laws of nature but because they still elude the grasp of formal science. (Most hallucinogens are derivatives of wild plants—mushrooms, cactus, a morning glory, many others— used for sacred purposes the world over; the ancients' soma may have been made from a poisonous mushroom of the genus *Amanita*.) Though frightening, the experience made clear that this family of chemicals (the phenol alkaloids) might lead to another way of seeing, and not in the slow labor of ascetic discipline but in cool efficiency and speed, as in flight through air. I never saw drugs as a path, far less as a way of life, but for the next ten years, I used them regularly—mostly LSD but also mescaline and psilocybin. The journeys were all scarring, often beautiful, often grotesque, and here and there a blissful passage was attained that in my ignorance I took for religious experience: I was a true believer in my magic carpet, ready to fly as far as it would take me. In 1961, in Thailand and Cambodia, on my way to an expedition in New Guinea, I experimented with a raw peasant form of heroin (sold to me as "opium") that frightened me to death, or a point close to it, one hollow night in an ancient hotel at the edge of black jungle and the silhouetted ruins of Angkor Wat. After a first ecstatic rush, I was stricken, paralyzed, unable to get my breath; with no one to call to, unable to call, I imagined that the End had come in this dead silent room under slow fans. Returning home a few months later, I treated drugs with more respect, working seriously with a renegade psychiatrist who was making bold, early experiments in the use of the hallucinogens in therapy. My companion was a girl named Deborah Love, who was adrift on the same instinctive search.

The search may begin with a restless feeling, as if one were being watched. One turns in all directions and sees nothing. Yet one senses that there is a source for this deep restlessness; and the path that leads there is not a path to a strange place, but the path home. ("But you are home," cries the Witch of the North. "All you have to do is wake up!") The journey is hard, for the secret place *where we have always been* is overgrown with thorns and thickets of "ideas," of fears and defenses, prejudices and repressions. The Holy Grail is what Zen Buddhists call our own "true nature;" each man is his own savior, after all.

> The fact that many a man who goes his own way ends in ruin means nothing. . . . He must obey his own law, as if it were a daemon whispering to him of new and wonderful paths. . . . There are not a few who are called awake by the summons of the voice, whereupon they are at once set apart from the others, feeling themselves confronted with a problem about which the others know nothing. In most cases it is impossible to explain to the others what has happened, for any understanding is walled off by impenetrable prejudices. "You are no different from anybody else," they will chorus, or, "there's no such thing," and even if there is such a thing, it is immediately branded as "morbid.". . . He is at once set apart and isolated, as he has resolved to obey the law that commands him from within "His own law!" everybody will cry. But he knows better: it is the law. . . . The only meaningful life is a life that strives for the individual Realization—absolute and unconditional—of its own particular law. . . . To the extent that man is untrue to the law of his being . . . he has failed to realize his life's meaning.
>
> The undiscovered vein within us is a living part of the psyche; classical Chinese philosophy names this interior way "Tao," and likens it to a flow of water that moves irresistibly towards its goal. To rest in Tao means fulfillment, wholeness, one's destination reached, one's mission done; the beginning, end, and perfect realization of the meaning of existence innate in all things.
>
> –Jung, 1954

This passage from Jung was the first hard clue to the nature of my distemper. I was sitting in a garden in the mountains of Italy when I read it, and I was so excited that for the first and only time in all my life I actually yelled and jumped out of my chair: this searching was not morbid after all!

Not that D and I considered ourselves "seekers:" we were embarrassed by such terms, and shied from people who employed them. We read and talked and read again, but what we needed was a teacher and a discipline. In those days, instant gurus were turning up as thick as bean sprouts, but true teachers were very hard to find. Finally D asked me to introduce her to the hallucinogens. I gave her mescaline on an autumn night of wind and rain.

On her first drug trip, D freaked out; that is the drug term, and there is no better. She started to laugh, and her mouth opened wide and she could not close it; her armor had cracked, and all the night winds of the world went howling through. Turning to me, she saw my flesh dissolve, my head become a skull—the whole night went like that. Yet she later saw that she might free herself by living out the fear of death, the demoniac rage at one's own helplessness that drug hallucinations seem to represent, and in that way let go of a life-killing accumulation of defenses. And she accepted the one danger of the mystical search: there is no way back without doing oneself harm. Many paths appear, but once the way is taken, it *must* be followed to the end.

And so, with great courage, D tried again, and sometimes things went better. I remember an April afternoon in 1962, when we had taken LSD together. She came out onto the terrace of a country house and drifted toward me, down across the lawn. D had black hair and beautiful wide eyes; in the spring breeze and light of flowers, she looked bewitched. We had been quarreling in recent days, and recriminations rose, tumbling all over one another in the rush to be spoken, yet as we drew near, the arguments aired so often in the past rose one by one and passed away in silence. There was no need to speak, the other knew to the last word what would be said. Struck dumb by this telepathy, our mouths snapped shut at the same instant, then burst into smiles at the precise timing of this comic mime of our old fights; delighted, we embraced and laughed and laughed. And still not one word had been spoken; only later did we discover that all thoughts, laughter, and emotions had been not similar *but just the same, one mind, one Mind*, even to this: that as we held each other, both bodies turned into sapling trees that flowed into each other, grew together in one strong trunk that pushed a taproot deeper and deeper into the ground.

And yet, and yet . . . an "I" remained, aware that something-was-happening, aware even that something-was-happening because of drugs. At no time did the "I" dissolve into the miracle.

Mostly D went on long, gray journeys, plagued by fear of death. I had bad trips, too, but they were rare; most were magic shows, mysterious, enthralling. After each—even the bad ones—I seemed to go more lightly on my way, leaving behind old residues of rage and pain. Whether joyful or dark, the drug vision can be astonishing, but eventually this vision will repeat itself, until even the magic show grows boring; for me, this occurred in the late 1960s, by which time D had already turned toward Zen.

Now those psychedelic years seem far away; I neither miss them nor regret them. Drugs can clear away the past, enhance the present; toward the inner garden, they can only point the way. Lacking the temper of ascetic discipline, the drug vision remains a sort of dream that cannot be brought over into daily life. Old mists may be banished, that is true, but the alien chemical agent forms another mist, maintaining the separation of the "I" from true experience of the One.

A SURVEY OF THE ENTHEOGENS ℮ Robert Jesse

Introduction

RELIGIOUS PRACTICES THROUGHOUT HISTORY have relied on certain psychoactive plants, as in the Eleusinian Mysteries of ancient Greece, Amazonian shamanism, and the peyote road of the Native American Church. As these plants were rediscovered and new substances were synthesized in the last century, they were mostly explored outside traditional contexts. In 1979 a group headed by classicist Carl A. P. Ruck sought a new name for this class of psychoactives. By that time, Ruck's group declared, the word "psychedelic" had become so contaminated by association with "deviant or revolutionary groups" and "the pop culture of the 1960s" that it had become "incongruous to speak of a shaman's taking a 'psychedelic' drug." The group proposed the term "entheogen" (from the Greek, *entheos*, god within).

In contrast to drugs such as alcohol, cocaine, and heroin, some of the entheogens, such as psilocybin, have virtually no addictive risk or physiological toxicity. What follows is a survey of the main entheogens.

Peyote

Peyote, a small, spineless cactus, contains the psychoactive chemical mescaline. Peyote has been used in Mesoamerica for at least 2,000 years and is still used sacramentally by the Huichol Indians of Mexico. Contemporary Huichol ceremonies are said to closely resemble pre-Columbian Mexican peyote rites little influenced by the Spanish Christian missionaries following the Conquest.

Beginning around 1880, ceremonial peyote use in the southwestern United States merged with Christian belief in some indigenous families in groups, evolving into ceremonial forms very distinct from those of the Mesoamericans. Since then, numerous US government actions have alternately prohibited and supported Native American use of peyote. The legal question appears to have been resolved by a 1994 federal law, the American Indian Religious Freedom Act Amendments, which requires all fifty states to accommodate the traditional, ceremonial use of peyote by American Indians.

In its report on the 1994 legislation, a US House of Representatives committee found that "peyote is not injurious," and that the "spiritual and social support provided by the Native American Church (NAC) has been effective in combating the tragic effects of alcoholism among the Native American population" (HR 103-675 1994:7). Occasional factionalism notwithstanding, it appears that the NAC has had a unifying and peace-promoting influence among Native American groups. Estimates of the number of peyote religion practitioners in the US range from 250,000 to as many as 400,000.

Psilocybin Mushrooms

"Mushroom stone" artifacts found in Guatemala and southeastern Mexico date religious mushroom use as far back as 1000 BCE. The Spanish conquerors reported *teonanacatl*, or "sacred mushrooms," to be of deep importance to indigenous religious life; their use continues to the present in some areas. In 1955, the ethnomycologist R. Gordon Wasson rediscovered the use of psilocybin-containing mushrooms among indigenous peoples in Oaxaca, Mexico. His 1957 *LIFE* magazine report on the nighttime mushroom ceremony of *curandera* Maria Sabina sparked Western interest in archaic and chemically assisted religious practices.

Ayahuasca

The name *ayahuasca* (also *hoasca*, *yagé*, *caapi*) describes "teas" or infusions made from combinations of Amazonian botanicals. The best-known form of ayahuasca is made from the vine *Banisteriopsis caapi*, containing monoamine oxidase (a digestive enzyme) inhibitors, and a bush, *Psychotria viridis*, containing the potent hallucinogen N,N-dimethyltryptamine (DMT). These entheogenic preparations are thought to be extremely ancient tools of Amazonian shamanism.

In the early part of this century, some Amazonian ayahuasca practitioners in Brazil migrated to the cities, continuing their old practices and blending them with Western beliefs. Out of this grew syncretic ayahuasca-using religions, most prominently the Santo Daime, founded around 1940, and the União do Vegetal (UDV), founded in 1961. Congregations drink the tea during services, usually held twice a month and for special observances.

UDV services, which combine contemplation, music, and instructive discourse, run about four hours. Santo Daime services often last all night, employing ritual music and dance. Each group has congregations in several countries in the Americas, Europe, and Asia. The Brazilian government granted permission, provisionally in 1986 and permanently in 1992, for the religious use of ayahuasca and its constituent plants.

India's Soma

One of the oldest texts known, the Rig-Veda, praises a mind-altering substance called *soma*. Of its 1,028 Sanskrit hymns, some 120 are devoted to extolling the virtues of soma and soma preparations; additional positive references are scattered throughout the other hymns. The identity of this revered plant was lost thousands of years ago. In 1968, Gordon Wasson published his research (in a splendid, leather-bound volume titled *Soma: Divine Mushroom of Immortality*) identifying soma as the psychoactive mushroom *Amanita muscaria*. While other scholars have proposed alternative psychoactive plants as candidates for the forgotten soma, the key point remains that an entheogen was central to a seminal Eurasian religion.

The Kykeon of Eleusis

Gordon Wasson later turned his attention to the Eleusinian Mystery rites held annually near Athens for nearly 2,000 years (until 395 CE when the Gothic leader Alaric destroyed the sanctuary). Wasson, in concert with Carl A. P. Ruck and Swiss chemist Albert Hofmann, developed convincing evidence, that an element of the culminating rite, the *kykeon*, was an entheogenic sacrament, made from ergot, a toxic fungus that grows on grain containing substances related to LSD. Many of the most influential Greek thinkers were initiates of this half-year program; they called themselves the "twice-born."

Iboga

Centered in the West African Republic of Gabon, a 150-year-old syncretic Christian sect called *Bwiti* is thriving. A Bwiti initiate is given the central sacrament, the powdered root bark of *Tabernanthe iboga*, in massive doses during a lengthy initiatory session. Enough of the predominant chemical, ibogaine, is ingested to ensure a profound sequence likened to a near-death experience, beatific vision, and subsequent rebirth. Thereafter, Bwiti congregants take the iboga powder in smaller amounts during night worship sessions held at intervals varying by sect from weekly to quarterly. These *ngoze* ceremonies are designed to achieve a shared sense of "one heart only," a mental state of goodwill and empathic understanding of others.

Colonial missionaries attempted to suppress the Bwiti, particularly between 1920 and 1940, destroying temples and killing religious leaders. But when Gabon became an independent republic in 1958, a Bwitist became its first president, giving the Bwiti nearly the status of a state religion. The practice has extended into other West African countries where it is regarded as a helpful unifying influence.

Cannabis

Cannabis (hemp, marijuana) is one of the oldest and most widely cultivated plants, valued in some cultures as fiber, food, and medicine. It is said to have been used as an adjunct to prayer in ancient Taoist, Vedic, and Sufi practices, among others. Cannabis is most often regarded today as a recreational drug; however, formal spiritual use continues among certain groups, including within Coptic, Rastafarian, and Hindu traditions. Reports indicate that more Americans use cannabis than all other illegal drugs combined; common contemporary use often defies neat classification as recreational, medicinal, or spiritual.

LSD

In 1943, Albert Hofmann, who had earlier synthesized d-lysergic acid diethylamide (LSD), discovered its psychoactivity. At first known only as an experimental psychiatric drug, LSD broke out of the medical profession and into an avid population of seekers and experimenters in the early 1960s. Accelerated by the ease of distribution and the low cost of LSD, potent chemical means for facilitating profound alterations of consciousness became available to dramatically increasing numbers of people throughout the 1960s.

Most people who took LSD did so outside any traditional cultural or religious context, although there were attempts to establish such contexts, some explicitly framed as religious. The difficulty of creating a new "psychedelic" religion became evident to Lisa Bieberman, who for two years published a newsletter to chronicle the birth and course of groups such as the League for Spiritual Discovery and the Neo-American Church. Reviewing this record, she wrote in 1967: "The collected back issues are a catalog of frauds and failures. . . . Most of the psychedelic projects I reported have flopped, even though the more obvious losers were screened out before printing. Those that remain are a caricature of the psychedelic vision, a mockery of the idealism of youth"(*New Republic,* 05 Aug 1967).

Still, the impact of LSD is not to be underestimated. Some contexts of ritual use, most popularly at Grateful Dead concerts, endured for years. Zen teachers in Europe and America have reported that many of their students were drawn to Zen training as a consequence of substances such as LSD.

MDMA

The German pharmaceutical firm Merck first synthesized 3,4 methylenedioxy-methamphetamine (MDMA) in the early 1900s, though Merck's patent does not report its pharmacology. Circa 1970, chemists, such as Alexander Shulgin, revisiting the compound discovered its unique psychotropic properties, described as empathogenic and "heart opening" more than hallucinogenic. In the late 1970s, an expanding community of psychologists and psychiatrists in the US and Europe began quietly using MDMA in psychotherapy. Shortly thereafter, MDMA emerged, with the name "Ecstasy," in dance clubs (later raves) and other unsupervised settings. The exponential growth of its use and the aggressive marketing associated with its distribution attracted attention that resulted in its being made illegal in the US in 1985.

MDMA is used very widely and for many purposes. Some religious leaders have reported that they have found MDMA to be a powerful adjunct to prayer and meditation.

Many MDMA users report that its effectiveness declines markedly with lifetime cumulative exposure, losing its "magic" after the first few experiences. Research since the 1980s has raised serious doubt as to whether MDMA, even used infrequently, has the freedom from neurotoxic risk which has been established for some of the traditional entheogens.

Current Practice

The historical and contemporary practices surveyed here demonstrate the spiritual significance of entheogens and indicate that at least some of them can be used with reasonable safety. The substances remain illegal in most countries, even when used in religious practice, on account of comprehensive bans on hallucinogenic plants and chemicals.

However, a few countries, including the United States, do accommodate certain entheogen practices, though the US drug law exemption for peyote is restricted to one racial group and one religious tradition. A genuine respect for religious freedom as guaranteed by the United Nations Universal Declaration of Human Rights and the US Constitution would seem to require that such accommodations be adopted *universally*, without regard to race or creed, for the traditional plant entheogens and other substances of comparable safety.

Well-crafted policies and practices would support the anti-drug abuse objectives of the current drug laws, mitigate the psychological risks inherent in profound religious experience, and limit the potential for abuses by individuals and organizations that offer such experience. If this can be accomplished, spiritual communities and individuals will be free to work out for themselves the proper role of entheogens to evolve beneficial contexts for their use.

CONCRESCENCE?

ENSŌ Eun, 17th century

VAJRAVISION ☺ Alex Grey

Startlingly clear inner visions often accompany our most profound and memorable meditative or psychedelic experiences. Distributed throughout *Zig Zag Zen* are images by extraordinary artists, offered to help visually contextualize the complex subject of the relationships between psychedelics and Buddhism. Some of the artists appearing in this volume have never done drugs, and some of these artists have probably never meditated. Nevertheless, their work is relevant to the themes of liberation of the mind, "altered states," and depictions of transcendental emptiness, and includes nontraditional images of the Buddha or Buddhist-influenced iconography. The works of Odilon Redon, Mark Rothko, Ethel Le Rossignol, Francesco Clemente, Mati Klarwein, Ed Paschke, Robert Beer, Paul Laffoley, Michael Newhall, Mariko Mori, Ang Tsherin Sherpa, Robert Venosa, Dean Chamberlain, Luke Brown, Amanda Sage, Carey Thompson, Android Jones, Randal Roberts, Sukhi Barber and Fred Tomaselli as well as pieces by my wife, Allyson Grey, and myself are woven throughout the pages of this book. Also presented are select examples from the Japanese Zen and Tibetan thangka traditions of Buddhist art. The connections and resonances between these diverse works are a quality of artistic consciousness I call *Vajravision*.

The *vajra* is a spiritual tool, a thunderbolt scepter owned by the Hindu god Indra. It was adopted by the Buddhist sages as a symbol of the diamond-like clarity and brilliance of the mind's true nature, and has come to stand for a special class of Buddhist teachings. These are known as the Vajrayana, which incorporate complex visualizations of deities, Buddhas, gurus, and sky-dancing dakinis. During carefully prescribed meditations, an exchange of transforming and enlightening energies takes place between the practitioner and the intensely imagined spiritual archetypes. Accomplishment in the Vajrayana approach depends on developing proficiency in opening the wisdom eye, navigating the subtle visionary realms, and confirming their luminosity, emptiness, and truth. Vajravision helps us see beyond the opaque material world to the spiritual reality behind appearances.

A dependable way to introduce one's self to the brightly colored and minutely articulated visionary inner worlds, to "see" with Vajravision, is through an entheogenic or psychedelic experience. Perhaps one of the primary benefits of psychedelics is their capacity to make the subtle realms explicit and inescapable to the percipient under their influence. To a consciousness familiar only with perception of the gross physical world, an immersion in the dynamic, overwhelming, and uncontrollable visionary imagination may result in ontological panic. Fear and paranoia then become infinitely magnified to hell-realm proportions; the classic "bad trip." But given the proper set and setting, a vast panorama of mysterious archetypal beings and highly articulated heaven realms becomes accessible. Visions of both heaven and hell are frequent for the intrepid Psychonaut.

As with many contemporary artists, my first encounter with Buddhist art was through the paintings and statues I'd seen in museums and art history books. Buddha's intriguing smile appeared even more mysterious than that of the Mona Lisa. It was only after I had taken LSD that the thangka paintings of Tibet and Nepal began to make sense, with their glowing beings surrounded by rainbow light and horrific many-headed, multi-limbed deities surrounded by patterned flames. My pursuit of the meaning of those images then began in earnest, with study of Buddhist scripture and my becoming familiar with the art's unusual perspective on existence. Thangka paintings interlace representations of the physical worlds with subtle visionary beings and geometrically dense mandalas that are familiar to those who have had psychedelic experiences. Only art in the visionary tradition begins to hint at the multidimensional glory the psychedelic voyager has experienced. Many people from the West who wind up studying Buddhism have had drug-induced altered state experiences that opened them for the first time to the infinitude and mystery of consciousness. Artists who have entered psychedelic states and are also practicing Buddhists are still something of a rare species, but are becoming less so. The confluence of these inspiring forces is helping fuel an underground artistic renaissance. Artists who have accessed deeper and higher aspects of their being via meditative disciplines or psychedelics are no longer content with the formal games and transgressionism of much contemporary art. A worthy subject is the most important discovery for artists—it's the magnetic passion that burns at the core of their work, attracting or repelling us, and determining whether they will attempt to evoke what is deepest and highest in us.

Visionary mystical experiences are humanity's most direct contact with spiritual reality and are the creative source of all sacred art and wisdom traditions. The best currently existing technology for sharing the mystic imaginal realms is a well-crafted artistic rendering by an eyewitness. Mystic visionary artists distill the multidimensional, entheogenic journey into externally crystallized theophanies, icons embedded with evolutionary worldviews. Since mystic visionary artists paint the transcendental realms from observation, their work offers a growing body of evidence substantiating the divine imaginal realms and by extension, Spirit itself.

Oscar Janiger's studies of LSD and creativity showed that many artists felt the work done while tripping or post-tripping was more inventive and inspired than their previous work. Keith Haring, one of the most celebrated artists of the 1980s, credited LSD with stylistic breakthroughs that brought him to his own unique work. I feel the same way about my art. This doesn't mean I recommend sacramental drug use for every artist, but I do think it should be a legal option for every freethinker.

The medical scientific verification of the mystic potency of psychedelics is now established by both Walter Pahnke's famous Good Friday Experiment from 1962 and Roland Griffiths's landmark psilocybin study reported in *Psychopharmacology* in August 2006. In both studies, sixty-five percent of those who took psilocybin had a mystical experience, full union with cosmic infinite love and transcendental reality. In each case the participants were "spiritually inclined" psychedelic virgins who were supported in an aesthetically pleasing, safe set and setting. The proof that psychedelics can catalyze mystical experiences establishes the credibility and repeatability of the insights, as though they were hardwired into the brain, awaiting awakening. Many indigenous shamanic traditions use plant teachers for gaining wisdom and uniting with spirit. Over the past decade, ayahuasca has spread throughout the world via traveling shamans and small church groups. Humanity is in the time of a worldwide sacramental psychedelic revolution, the re-emergence of an ancient tool to sacred reality.

Since visionary mystical experience is at the foundation of all religions, imprisoning those who take mushrooms to see God is clearly suppression of religious freedom. Despite a worldwide war on drugs, some artists have dared journey into the higher heavens by using psychedelics, confirmed the mystic truths of all ages for themselves, and have then attempted to bring their revelations into form. The world is better for this work because it helps people open their minds to positive influences. Psychedelics are ancient sacramental tools for bringing humanity into alignment with higher wisdom. For many people psychedelics are the reset button for a meaningful life. It was that way for me.

The mystic state described by visionary artists includes images of unity, cosmic oneness, transcendence of conventional space and time, a sense of the sacred in having encountered ultimate reality, positive affect, vivid color and luminosity, symbolic pattern language, imaginal beings and infinite geometric jewel-like vistas. Much of traditional Buddhist Art could be similarly described. For pilgrims to the sacred inner dimensions, visionary art provides validation for their own glimpses, and proves the universal nature of the imaginal realms. Reflecting the luminous richness of higher spiritual worlds, visionary art activates our light body, empowers our creative soul, and stirs our deepest potential for positive, transformative action in the world.

One of the difficulties after attending meditation retreats and the psychedelic experience alike is the integration phase—after you've visited infinitely beautiful spiritual dimensions but feel unable to revisit the state or share your visions with others. This is where both sustained Buddhist practice and art can play a role. Buddhism and other contemplative practices can help us reconnect with the truth on a daily basis, and art can help us bring our visions to form and share them. For the visionary artist this is a somewhat straightforward translation of mystical experience into artworks that transmit the depth of feeling and perception of the subtle inner worlds. Some visionary domains are, of course, unique to each individual, yet there are deep archetypal states of Being experienced by large numbers of seekers and seers that can be summoned and described through art. In 1928, Heinrich Klüver published his book *Mescal and the Mechanism of Hallucinations*, wherein he reported certain visionary "form constants" that recur in the effects of mescaline on normal subjects. These shapes inform many entheogenic Buddhist artistic visions. The "form constants" are the spiral, the lattice or fretwork, and imagery of tunnels, funnels, or passageways. There is a perception of "greater dimensionality," both visual multidimensionality and ontological dimensions of meaning. Iridescent and finely filigreed organic and complex geometric shapes evolve and dissolve, referencing seedpods, flowers, butterflies and seashells, infinite natural forms and sacred architecture. Colors appear more brilliant and overwhelming. Light itself takes on a palpable if plasmic character. Luminosity is everywhere present, holding everything together. Many of the artists in *Zig Zag Zen* use these forms. Think of Klarwein's spirallic beings, Tomaselli's web-like leaf patterns, or Le Rossignol's brilliant colors.

In the thirteen years since the first publication of *Zig Zag Zen* in 2002, a strong new generation of psychedelic artists has emerged, some of whom appear in this updated volume. Many of them cite the original book as an inspiration. Today in 2015, an expanded taxonomy of psychedelic visual effects and an encyclopedia of subtle beings are being created by the worldwide visionary artists' movement being spread through festivals, the electronic music scene and a thriving online community eager to decode their heavenly messages. Amanda Sage bridges her American psychedelic roots with training from Ernst and Michael Fuchs, masters of the Viennese Fantastic Realist School, and meditative spiritual development to craft her light-infused figurative oil paintings. Android Jones paints both dynamic abstractions and socially charged glowing bodies in higher dimensional fractalscapes while onstage at concerts by drawing with an electronic pen and projecting his light art on screens at events around the world. Luke Brown is equally comfortable with pen and ink, oil painting and digital tools, which he uses to build some of the "trippiest" dharma-informed art ever made. Carey Thompson is an extraordinary visionary artist who melds archetypes and motifs into new icons shining with light of the divine. Carey, being of the same generational wave as Amanda, Android, and Luke has joined forces with these artists and built sculptural stages for music festivals like Boom in Portugal and Burning Man's Fractal Planet. The visionary tribe has evolved a collaborative and community serving ethic, a spiritual worldview supported largely outside the conventional art marketplace. It takes bravery, tremendous discipline and skill as an artist to express one's inner theophanies with the clarity and directness of these new visionaries.

Sukhi Barber is perhaps the perfect fusion of serious Vajrayana practitioner, psychedelic explorer and classically trained figurative sculptor. She has been working for more than a decade on translating her visionary experiences onto her Buddha-like statues. Though the figures sit in lotus posture, the body, and thereby the ego identity associated with it, is dissolving, unraveling, breaking down, revealing emptiness and continuity with infinite openness.

Ang Tsherin Sherpa is an artist from Nepal who has integrated some western approaches to design with ancient Buddhist iconography, and it is a delight to share his work as a counterpoint to all the Western artists integrating Buddhist iconography.

In one of his essays on the visionary experience, Aldous Huxley proposed that the mundane attraction to jewels is based on the similarity of gemstones to the sparkling jewel-like nature of the Heaven Worlds. It's one of the unconscious reasons for the strangely high valuation given to these little shiny pebbles. *The Revelation of St. John* refers to the Holy City as "having the glory of God, its radiance like a most rare jewel," and all through the *Avatamsaka Sutra* there are references to infinitely jeweled Buddhafields. Many who have tripped have seen them. The subtle beings are alive. They are self-illuminating. A densely patterned jewel-like fire-fluid is the epidermis of angels. Portrayals of luminous glass-like forms that Venosa, Klarwein, Ernst Fuchs, and I paint are cousins and close visual analogs to thangka paintings, which portray the subtle spiritual realms. Tibetan artists are known to grind gemstones into their pigments to help them recreate the luminous visionary worlds.

Each stage of higher consciousness and the subtle inner worlds can be depicted and evoked through art. In the early stages of the psychedelic experience we feel a heightened sensitivity to colors and notice wavy or slowly billowing distortions of our outer-world perceptions. When we look inward, we begin to perceive dynamic geometric forms and cartoon-like figures morphing into strange and inventive shapes. The art that relates to this stage of tripping could be Op art, or works that depend on densely colored patterns related to phosphenes, and some cartoon-like surrealist works. Randal Roberts, one of the new generation of visionaries, shows the beckoning of the psychedelic DMT portal in his 2007 oil painting, *Divine Messenger of Truth*.

Deeper into the trip there arises a symbolic importance to everything in life. The perception of beauty and meaningfulness is mingled with ecstatic rushes of bliss and laughter. You lucidly interpret your life in a more holistic framework. Everything is okay, even if it is out of our control, for we are beginning to surrender to a higher power. A connectedness with beauty, meaning, and the rhythms of the cosmos in everyday reality is the state of consciousness that is suggested by John F. B. Miles in such paintings as *The Room When No One is There*. For some people, psychodynamic visions of unresolved repressed emotions emerge via dramatic, personally meaningful imagery. The visionary biopics of Frida Kahlo or Francesco Clemente may relate to these phases.

Then come the truly transpersonal stages, the birth, death, and rebirth experiences. The ego or small self is frightened, crushed, overcome, and reborn through intense chthonic and cathartic visions. Here the Northern Renaissance masters portrayed stunning visions of hell, but so did contemporary artistic demonologist, the painter H. R. Giger, or we could just as easily reference the Tibetan Yamantaka thangka paintings with bull-headed wrathful deities surrounded by flames and crushing egos underfoot. The entire pantheon of spirits, gods, and demons can be encountered in altered states. Several of the artists included in this book point to this archetypal realm: Paul Laffoley, Ed Paschke, Ethel Le Rossignol, Michael Newhall, Mariko Mori, Odilon Redon, and Robert Beer. Continuing with the description of altered state experiences, Vajravision can reveal subtle energetic movements in the body—chakras opening—strands of energy systems weaving throughout the body and world. Like me, Randal Roberts and Amanda Sage have painted human figures emanating and interlacing energetic tendrils. Depictions of the astral worlds and heaven worlds can be found in the works of Robert Venosa, Dean Chamberlain, Fred Tomaselli, and Allyson Grey. Ultimately, the Universal Mind—an experience of complete cosmic Unity—comes to the experimental mystic, which can also manifest as the classic Zen *satori* of voidness or emptiness as the ground of being beyond polarities. The structure of underlying reality has been mapped in complex Tibetan mandalas using sacred geometry, visions of worlds inside of worlds, and charts of the entire cosmos. These ultimate states of being are also evoked in the extraordinary works of Mark Rothko, the various Zen *Ensos,* as well as some of Mariko Mori's and Mati Klarwein's masterpieces.

Odilon Redon, the French symbolist, was probably one of the first European artists to use the Buddha as a subject in his art. In his first interpretation of Buddha, included in the third version of his *Temptations* lithograph albums, Buddha is a scary hybrid of a sinister-looking man with a turban and a snake's tail: an idol from an exotic religion, competing with Christianity. Later, as art historian Claudia Müller-Ebeling pointed out to me, Redon changed this presentation into one of a peaceful teacher and wanderer amid lush vegetation and shiny flowers.

I've never been able to find credible historical evidence to confirm whether Redon went to Paris's Latin Quarter and visited Le Club des Hashischins like his friend Baudelaire and other "decadent" poets of that era. Certainly, however, Redon would have been familiar with descriptions of hashish's effects.

Baudelaire noted in *Les Paradis artificiels*,

> . . . The man gratified with this sense of loveliness, unfortunately so rare and so transitory, feels himself more than ever the artist, more than ever noble, more than ever just . . . The eyes have a vision of Eternity . . . Sounds take on colors and colors contain music. . . . Suppose you look at a tree gracefully waving in the wind . . . you attribute to the tree your passion, your desire or your melancholy, its murmurs and its writhing becomes yours, and before long you are the tree. In the same way, a soaring bird first represents the immortal desire to fly above things human, but already you yourself are the bird . . . (1860, 1967).

This quality of becoming one with the artistic subject is the recommended state of consciousness for the Zen painter, "One must first become the mountain in order to paint the mountain." Due to their visionary richness, both the meditative and entheogenic experiences have great importance for fueling artistic and cultural renewal.

The Dalai Lama has stated, "I believe deeply that we must find, all of us together, a new spirituality. This new concept ought to be elaborated alongside the religions in such a way that all people of goodwill could adhere to it." In the new millennium, a universal sacred art can accompany this developing spirituality. Our art—painting, sculpture, film, web design, and architecture—can help foster, as Huston Smith advised, "the transformation of altered states into enduring traits." Iconic and symbolic transmission of wisdom can be equal, if not more effective, than oral transmissions when based on authentic and mystically valid visionary states. Under the proper circumstances, the depths of Being glimpsed through psychedelics open a person to the infinite compassion and wisdom at the basis of all religions. Art that is catalyzed by such Vajravision speaks to the heart of an individual and orients a person toward interconnectedness with the cosmos, and ultimate identity that lies beyond representation but can be pointed to when inspired visions are powerfully transmitted.

Humanity's materialistic worldview must transition to a sacred view of Oneness with the environment and cosmos or risk self-destruction due to continued abuse of the life-web. Great works in the creative arts call us to imagine our higher unity as humanity evolves toward a sustainable planetary civilization. Mystic Visionary Art is a manifestation of the Primary Religious Experience. The word religion comes from the Greek meaning "to tie back." The Primary Religious Experience is a personal connection with Source that "ties us back" to our own divinity. The Vajravisions shared by the artists in *Zig Zag Zen* point to humanity's common transcendental source.

DMT DHARMA ❧ Rick J. Strassman, MD

IT IS JANUARY 1991, twenty-three minutes after I injected a large dose of DMT (N,N dimethyltryptamine) into Elena's arm vein. Elena is a forty-two-year-old married psychotherapist with extensive personal experience with psychedelic drugs. DMT is a powerful, short-acting psychedelic that occurs naturally in human body fluids, and is also found in many plants. Elena has read some Buddhism, but practices Taoist meditation. She knows of my long-standing Zen practice.

She lies in a bed on the fifth floor of the University of New Mexico Hospital General Clinical Research Center. The clear plastic tubing providing access to her vein dangles onto the bed. The cuff of a blood pressure machine is loosely attached to her other arm, and the tubing snakes its way into the back of a blinking monitor.

Within thirty seconds of the injection, she loses awareness of the room, and us in it. Besides myself, Elena's husband, who had just undergone a similar drug session, and our research nurse sit quietly by Elena's side. I know from previous volunteers' reports that peak effects of intravenous DMT occur from two to three minutes after the injection, and that she will not be able to communicate for at least fifteen minutes, by which time most effects will have failed. Her eyes closed, she begins spurting out laughter, some quite uproarious, and her face turns red. "Well, I met a living Buddha! Oh, God! I'm staying here. I don't want to lose this. I want to keep my eyes closed to allow it to imprint itself. Just because it's possible!"

Elena felt great the next week. "Life is very different. A Buddha is now always in the upper right-hand corner of my consciousness," she says. "All of what I have been working on spiritually for the last several years has become a certainty. Left hooks from the mundane world continue to come up and hit me, but the solidity of the experience anchors me, allows me to handle it all. Time stopped at the peak of the experience; now everyday time has slowed. The third stage, that of coming down from the peak, was the most important; if I had opened my eyes too soon I wouldn't have been able to do as much integrating of the experience as I have."

Two years later, Elena rarely takes psychedelics. Her most positive recollection of the DMT session was the "clarity and purity of the medicine." The most negative: "The absolute lack of sacredness and context." Many of the changes in her life, particularly a deepening shift from "thinking" to "feeling," were "supported" by the DMT session, but were underway before it, and continued after it.

Elena's experience, repeated by ten to twenty percent of the volunteers in our psychedelic drug trials, represents the most gratifying and intriguing results of our work in New Mexico. My own interest in Buddhism and psychedelics meet in the most beneficial way in her DMT-induced "enlightenment experience."

Ours was the first new project in twenty-five years to obtain US government funding for a human psychedelic drug study, the research a result of eighteen years of medical and psychiatric training and experience. I also have been practicing Zen Buddhism for over twenty years. In the molecule DMT, these two interests finally merged.

There are important medical reasons to study psychedelic drugs in humans. The use of LSD ("acid") and "magic" mushrooms (which contain psilocybin) continues to climb. Understanding what psychedelics do to brain function, and how, will help treat short- and long-term negative reactions to them. Since there is some similarity of symptoms between psychedelic drug states and schizophrenia, such research also may shed new light on this devastating mental illness.

Other less "medical" reasons to study hallucinogenic drugs also relate to health and well-being, especially in the overlap between psychedelic and spiritual states. I was impressed by the "psychedelic" descriptions of intensive meditation practice within some Buddhist traditions. Since their scriptures did not mention drugs, and the states sounded similar to those resulting from psychedelic drug use, I suspected there might be a naturally occurring psychedelic molecule in the brain that was triggered by deep meditation.

I was led to the pineal gland as a possible source of psychedelic compounds produced under certain unusual mental or physical states. These conditions would include near-death, birth, high fever, prolonged meditation, starvation, and sensory deprivation. This tiny organ, the "seat of the soul" or "third eye" of the ancients, might produce DMT or similar substances by simple chemical alterations of the well-known pineal hormone melatonin, or of the important brain chemical serotonin. Perhaps it is DMT, released by the pineal, that opens the mind's eye to spiritual, or nonphysical, realities.

The pineal gland also held a fascination for me because it first becomes visible in the human fetus at forty-nine days after conception. Also this is when the gender of the fetus is first clearly discernible. Forty-nine days, according to several Buddhist texts, is how long it takes the life force of one who has died to enter into its next incarnation. Perhaps the life force of a human enters the fetus at forty-nine days through the pineal. And it may leave the body, at death, through the pineal. This coming and going would be marked by the release of DMT by the pineal, mediating awareness of these awesome events.

In addition to the scientific puzzle presented by the similarities between psychedelic and mystical consciousness, there were issues of healing that also drew me to both. The sense of there being "something greater" resulting from major psychedelic episodes led me to think that psychedelics might be helpful to people with psychological, physical, or spiritual problems. It seemed crucial to avoid the narrowness that often spoiled claims for the drugs' usefulness or dangers, and to hold a broad view. My emerging worldview resembled a tripod supported by biological (brain), psychoanalytic (individual psychology), and Eastern religious (consciousness and spirituality) legs. The first two legs were important in my decision to attend medical school. The third pushed me deeper into Buddhism.

Disheartened by the lack of spirit in medical training, I took a year's leave of absence from medical school and explored Zen in a series of retreats. Zen's emphasis on direct experience, its evenhanded approach to all mental phenomena encountered during meditation, and the importance of enlighten-ment all fit with my image of an ideal religious tradition. During my four-year psychiatric training, I helped found and run a meditation group affiliated with my long-standing Zen community. I was ordained as a lay Buddhist in the mid-1980s. This was the same year I trained in clinical psychopharmacology, learning to administer psychoactive drugs to human volunteers in controlled scientific studies.

The form our New Mexico research took was a traditional biomedical one, monitoring effects of several DMT doses on blood pressure, temperature, pupil size, and blood levels of several chemicals indicating brain function. We recruited experienced hallucinogen users who were psychologically and medically fit. This was because they would be better able to report on their experiences, and less likely to panic or suffer longer-lasting side effects, than drug inexperienced volunteers. Volunteers believed in the ability of psychedelics to help "inner work," and volunteered, at least in part, to use DMT for their personal growth.

Was there a spiritual aspect to the DMT experience? And, if so, was this helpful in and of itself? This was one of my deeper reasons for developing our DMT research program.

Supervising sessions is called "sitting," usually believed to come from "baby-sitting" people in a highly dependent and, at times, confused and vulnerable state. But, in our minds, Buddhist practice is as relevant a source for the term. Our research nurse and I did our best to practice meditation while with our volunteers: watching the breath, being alert, eyes open, ready to respond, keeping a bright attitude, and getting out of the way of the volunteer's experience. This method is very similar to what Freud called "evenly suspended attention," performed by a trained psychoanalyst who provided support by a mostly silent but present sitting by one's side. I experienced this type of listening and watching as similar to Zen meditation.

Another example of how psychedelic and Buddhist meditation converged was in the development of a new questionnaire to measure states of consciousness. Previous questionnaires measuring psychedelic drug effects were not ideal for many reasons. Some assumed that psychedelics caused nothing but psychosis, and emphasized unpleasant experiences. Other scales were developed using volunteers, sometimes ex-narcotic-addict prisoners, who were not told what drugs they were given or what the effects might be.

I had always liked the Buddhist view of the mind being divided into the five *skandhas* ("heaps" or "aggregates") which, taken as a whole, give the impression of a personal self who experiences. These are the familiar "form," "feeling," "perception," "consciousness," and "volition." I looked into several guides to the Abhidharma literature, the Buddhist "psychological canon," with over a thousand years of use monitoring progress in meditation. It seemed a *skandha*-based rating scale could provide an excellent basis for a neutral, descriptive understanding of psychedelic states.

I let it be known I was interested in talking with people who had taken DMT. Soon, the phone was ringing with people wanting to describe their experiences. Most of the nineteen people were from New Mexico and the West Coast, and nearly all were involved in some therapeutic or religious discipline. They were well-educated, articulate, and impressed with DMT's ability to open the door to highly unusual, nonmaterial states, which was greater than that of longer-lasting psychedelics like psilocybin or LSD. After completing these interviews, I decided to add a sixth "*skandha*" to the questionnaire, called "intensity," which helped quantify the nature of the experience.

We gave and analyzed this new questionnaire, the Hallucinogenic Rating Scale (HRS), almost four hundred times to more than fifty people over four years. The grouping of questions using the *skandha* method gave more sensitive results in our DMT work than did a large number of biological measurements, such as blood pressure, temperature, or levels of certain chemicals in the blood.

Besides informing our style of sitting for and measuring responses to drug sessions, Buddhism helped make sense of the experiences people had in our relatively sparse but supportive environment. For many volunteers, even those with prior DMT use, the first high dose of intravenous DMT was like a near-death state, which in turn has been strongly linked to beneficial mystical experiences. Several were convinced they were dead or dying. Many had encounters with deities, spirits, angels, unimaginable creatures, and the source of all existence. Nearly all lost contact with their bodies at some point. Elena's case is a good example of an enlightenment experience—sounding identical to reports in the Buddhist meditative tradition—brought on by a high dose of DMT.

On one hand, a Buddhist perspective might hold all of these experiences to be equal. The matter-of-fact approach to nonmaterial realms in Buddhism provides firm footing for accepting and working with those experiences. It also does away with judging nonmaterial realms as better (or worse) than material ones—a tendency in some New Age religions. The experience of seeing and speaking to deva-like creatures in the DMT trance was just that: seeing and speaking with other beings. Not wiser, not less wise, and not more or less trustworthy than anyone or anything else.

On the other hand, how to meet head-on the volunteer who had a drug-induced enlightenment? Certify him or her as enlightened? Explain away by pharmacology the earth-shattering impact of the experience?

It was confusing. At first, it seemed as if a big dose of DMT was indeed transformative. As time elapsed, though, and we followed our volunteers for months and years, my perspective radically changed. While some, as Elena, had profoundly beneficial results from her participation, a small number had frightening, negative responses that required some care afterward. Other, more subtle adverse effects also crept in (as may happen with Buddhist practice) in the form of increased self-pride—that is, a division of people into those with and without "understanding." In addition, "solving" problems while in an altered state particularly common with high-dose psychedelic use—but then not putting the solution into practice, seemed to me worse than not even trying to work on the specific problem.

I have concluded that there is nothing inherent about psychedelics that have a beneficial effect, nor are they pharmacologically dangerous in and of themselves. The nature and results of the experience are determined by a complex combination of the drug's pharmacology, the state of the volunteer at the time of drug administration, and the relationship between the individual and the physical and psychological environment: drug, set, and setting.

The volunteers who benefited most from their DMT sessions were those who probably would have gotten the most out of any "trip"—drug or otherwise. Those who benefited least were those who were the most novelty-saturated. The most difficult sessions took place in combinations of two factors, the first being an unwillingness to give up the internal dialogue and body awareness; and the second being uncertain or confusing relationships between the volunteer and those in the room at the time. Therefore, the "religious," "adverse," or "banal" effects resulting from drug administration depended more upon the person and what he or she and those in the room brought to the session, than on any inherent characteristic of the drug itself.

Thus, the problem with depending on one or several transformative psychedelic experiences as a practice is that there is no framework that suitably deals with everyday life between drug sessions. The introduction of certain Amazonian hallucinogenic plant-using churches into the West, with their sets of ritual and moral codes, may provide a new model combining religious and psychedelic practice.

In the last year of our work, a more difficult personal interplay of Buddhism and psychedelics appeared. This involved what might be described as a turf-battle developing between my Zen community and me. For years, I had been given at least implicit support to pursue my research by several members of the Zen community. These were senior students with their own prior psychedelic experiences. In the last year, I described our work to psychedelic-naive members of the community, who strongly condemned it. Formerly sympathetic students appeared pressured to withdraw any support for my studies. This concern was specifically directed at two aspects of our research. One aspect was a planned psychedelic-assisted psychotherapy project with the terminally ill, research that demonstrated impressive potential in the 1960s. That is, in patients who were having difficulty with the dying process, a "dry run" with a high-dose psychedelic session might ease the anguish and despair associated with their terminal illness. The other area of concern was the potential for adverse effects, both the obvious and more subtle ones previously described.

Scriptural and perceptual bases for this disapproval were given, in addition to community members' own and others' experiences. However, it appeared to me that the major concern was that it would be highly detrimental for them, as a Buddhist community, to associate Buddhism with drug use in any way. It appeared that students who had their own psychedelic experiences (and had found them to stimulate their interest in a meditative life) had to close ranks with those who did not.

What I experienced as the friction between disciplines is not uncommon in the world at large, and perhaps within the Buddhist community in particular. That is, is it "Buddhist" to give, take, or otherwise occupy oneself with the psychedelics as spiritual tools?

While there are abuses possible of anything by anyone on the relative level, at the absolute level, how is this possible? One of our volunteers succinctly stated how these issues might have been more openly put into context: "Meditation can be applied to anything, meditation can be strengthened by anything, meditation can be afraid of nothing."

Several research projects are being planned across the US, using psychedelics to treat intractable drug abuse, a condition with a high mortality rate if untreated. I understand Buddhist precepts to condone the use of "intoxicants" for medical purposes (e.g., cocaine for local anesthesia, narcotics for pain control). Whether a Buddhist who gives or takes a psychedelic "intoxicant" for the treatment of a medical condition faces similar criticism will be important to note. Complicating this case is the point that the psychological/spiritual effects of a properly prepared and supervised psychedelic session might be seen as curative.

In a final area of possible overlap, I believe there are ways in which Buddhism and the psychedelic community might benefit from an open, frank exchange of ideas, practices, and ethics.

For the psychedelic community, the ethical, disciplined structuring of life, experience, and relationship provided by thousands of years of Buddhist communal tradition has much to offer. This well-developed tradition could infuse meaning and consistency into isolated, disjointed, and poorly integrated psychedelic experiences. The wisdom of the psychedelic experience, without the accompanying and necessary love and compassion cultivated in a daily practice, may otherwise be frittered away in an excess of narcissism and self-indulgence. Although this is also possible within a Buddhist meditative tradition, it is less likely with the checks and balances in place within a dynamic community of practitioners.

Dedicated Buddhist practitioners with little success in their meditation, but well along in moral and intellectual development, might benefit from a carefully timed, prepared, supervised, and followed-up psychedelic session to accelerate their practice. Psychedelics, if anything, provide a view that—to one so inclined—can inspire the long, hard work required to make that view a living reality.

PSYCHOACTIVISM ☯ David Chadwick

IN THE EARLY SEVENTIES at a meeting of fifty students at Tassajara Zen Mountain Center, the agenda had been covered and there we all were sitting around the dining room, enjoying the energy of being together. Our faces were highlighted by the flickering light from the kerosene lamps as someone broke the silence by asking "How many people here have taken LSD?" There was a moment of silent confusion followed by interest in the results of this sudden poll. Most hands shot up. The room filled with laughter.

It's undeniable that psychedelics played a central role in the hippie counter-culture revolution of the late sixties and early seventies, but sometimes we forget that the same is true of the influence psychedelics had during that same period on the emergence of Buddhism in America and a generation's search for spiritual experience. To the uninitiated, the word "psychedelics" might conjure up media-inspired images of colorfully dressed, long-haired hippies adorned with flowers, beads, and blissed-out smiles tripping around Golden Gate Park in San Francisco, dancing kids taking a break from the responsible course of their lives, or worse, destroying themselves. One might think about the bad trips, the freak accidents when someone decided they could walk in front of traffic free from harm, or when Art Linkletter's daughter died jumping from a building while on LSD. All of that may be true, but it's a distorted image that neglects the sacramental role of these substances, and ignores the myriad of people who were encouraged on their spiritual journeys by one or more mind-expanding experiences with psychedelics, or entheogens, as they are often called by scholars these days.

After thirty-five years of being around a diffuse subculture of Buddhist, Hindu, shamanist, New Age, Sufi, Christian, and what-not enlightenment seekers, I am familiar with the formative role psychedelics has often played in their lives. This has been brought home again in the course of years of interviews while working on the biography of Shunryu Suzuki Roshi, the founder of the San Francisco Zen Center and Tassajara Zen Mountain Center. Though many of the people I've known and interviewed have told me that their psychedelic experiences, like mine, were a prime factor in the early stages of their spiritual paths, most of them did not continue psychedelic use. Many people just mention it in passing, as in "I took LSD, read Alan Watts, and came to San Francisco looking for a spiritual community." Recently, I received a letter in which a retired professor of English wrote: "I still think LSD saved my life—breaking me out of the Berkeley existential, druggie, deluded, fashionable despair of the Beats." (The Beat writers were, of course, also major contributors to the West's new openness to Buddhism and Eastern thought.) In a few cases I know of, an Asian priest tried LSD. One Japanese Zen priest who took LSD in the sixties called it "spiritual masturbation." Another took it and kept taking it for years (until he got arrested in Japan) and calls it "powerful medicine." Regardless of whether we view these psychoactives as helpful in the short or long haul, it's clear they have been and continue to be pivotal catalysts in the spiritual journey of a multitude of seekers. They sure were for me.

I was unusual at the Zen Center in that I'd been brought up in a family whose religion had much in common with Buddhism. My parents were my first spiritual teachers. I was taught that God was not a being, but infinite and perfect mind. We didn't use the word "God" a lot, but we were Christians. My father had been a reader in the Christian Science Church but dropped out because he felt that they elevated Jesus too much beyond being an extraordinary human who had realized his divine nature.

In Mexico at the age of twenty I discovered marijuana. It was an exciting, epiphanous year; there were endless insights. My friends and I thought that marijuana was the answer to all of the world's problems and was all that was good. We liked to get stoned and ride the roller coaster in Mexico City, which I'd thoroughly enjoy as long as I didn't start wondering about how well it was being maintained. At times I would get high, lie down, close my eyes, and look for the kernel of my self and sometimes I thought I'd found it. Then one day I ingested vile-tasting peyote with some friends, vomited, and went out walking on the streets. Everything was moving, alive, newborn, and I remember holding the galvanized pole of a traffic sign and saying that peyote had taken away all the cultural overlay and I could see the pole for what it was (I was studying anthropology at the time). I also discovered speed that year, in the form of Dexedrine and Benzedrine (which you could get in pharmacies without prescription) and took it quite a bit until it was clear that I had to stop. I observed my complexion worsening, a tendency to get manic, and the reluctance of people to listen to me. It was hard to stop taking it.

Thinking I'd gone about as far as I could with marijuana (though I didn't stop smoking it), I was eager to plummet deeper into my being with the aid of LSD, which I'd heard so much about—both wondrous promises and dire warnings. On a return to the States I bought a copy of *The Psychedelic Experience* by Harvard psychedelic pioneers Timothy Leary, Richard Alpert (later to become Ram Dass), and Ralph Metzner. To many, psychedelics were dangerous drugs that should be illegal, and those who promoted them were a scourge on society, Pied Pipers leading America's youth into a bottomless pit of ruin. To lots of us though, those men brought good news, and were the voices of new possibilities who, through their books and lectures, actually suggested a responsible way to take psychedelics so as to avoid the pitfalls and awaken briefly to truths perennial. This was far more wonderful than the materialism and narrow worldview we were being home-, school-, and media-fed. I took the book back to Mexico, studied it carefully, and did not take any more speed.

A year later I went to San Francisco. In the carnival atmosphere I tripped around smoking grass and met lots of new people who'd taken the pilgrimage to that hub of the hippies. That summer I had to go back home to make an appearance for my draft induction physical, to convince the army they didn't want me. I had an acid trip while in Texas at that time that was most powerful. I followed the advice in *The Psychedelic Experience* closely. The book was modeled after the *Tibetan Book of the Dead;* the point of both was to guide one toward an experience of the clear light. I had been told by people who'd been there, that to experience the clear light was to meet God, Buddha, ultimate truth, the absolute ground of being. I believed them. I still do. On that day I reread the book beforehand, fasted all day, meditated, and as the sun went down, took five hundred micrograms of LSD. There were two friends with me who served as guides. Their job was to be a reference to reality if I got paranoid or confused, and to remind me that we had an agreement to be quiet (my studies and prior experience had indicated that almost all the problems one encountered in a psychedelic experience were caused by social interaction). My friends were also to read me brief sections of the book when I showed an interest in communicating too much or needed to be gently nudged off a negative course.

This was not a frivolous event. I was trembling with anticipation and knew the gravity of what I was about to do. Leary said that he experienced the clear light on about half his weekly trips, but he also said that he descended into a hell realm (there are endless options there) about one out of five times. I knew from what I'd read, talking to others, and a few skirmishes with lower realms on prior trips that being in the grip of seemingly eternal, fantastically paranoid, hideous horror was a possibility that I faced. When the pill washed down my throat I knew my ego was about to die and gave in immediately. As the LSD started to come on strong, my friends played, at my prior request, the Beatles' perfectly appropriate: "Turn off your mind, relax, and float downstream," and then there was only the sound of the gentle waves of Lake Worth outside the screened porch as I lay on a cot, and I did float downstream, leave my friends, the bed, the waves, myself, and the universe as I had known it, and passed through progressive visions each more ecstatic, powerful, and subtle than the prior ones. The deeper I went, the more familiar and wonderful it was. I felt I was going to my eternal home.

Leary advised taking a strong dose under these types of controls for early trips because it got one quickly beyond the transitional states where problems could come up with one's ego fighting to maintain control. I had not a stitch of a chance to fight or maintain any type of control. I died, it seemed, as completely as one can die and found myself at one with all that is, beyond space and time, birth and death, bathed in love—it was always changing—and then, the dualism even of this oneness gave way and mind opened to the experience of the clear light, of which, later, I could really say nothing but that the experience seemed to be the crowning glory of all that is and isn't. I felt that I had experienced what a Hindu text described as greater than if ten thousand suns were to explode in the sky. I don't know how I can say this because none of these experiences can be remembered any more than the Pacific Ocean can fit into a thimble, but I came back saying that the clear light was pure, unborn, ecstatic—things like that. On that evening I emerged from the clear light into a calmer, perfect, absolute, vast clarity with no sense of identity or physicality in it, a state not characterized by any mundane attributes such as existence, experience, or anything.

I remember some time later opening my eyes and seeing the stars through the screened porch, then realizing that I had returned to awareness of this universe, which seemed dreamlike compared to the powerful bliss I had died into. I thought, "oh yes, space, time, stars, and I'm on a planet—this sort of reality." It seemed like one of an infinite number of possible dream places I could have landed, and it was beautiful. I soon realized I was there because I was tied in some way to a body which seemed to me like an idea which kept repeating itself, all this being experienced as a reflection in a mind beyond dimension—not located in space or time but that which imagined space and time.

I felt as if I'd just been born, didn't remember anything about myself and didn't know who the people were who were with me. I told them that if I was in the way they should feel free to dispose of me. They gently urged me to lie back down and read me a few lines which cleared my mind. I experienced spectacular visions gradually reentering into lower though still quite exalted, brilliantly colorful states of mind. Every now and then I'd sit up. I remember looking at my friends and seeing our bodies as energy fields which grew out of the same base, like we were fingers on a hand. I saw they thought they existed as independent beings and I told them, "We don't exist in any way." No wonder so many people were irritated by hippies.

In the days that followed I contemplated the experience I had had on the lake and knew that there could be no purpose in my life to compare with awakening to the essence of being I had kept company with that night. I also thought that taking more LSD or more of anything would not be the way to get there. I picked up some of the books I had on Buddhism and Hinduism and they made a lot more sense to me than before. I saw my normal state of mind as being tiny, confused, and filled with giant mountains that blocked knowledge of higher states. I knew LSD could evaporate these mountains but was sure that they'd just return. It seemed that books alone wouldn't get me there either. I thought that I needed to learn to meditate so as to gradually wear the mountains down and thought that possibly there could be a breakthrough *satori* experience after they'd been well eroded. I decided to travel the world looking for a teacher and had some idea of finding a community to meditate with. So I was off—first stop, a return to California. Soon I was meditating regularly at the San Francisco Zen Center.

Ministers, priests, psychologists, and various types of spiritual teachers back in the sixties had an interesting situation to deal with. Lots of people were coming to them who'd had psychedelic experiences and who were looking for an explanation of what they'd experienced, or seeking a more grounded and lasting way to meet the vastness of higher consciousness. Many of these counselors had no idea what to say or summarily dismissed these experiences as bogus. Some, like Shunryu Suzuki, were more helpful. Suzuki had a way that worked well with such seekers. He told us that enlightenment was not a state of mind, was not contained in any experience, and he guided us away from trying to recreate past profound events and toward accepting ourselves as we were. He taught a disciplined life of zazen meditation, attention to the details of life, not wanting too much (especially another state of mind), and not getting too worked up. He said that people will have enlightenment experiences without spiritual practice, but only with such practice will their revelation continue and not come and go like psychedelic experiences. He made us feel confident that we could wake up to who we were without any chemical aids, and he did it without taking any strong stand against marijuana and LSD, though he really didn't want his students taking them. He appreciated psychedelics as an initial impetus, but not as a way of life.

In the Buddhist circles I'm familiar with, psychedelics are mainly seen as something to forget about and move on from, and a story like the one I just told might elicit a been-there-done-that type of response. But I remember these substances fondly because they gave me what I felt was empirical evidence of the perennial goal of religion and philosophy and helped me to get on the path. And to think that what I did is now illegal.

To me, psychedelics are best used as a sacrament in an initiation ceremony which is what my experience seems to have been. It may be better for initiations to be conducted by elders or guides, but young people have for years been self-initiating because their elders or their society are not there for them in this way. Society seems mainly interested in shielding youth from anything that would challenge consensus reality, molding them into good workers and consumers, and chastising them if they get caught being too out of line. I know that my views on this are hopelessly astray from the norm, but I don't think that I or others or the state should have the right to tell anyone whose body has pretty much stopped growing that they can't do psychedelics or any psychoactives. It's telling people that the government, which has not set a very high moral or spiritual example, can regulate spiritual inquiry and which states of mind are legal.

News of all the violence from the inner city turf wars over drugs, and people's real or media-driven fear for their safety, help to fuel the war on drugs, whose propaganda lumps all illegal psychoactives together and goes after them in an uneven blitzkrieg. Alexander Shulgin, sometimes called the grandfather of Ecstasy, wrote that "the entheogens are the dolphins caught in the tuna net of the war on drugs." Aside from all those incarcerated for narcotics and stimulants, there are lots and lots of people being arrested, prosecuted, and locked up for dealing and using Ecstasy, LSD, and especially marijuana.

I wonder sometimes why more people don't come out against the war on drugs in its present form. It's so extremely costly, ineffective, and causes more harm than the problem. A quick look online reveals interesting statistics about current US drug policies. One million people, almost entirely nonviolent offenders, are in the slammer for some psychoactive or other, representing about forty percent of all those incarcerated in the US. The NORML (National Organization for the Reform of Marijuana Laws) site tells that, according to government figures, seventy million Americans have smoked marijuana since 1972 and ten million of them have been arrested since then. That was the year the National Commission on Marijuana and Drug Abuse issued its recommendation to Congress to decriminalize marijuana. I couldn't find how many people are in prison for life without possibility of parole for pot, but I read in *Atlantic Monthly* years ago that it was hundreds. Under President Clinton's watch, marijuana arrests were up sixty percent—an arrest every forty-five seconds.

Funny thing is that there seems to be an epidemic of giving legal drugs to kids. A young woman I know tells of how her parents and doctor put her on Ritalin when she was six because she was considered hyperactive. By the time she was twelve she had developed ticks and nervousness to a degree that she was diagnosed with (and medicated for) Tourette's syndrome. In high school she was on so many prescribed drugs that she was supplementing her allowance by dealing them at school. On her eighteenth birthday she announced to her parents, "No more of your drugs!" She tried drink and tobacco but didn't take to them. She even found that coffee was too stimulating. Now she only smokes pot and takes Ecstasy or mushrooms occasionally and is glad to be free of all the legal drugs that made her so miserable. She is a libertarian and has absolutely no respect for authority. And now, because of the choices she's made, she can get arrested.

Lots of people have no respect for authority because of how the powers that be are behind legal drugs and demonize all illegal drugs. There's nothing quite as effective in undermining a young person's respect for the law as when they try pot and find it to be benign and fun and at times profound.

The war on drugs also, in the eyes of many, makes criminals out of those in law enforcement, people who we want to respect and support. Steve Kubby, a past libertarian candidate for governor in California, and a leader in passing the state's medical marijuana initiative of 1996, publicly opposes the war on drugs. It's well known he has a prescription for medical marijuana. In 1998 twenty heavily armed officers invaded his home, arrested him and his wife, and terrified their three-year-old daughter. This type of thing is happening daily all over America. There's an endless list of sickening statistics and horror stories. Citizens have had to choose between testifying against their spouses or going to jail and losing their children.

The war on drugs can be seen as a power drug the government is addicted to. I think it's just old-fashioned persecution and the poor and disempowered are the main ones being persecuted. In the case of psychedelics, it's religious persecution.

No one I know wants their kids or friends to take strong stimulants or narcotics, just like we don't want them to be constantly stoned-out potheads or excessive drinkers. But a lot of us have done these things to some extent without robbing people or getting violent, and have grown out of it. It seems that in our eagerness these days to protect ourselves from worst-case scenarios, we have turned a blind eye to the suffering we've caused. I remember the cover of a Northern California weekly newspaper with a headline that read "Gulag California" above a photo of a long concrete hall overcrowded with depressed-looking prisoners milling about in and out of the cells. One point of the article was that many of those in jails and prisons are there just for possession of illegal drugs, and not for being violent, stealing, or breaking any other law. I gazed at the faces and could not believe that they were all dangerous people who should be locked up. I was reminded of the line from Bob Dylan's song, "Chimes of Freedom:" "And for each unharmful, gentle soul misplaced inside a jail."

Some engaged Buddhists currently work in the prisons, or with homelessness or other social problems, bringing them in touch with the victims of drugs and the war on drugs. I salute these active Buddhists, and non-Buddhists too, who are doing what they can to reduce all suffering and confusion. But most of us don't know what to do and aren't doing anything. We've got zazen at Auschwitz and peace ceremonies on Hiroshima Day; we remember these high-ticket items and nobly proclaim may it never happen again while all around us something very bad is happening now.

It's a lovely day in late September. I sit outside and see the clear blue Northern California sky. I wish for such clarity in how American society deals with the use and abuse of psychoactives. I wish there was such clarity in my mind about what, if anything, I could do. I pray to be alert for any opportunities that present themselves. I doze off and dream. My nightmare is Gulag America, the war on drugs finally won by turning this shining land into one giant prison where we are all born and die, never to know there ever existed any such things as privacy or personal rights. My sweet dream is that I fly around the country miraculously freeing all those who've lost their freedom to drugs and prisons, and on the day following this gallant act of psychoactivism we all celebrate together in harmony, enjoying our natural minds and the good earth's fresh air and sunshine.

LEANING INTO RAWNESS ⊘ Trudy Walter

I USED TO LOVE GETTING STONED. I especially loved to get stoned and read Dharma. When stoned I was never bored: Every single piece of my world was reliably fascinating. My curiosity and delight with any and everybody was palpable. I could read the newspaper and not have my blood curdle. Trees would twinkle and wave especially at me. It felt as if the miracle of my life was familiar and accessible again: Here I was once again in this cozy space. I got so into the addiction that I could hardly go for a walk without getting buzzed. Almost every high brought that tremendous feeling of contact—that feeling of being a part of every crack in the sidewalk, every mosquito trying to make its way in the world. Exhaustion was buoyed and did not weigh so heavily. With gratitude, not annoyance, with humbleness, not resentfulness, I could carry on domestic routines: the care of two small children, a husband, and a dog, and I could attend to a widening array of friends and participate in Buddhist practices that took daily attention, most of every weekend—sangha, driven with the abundant and never-ending celebrations, practices, feasts, and training programs. Getting stoned brought perceived relief but no real rest. I was part of a life-transforming scene that would change the world, and I didn't want to miss it.

I had heard stories from first- and second-wave practitioners from Tail of the Tiger that Chogyam Trungpa Rinpoche had held a special ceremony one evening where all who lived there were asked to bring their stashes of dope and burn them up in the campfire while he proclaimed "the end of illusion." It didn't make any sense to me, since I knew how much alcohol and other substances were being consumed there. It especially didn't make sense when it seemed that my drug of choice was being condemned, while my husband's drug of choice (alcohol) was being celebrated. Drinking lessons were held as we were taught about bringing awareness to inebriating the senses. Alcohol was sanctified during feast practice as our usually chaotic mind was redirected in "sacred space." Why was my smoke not able to be in sacred space also? I had only one personal interview with Rinpoche, and I hungrily begged for an explanation of why he thought it was alert to use alcohol and not marijuana. Stoned or drunk, my friends and I seemed to get to the same psychic places. Why couldn't he bless my chosen substance? Rinpoche paused for a long moment and then quietly told me that when I relaxed into living my life I would be a terrific drinker. That certainly slowed down my momentum—it made no sense to me whatsoever. Perhaps it even stopped my mind, which, instead of just solving our problems, was what the teacher was supposed to do.

From that point of contact with Rinpoche it took many more years of smoking—at least every afternoon, and on bad days from early in the morning—for me to come to my own realization. Without fail every morning, I would rise with the fervent vow that this would be the day I would quit, would no longer use this route to cope. Later, it took someone in my addiction recovery unit to tell me how this vow itself was the setup for using. Somehow it would trigger the glee and defeat of getting to a level of tension or frustration and then fold into "Fuck it. I'm smoking. I deserve this and no one can stop me."

It took one wretched near-fight with my husband, where my trembling rage leaked into my awareness, to crack the momentum of my habit. I was already as stoned as I could get. It was a batch of fabulous weed. I felt something rise up in me that was so powerful it was undeniable. Instead of screaming and yelling, expressing and exploding, I felt myself implode. I took my vibrating rage and found myself, as I came to, desperately sucking my special pipe in order to make this ignition disappear. It was too late. The realization had seeped through beyond denial and confusion. Something had soundlessly snapped. The hypocrisy of living half of my life trying to wake up by meditating and the other half trying to anesthetize myself was overwhelming. I knew I needed help.

By myself I could not overcome the underlying desire to feel only the good stuff. No matter what I had learned from the Dharma, I really wanted out of the violence of my anger, confusion, helplessness, hunger, and fear. With just a puff or two, anger simply got fuzzy and rounded off. What was so unutterably irritating just moments before, would vanish. I had labeled the force of anger as small-minded, tightly wound up, territorial, uncompassionate, and surely unevolved. Somewhere along the way the word got out that losing your cool erased the karma of an entire month of sitting. This was not Rinpoche's example. He did get angry and did display it. I always had the impression, from the infinite stories of those who were closer to him, that his anger was pure energy and not attached. He simply roared at someone and then it was over. My delusion was that if I got angry the world would fall apart, people would leave me forever and finally know how awful a human being I was. I was not and am not now unattached. My anger resounds for years. Letting it go is an aspiration, not something that seems to work. Not expressing anger did not originate solely from our sangha: this was the way my parents had operated as well. Also, beginning long before I was even conceived, both parents never let a day go by without a cocktail hour. Thus, on a cellular level, my being was accustomed to daily inebriation. Both parents were socially acceptable drinkers, active participants in their busy worlds. Here in this Dharma world, the sangha recreated the atmosphere.

Almost. There was a difference. When Rinpoche taught us about co-emergence he had two of us walk together to the front of the room and then suddenly split off in opposite directions. This was a stunning enactment of how closely the neurotic state of mind arises right along with the enlightened. There is no guarantee of choosing the awake route. It is only the vow to lean into the rawness of experience, without filter and without props, that we have to count on. I have found that every vow I have taken as a twenty-year practitioner is a fumbling attempt to stop the perpetration of illusion. I still scrape along on my knees a lot. In the dozen years since I quit using dope regularly, I have experimented a handful of times—"done more research," as they say in the recovery business. It always fails. I am relentlessly stuck back in the realm of anxiety or frustration that couldn't be smoked away. The connection to each step beneath my feet—to the place where things are allowed to simply be as they are—is what meditation practice works with. The illusion is that this contact is brought about by the drug itself, and it always fades as the THC passes through.

The struggle for a practitioner lies in the infantile yearning for only the good stuff and not being able to hang out with the bleakness. Great ecstatic meditation periods have never been celebrated by teachers; we're always told to go back to the cushion, to let go of all that arises. Those grungy black emotions come and go with a will of their own. The commitment is to the entire mandala, not just the part where there are only downhills and the wind is always gently blowing at my back. Far more often than I'd like to admit, I still actively yearn for the moments of joy and oblivion that dope provided. It's embarrassing to find that my longing for spirit or connection the fast way hasn't really disappeared that much over time. I get caught sometimes in the dualism that pokes an annoying finger in my moralistic stance: "What a good girl I am for not smoking. Why don't I just give myself a tiny little break. Is it imperative that I be gentle and kind and lighten up? Light up! Where's my *maitri* (benevolence)? Where has not smoking gotten me? I am no more awake or aware than I was when I was smoking. What is my problem?"

It's stark how much the ol' hair in the eyeball stings, and what treachery the mind pulls when it wants a break, and you know that giving it that break is destructive. The fire that Rinpoche lit to burn up illusion is still burning away in me.

HARMONY OF THE DRAGONS Android Jones, 2012

ENLIGHTENMENT CAPSULE Mariko Mori, 1996-1998

BURNING DESIRE Mariko Mori, 1998

RELATIVE TRUTH ☙ Brigid Meier

My first plant medicine experience was in 1974. I asked the *Vidyadhara* Chogyam Trungpa Rinpoche what he thought about me taking some of the many fresh peyote buttons circulating around Boulder that summer. "If you're going to do it, do it right," he admonished me in his Oxonian accent. I took that to mean that I should investigate how peyote is used traditionally as a sacrament, as a tool for awakening. I did this to the best of my ability; I fasted, meditated, and prayed—and created a supportive, safe setting. My set—what I brought to the experience—was an eclectic mix of reverence, curiosity, warriorship, and leftover beatnik/poetic anarchism. My intention was undoubtedly influenced by having read Carlos Castaneda and resonating with Don Juan Matus's proclamation that "peyote could teach you the right way to live."

It was with a similar inquiry that almost twenty years later I returned every six months for three years to a sacred plant medicine circle. I apprenticed to the realm of plant medicines to seek teachings from a stratum of nonhuman consciousness in order to open to the direct felt experience of Gaia, to the experiential knowing, not simply the insight, of the interdependence of all beings.

Despite not attending the circle for the past several years, it remains my belief that sacred plants, as a frequency of planetary intelligence, have offered themselves as emissaries from the increasingly ravaged natural world. Their intention seems to be to get inside and convert as many mobile humans as possible—a critical mass—in order to do their subversive work of infiltrating then dismantling the cancerous human ego that is destroying the planet and their ecosystem. This notion feels intuitively accurate—the organism of the Earth is healing itself, coming into balance in a state of being that is not focused on human history and human culture. As one whose heart and soul are aligned with this evolutionary mission, I feel that having had the opportunity to scrape some accumulated barnacles of mass consciousness off my psychic boat was a profound blessing. The medicines' teachings became another "turning of the wheel" of wisdom—an invitation to become a member of the sangha of ALL beings, not only of a human-centric universe. The message of genuine interdependence and empathy that the medicines impart—in their multidimensionally holographic way—seems to be utterly specific to the living spirits of the beings—the plant people, the rock people, the tree people, the devas—of each bioregion. The medicines allow one to finally hear the voices of one's neighbors—on every level—all my relations. I found that Buddhism and native wisdom often vector in the plant medicine experience. And the gestalt of "Buddhism"—moment to moment enlightenment of "what is" beyond grasping—came alive for me in a way that was surely once accessed through the shamanic use of plants or fungi in the early Vedic era.

The real work, with both meditation practice and the use of plant substances, is to transmute the grace and insight received into compassionate, skillful action in one's ordinary life. Neither discipline on its own has made me a more generous person. Nor do they do my work for me—they both simply point toward what needs to be done. I have experienced meditation and plant substances as each having its own morphogenetic field which rises up to meet me the deeper and more committed I venture. I've encountered beings from many realms throughout time that have preceded me, who've invited me to tap into their experiences and insights. They can become a lineage and a transmission to impart if one chooses to follow. The task, as always, is to navigate the sea of awareness—Mind!—which unfolds ceaselessly in the present moment. And there's a way in which medicine practice, like meditation practice, feels like preparation for death. One simply cannot hold on and proceed at the same time. Every time I journeyed I ran into Trungpa Rinpoche out there in hyperspace and he asked me, "Are you having fun, sweetheart?" or "What do you think you're doing now?" The truth of No Escape holds up—the guru is everywhere—inextricably lodged in the practitioner's Being.

But like anything else, taking plant medicines indiscriminately and carelessly can become a frivolous trip—fertile ground for ego to form. It can be a fairly dangerous trip; people get stuck for years in what Ken Wilber calls "the green meme." It is crucial to have a qualified guide, one who is experienced and who is also impeccable. The best guides admit they know nothing themselves and have no desire to lay a trip on you; they simply create a safe, mindful set and setting conducive to further awakening. They are more like midwives gently encouraging you to explore and/or release while possessing the knowledge of how

DHARMA DRAGON Android Jones, 2012

DIVINE MESSENGER OF TRUTH Randal Roberts, 2007

to perform psychic triage should the need arise. These guides have unfathomable trust in the medicines, in the sincere seeker, and in the spirits to create a sacred healing alchemy for the highest good.

The first formal medicine circle I attended was held over a weekend during the early nineties at a remote New Mexico setting in a zendo-like hall complete with zafus and a candle shrine to the four directions in the center of the room. After setting our intentions for healing and vision, then sharing them with each other on Friday night, all twelve of us participants spent Saturday alone, fasting outdoors, opening to nature. Saturday night we each took the medicine we felt more aligned with. We were offered the choice of ayahuasca, psilocybin mushrooms, San Pedro cactus, or iboga root. Alignment was determined by many factors but primarily it had to do with which axis on the medicine wheel you felt you were on at the time, which energy you most wanted to connect with. Mushrooms, called "the little children" by the Mazatec *curandera*, Maria Sabina, were in the east and were taken to invoke new beginnings. Ayahuasca, a powerful rainforest concoction which activates the lower chakras or primal instinctual energy, was in the west and was taken in order to let go of what is no longer needed. Iboga, a root from Africa, held the northern position and is taken to invoke the ancestors or masculine energy. San Pedro cactus from South America is in the south and represents rejuvenating, nurturing feminine energy. This is a loosely constructed schema but it seems to hold up energetically.

Saturday evening we gathered in the meditation hall, invoked the plant, animal, and ancestor spirits and the spirits of the earth. Then we each took our respective medicines. For several hours we alternated lying down, heads toward the center shrine, led verbally by the guide and having time to be with our own individual experiences. We then sat up and passed a staff and sang our journeys. We did this sequence three times. It was an extraordinary combination of personal biographical exploration, a guided archetypal journey, and the retrieval of information relating to our intention which we brought back to the collective. Because everybody's ass was on the line, there was an incredible atmosphere of unconditional love for each person's courage to be psychically unmasked before the group. A feeling of true sangha flowed throughout my experience, something I had not been able to find during all those years of practicing at different Buddhist centers.

On that particular journey I tried ayahuasca for the first time. My life was at a crossroads and I was feeling as if the wind had gone out of my sails; on many levels I was ambivalent about life. Ayahuasca most assuredly cut through that conceit in a hurry and I got my butt kicked by the ruthlessly uncompromising love of the plant spirits. I experienced the same quantum leap in consciousness with ayahuasca as I did when I first took LSD in San Francisco, 1967. I had the same infusion of gratitude to be alive and a similar certainty that "my world will never be the same."

Although they can sometimes be heavy-handed, many journeyers appreciate the tryptamines—mushrooms, ayahuasca, DMT—for the visual hallucinations they elicit. I found the phenethylamines—San Pedro cactus and peyote—to be true teachers for my particular biochemistry and spiritual inclinations—less form, more emptiness, perhaps.

San Pedro has an uncanny ability to impart its wisdom in a particularly gentle yet firmly ineluctable way. I did a painting of a San Pedro journey I had in the circle depicting myself being held in the loving hands of Our Lady of Guadalupe, who feels to me like the Western hemisphere's Kuanyin or Green Tara. During the journey, which I experienced as deep waves of energy coming up from the earth and through my belly, I felt as if I was being shown, in innumerable ways, how the specificities of my life are not separate from the perennial teachings—how my life lessons are exquisitely "tailored" for me but are simultaneously universal. All this was revealed with profound love for how human I am. It felt like a direct encounter with Gaia, the mother, the earth, offering her child healing on a cellular level—the Relative Truth of the biological substrate of compassion: deoxyribonucleic acid—DNA as Prajnaparamita.

YAGÉ AND THE YANAS ⊘ Allan Badiner

(Fall 1996 – revised November 2014)

WITH MORE THAN A LITTLE TREPIDATION, my girlfriend and I boarded a flight to Hawaii. Once buckled in, I fell into a deep and unusually restful sleep. Hours later, I raised the shade and, overcoming a blast of near-blinding light, peered out the small window. The palm-fringed handful of islands strewn in a random arc in the middle of the blue Pacific looked like the last grains from a weary sower's hand. I remembered that it wasn't for the black sand beaches and helicopter rides over volcanoes that I had made this journey. It was 1987, and my moment with a shaman was coming near. I had an appointment with yagé, or ayahuasca, the "vine of the soul."

Walls of red sugarcane stalks lined the highway from the airport as we sped to the place of my appointment: a botanical reserve amidst climax rainforest on the slopes of the Mauna Loa volcano. The placid blue ocean stayed constant, while the scenery on the other side of the road turned dryer, harder, and darker, and the mileposts whizzed by. Finally, the land was just a solid black crust of once-liquid lava beds as far as the eye could see, resembling a black version of a lunar landscape. A volcanic haze called "vog" hung high in the horizon above the still-fiery Pele some twenty miles farther to the south.

We turned up an inland road, parked, and boarded a waiting jeep. As we climbed the bumpy road, we noticed hints of vegetation appearing here and there, leading to persimmon bushes, and then groves of ginger flowers, mango trees, and macadamia trees. As we entered the reserve area we found ourselves on the edge of a jungle, an overgrown thicket of kukui grass with spectacular ocean views peering between tall trunks of blossoming ohia trees.

The shaman, with a gray beard and wizened features, greeted us with some Kona coffee and showed us to our quarters. The appointed hour was drawing near, and after a short rest, we assembled on the porch where I was to drink the ayahuasca—a catalyst for perhaps the most powerful and intensely visionary experiences ever known.

The sun was setting over the jungle as I contemplated my glass of the pungent brew. An incredible amount of work went into producing this thick, dark chocolate-colored drink. Ayahuasca is brewed from the *Banistereopsis caapi* vine mixed with the leaves of the DMT-rich *Psychotria viridis*, plants that originate from the Amazon rainforest, but also thrive in Hawaii. They are boiled first separately and then together for over a week, requiring constant stirring and removal of pulp. The origin of the recipe is itself a mystery, and I wondered what the odds were on the Amazon Indians discovering this formula randomly through trial and error.

I had read the descriptions of encounters with ayahuasca by contemporary Westerners in William Burroughs and Allen Ginsberg's *The Yagé Letters*, the McKenna brothers' *The Invisible Landscape*, and Andrew Weil's *The Marriage of the Sun and the Moon*. Nothing, however, except perhaps Buddhist meditation practice, had prepared me for what followed after emptying my glass.

I kissed my companion goodbye and was shown to the tent that the shaman had set up for me farther into the jungle. He wished me luck, reminded me not to cling to any visions, delightful or horrifying, and disappeared into the night. The stars above were so bright and numerous that I couldn't take my eyes off the night sky. I remembered a bit of unfinished business to do before losing motor control, and picked a spot in the ground in which to deposit my vomit when it came time. Still feeling normal, my gaze returned to the starry heavens.

I was expecting all hell to break loose at any second, but what ensued was so subtle that I could hardly believe it was a function of the ayahuasca. As I stared at the star formations, I could suddenly see that these were not isolated stars but points of light on a giant body—the body of a massive spider. She moved her body ever so subtly, as if to offer confirming evidence of her existence. When the spider moved, all the sky moved in relation to her, and in scale the way the many legs of a real spider would actually move.

This didn't feel like a hallucination at all, but more like a filter had been removed, and I was suddenly able to see the true nature of the sky. I was ecstatic, not from the drug, but from the honor and thrill of seeing the heavens in its true living integrated form, power, and beauty. My preoccupation with the animated, breathing sky above me was interrupted by a powerful feeling of being lifted off the ground. The next thing I knew I was staring closely at the dirt and hearing a torrent of matter fleeing my body, its stream forming one leg of a tripod, my hands the other two, as my legs flailed about straight up in the air. The sound of my retching reverberated through the jungle like a call to the spirits for help. I had expected the vomit, but what mystified me was how I was being supported upside down as it gushed from my mouth.

The feeling of being drugged was definitely kicking in now, and I quickly found my way into the tent and lay down. Just before I was able to get horizontal, a light and color show began. I laid back and watched the most extraordinary colors vibrate and gyrate into fractals. The colors were unlike any I had ever seen, and they displayed themselves with the most remarkable intensity. They seemed unaffected by whether my eyes were open or closed, and the first inkling of fear set in. Was I blind? Would I ever see the real world again?

Growing weary of the swirling colors, I longed to see my raised hand or the inside of the tent. How could I have done this to myself? I kept wondering. Please let it be over, I prayed. But the journey had just begun, and the light show was the fun part. I struggled to turn my mind away from the compelling visions to the steady rhythm of my breath. Suddenly the sound of my breathing became almost ear-shatteringly loud, as if it was blowing across the surface of a distant planet, like a giant windstorm.

I became aware, quite suddenly, that my body had vanished, and only my mind and sensory impressions remained.

Gradually the true meaning of this experience became clear—I was journeying to the end of my life. In the process, I came to grips with something I had no idea was true about myself—that I was completely unwilling to believe that death was real. Intellectually, I was aware, like everyone else, of the inevitability of death. But the reality of the very moment of death, the moment of my last breath, was not something I was willing to see. And then I saw it.

I was back on Earth, standing in the mud outside my tent and staring disbelievingly at a corpse—my own. I picked up a hand and felt the cold weight of an arm that would never again move on its own, and dropped it back into the mud. I noticed a small trail of blood from its mouth across an unshaven and pale cheek dripping into the mud. All the while I heard my mind saying, "No, it's not real, it's just the drug," but my eyes saw my lifeless body lying there, real as could possibly be.

As if this wasn't convincing enough for my persistent ego, I flashed on a scene in which I was driving by a cemetery, only to notice one particular tombstone standing out among the others. I read with total horror my own name chiseled across the tall granite slab. Images from my life flickered before me, first slowly, then in hyperspeed, and finally there was just blackness. Death was finally real and surrender was the only option. But why didn't this voice I was hearing stop, and who, or what, was listening to it?

I didn't have much chance to reflect on these important questions before facing yet another struggle. The scenery had changed. It was more fantastical, more dark, more frightening. Dead as I was, I still found myself on the run, this time from a classic fire-breathing dragon. I almost laughed at the clichéd imagery when the surroundings grew increasingly more macabre. The world became a series of caves, populated by bizarre forms of life.

Mechanical and yet biological, these machine-like beings twisted and turned in mathematical precision with each other as if I were peering into some nanotechnological microcosm of the dark forces of nature. A strange haunting melody accompanied their gyrations. Whenever I found myself fascinated with some aspect of what was undoubtedly the underworld, a blast of fire from the dragon curled around me and singed the hair on my legs. The verisimilitude of this vision and the smell of burning hair had me biting my lip so hard I could taste the blood.

Suddenly I unsheathed a giant sword and stabbed the beast repeatedly in every part of its scaly body while narrowly avoiding being burned or swallowed. I thrust the final blow to the throat and watched the torrent of blood pour from his wound until the thrashing of its long powerful tail finally ceased. As I stared into the closing eyes of the now slumped dragon, I could see a glimmer of recognition. Slipping out of consciousness, its face slowly metamorphosed into a more human one, and gradually it became clear that the face the dragon was wearing was my own.

I stared at the dead dragon and felt a tremendous upwelling of sympathy and compassion. As a tear slid down my virtual cheek, I reflected on what a fantastic lesson in self-as-other this experience was: here was a despicable, horrible beast intent on crushing me between its teeth or burning me to a crisp, yet I was able to widen my circle of compassion to embrace it. What enemy could I have, what unspeakably vicious act could I not forgive after this? The lesson was swift and immediate.

Then, for what seemed to be an eternity, I experienced a complete and total void of any sensory input. There was no time, no place, no visions, no sounds, no feelings. Even my thoughts, which had been intact throughout the ordeal, seemed less forthcoming and harder to grasp. I tried to muster enough mental energy to form at least the desire for life. Something in my essence was pleading for life, some kernel of consciousness was intent on seeking an animated state. Muscles and nerves seemed to create themselves anew, attempting to generate at least a tingle of sensation.

Perception of my surroundings—the dull gray color of the tent and the moon shadows dancing on its surface—crept into my field of vision so gradually I hardly noticed they had been absent. The world I had just visited still felt very much present, separated from me by no more than the flimsiest of veils. My thoughts returned, and the first one was gratitude. The sensation of being distinct from the mud, of having a community of bones and sinews with which to feel the damp canvas floor against my back was quietly thrilling. To see the play of light and dark along the tent walls and hear the throaty call of nearby insects was indescribably joyful.

Slowly I raised my tired body and stepped out into the night, inhaling what felt like something very alive itself—the sweet and perfumed night air. I was grinning so hard I thought the corners of my lips might crack. I sank to my knees and practically buried my face in the mud, examining closely the surface of the earth and tasting with the tip of my tongue the richness of her soil. My thoughts turned to my girlfriend, and how delicious it would be to hold her and to be held. I stumbled along the roots of vines and carelessly brushed past the blades of the bush to find my way back to the main house.

Immediately after coming through the kitchen door I confronted the shaman, who was busy stirring a large pot of the foul-smelling brew. "How could you do that to me?" I asked. The shaman stopped stirring, brought me some water, and sat down at the table with me. "Did you suffer?" he asked. Although I felt as though I had never in my life suffered so intensely as in the last few hours, at that moment I was aware of much greater space in my mind around the very notion of suffering itself. Buddhism teaches us that suffering is an inevitable part of life, but to have experienced so concentrated an episode of mental torture was like bringing the teaching into my cells and making it an organic truth of my life.

Although suffering exists, I deeply understood for the first time that no sufferer really exists. Throughout my journey I was actively doing and thinking, but having confronted the truth of my demise over and over, it was painfully obvious that I had no actual inherent existence. I was astonished that as he asked me the question, I no longer seemed to have any aversion or charge about suffering itself. As a graduate of the journey, I demonstrated my willingness to suffer and die. I reflected on the words of a gentle Buddhist monk from Sri Lanka now living in Brooklyn: "People are at their cruelest when they are intent on avoiding suffering." So in response to the shaman's query, I found myself smiling and I uttered simply, "Yes, but I recognized the emptiness of it."

As I looked into the shaman's eyes I found myself staring into the face of a dead man. It felt miraculous that we were animated, breathing, and making sounds. I looked at my hand for a few moments, and it seemed like a stranger's hand—belonging more to my parents and my ancestors than to me. My eyes shifted to the flame under the pot, and then they narrowed and closed. The shaman and I spontaneously began to meditate, sitting totally still and silent for at least fifteen minutes. I have observed that my meditation practice jumped to a new level since the journey, and I find it easier to stay concentrated on my breath. Perhaps the reason for this is simply that the breath itself is more interesting to me, and I remain amazed that we have this capacity to exchange gases in the invisible soup of life within which we live.

The most powerful and obvious transformation resulting from this appointment with the shaman was in my relationship to death. I was dramatically aware of how diminished my fear of it was, and that not only could I hold thoughts of death while remaining in a pleasant state of mind, I was actively looking at death and the reality of dying for inspiration, clarity and a deeper context for my life. Beyond my new respect for death, the nature of my relationship to Buddhism also felt very different. Whereas Buddhism used to seem more like a vehicle with which I was seeking a destination, it now seems like a clever way to enjoy the present moment. I'm not sure I have any hopes for ultimate realization, but I do have a stronger interest in spending more of my life in Buddhist practice.

The shaman asked me if I would consider taking the ayahuasca again. I had to laugh. A chuckle turned into bellows of belly laughs followed by sharp cries of uncontrollable laughter. The notion of taking the vine or any other psychedelics again seemed absolutely preposterous. "No way, José," I replied. The morning sun would soon be upon us, and I thought of how its light would allow me to see the multitude of flowering plants in the area. I thought of how psychedelic it would be just to see the flowers and bring them to my nose. Suddenly the prospect of having a baby seemed far more exciting than dropping a neurochemical bomb in my system to see endless parades of colors and forms.

"You had a good journey," the shaman said as we left the table and prepared to take a nap before the dawn. "Why?" I asked, "'That which does not kill you makes you stronger,' as the saying goes?" "No," the shaman replied with the liveliest grin I had seen on his face so far, "that which kills you makes you stronger."

JUNGLE DHARMA: The Interweaving of Buddhism and Ayahuasca
David Coyote

"As long as there are practitioners who go to the forest to practice,
the way of the awakened ones will never die."

—The Buddha

IT CAN BE USEFUL TO THINK ABOUT spiritual and cultural traditions, such as the Buddhadharma, as spontaneously arising, self-organizing, living beings of their own: in other words curiously similar to plants. They have roots in the Earth, they grow and their branches spread, they flower and fruit and drop their seeds, sometimes quite far from the original soil. The seeds sprout, flourish and adapt to new conditions. Seeds of the Buddhadharma have dropped into many contemporary hearts. We are as gardeners doing our best to cultivate them, each in our own way: in Sangha, in lineage, in our daily lives and in our own native cultural soil.

For me, this process has led to over thirty years of intensive study and retreat, which has included ordination in Asia and lay practice in America. I've learned several languages, received numerous initiations, practiced yogas and have lived in many communities as well as alone in the woods. Like many others, my spiritual journey began with the intense shock of suffering: in my case, the death of both parents. This gave rise to a deep questioning about the purpose of life and a search for teachings and a path—a deep thirst for healing and liberation and a willingness to try any means that worked well and skillfully—preferably one with roots. I was quickly drawn to Buddhism.

My first teacher was a Korean Zen master. He had arrived in the West in the early 1970s and his first students were young hippies and seekers. He introduced them to *koan* practice, bowing, sitting and chanting. At one student's request he even tried LSD. He called it "special medicine" and thought it might have some use for practitioners, maybe used once to break the hard shell of their concepts. But his own tools were "the great question," hard training and a deep Bodhisattva vow—not medicines, however special they might be.

My second teacher was a Tibetan Vajrayana master. Through him, I was introduced to the intense devotion of the way of the Tibetan yogi and the vast array of skillful means available in the lineage. Rinpoche's teachings were tantric and at times our practice included the transformation of alcohol into *amrita*. Having been requested, he too tried LSD. His comment was, "Good for visualization practice." As with my Zen master, Rinpoche saw these substances as interesting and possibly useful, but nothing he was interested in pursuing.

I met a third teacher many years ago and she is just as strict and demanding as a Zen master or Rinpoche. Sometimes wrathful, sometimes peaceful, she has her own lineage and wisdoms, her own gifts to offer. She is the plant teacher Ayahuasca. Through the guidance of various *ayahuasceros* and many travels south that have come to total several years' time spent in the Amazon jungle, her medicine has been part of my Dharma practice ever since. I have needed this "bitter practice" to take me deeper into my body and to clarify my emotions; to actually feel the Earth I'm living on.

Siddhartha Gautama walked into the jungle where he lived and practiced for six years. Finally, he sat under a tree for days until one dawn, as the morning star appeared in the sky, he awoke to his true nature. Imagine being that intimate with the trees, the plants, the animals, the waters, and living that closely with the Earth for so long. The Buddhadharma arose in the wild and since that time has produced a tradition of practitioners who have also lived and practiced deep in nature—in forests, on mountains, in deserts and on islands. What could be more fitting than the Dharma meeting and interacting with another tradition that also arose in the jungle? A tradition of indigenous peoples, almost destroyed, and then ignored by their conquerors? Maybe having the humility to receive their tradition and its sacred plant medicine can help post-industrial people to finally arrive on this land; to finally come home.

I share my perspective, thoughts and experiences because the dharma seeds in some practitioner's hearts may flourish as mine did in Ayahuasca's wild and indigenous love. I have come to feel that a clear and openhearted engagement with this native tradition (which like the Dharma is both thousands of years old and has come a great distance to meet us) can help those of us who are in need of roots and brave enough to receive her teachings. It can deepen our dharma practice and help us to truly find our own seat on the Earth.

This isn't the first time that the Dharma has traveled and met with other traditions. When Dharma teachings came to Tibet as Vajrayana they met the indigenous shamanic tradition of Bön and a uniquely Tibetan Buddhism appeared. Arriving in China, the Dharma "met and married" Taoism with its nature worship and alchemical roots and the child of that union lives on as Zen. In coming to a new place there is always a meeting, always an exchange of gifts, always new growth.

The Practice

Like the Buddha Way, Ayahuasca is fundamentally a practice, an experience, something that we do. In so doing we are transformed, purified, and opened to the essence of our body, heart and mind. As with meditation, there are lessons to be learned, concepts to release and a balance to maintain. For those who are ready, this ancient practice is an immediate and powerful embodiment of Dharma teachings.

Ayahuasca is perhaps different from other entheogens in that it is a very embodied *Nirmanakaya* experience, partially because the brew is a purge. The native healers' explanation is that Ayahuasca works by finding the crossed energies, the blockages, the illnesses of body and mind and clearing them out of the system physically and energetically. This energetic opening can be experienced in a very yogic manner. We may become aware of energetic blockages in the body that are released and result in involuntary *kriyas* or movements. We may feel the *chakras* and *nadis*—the energy system of the subtle body. Sometimes the channels open easily; and other times, there may be an extended and painful process of contacting blocked emotional energies or life experiences that led to one's energy body having shut down.

Often there are powerful *Sambhogakaya* visions, which offer healing or give teachings. These visions can be the traditional jungle spirits of Jaguars, Anacondas, plant spirits or of Ayahuasca herself. (In the tradition of my indigenous teacher, she is embodied as a beautiful woman.) Practitioners may also have visions of their dharma teachers, of Buddhas and Bodhisattvas and teaching deities such as Tara or Kuanyin. There can be experiences of karmic life review which may be biographical or may resemble the past life remembrances that experienced yogis report. We may have visionary conversations and interactions with friends, enemies or family members that lead to forgiveness, clarity and openheartedness.

For people with proper training, the end of an ayahuasca ceremony can be an amazingly fruitful time. After the powerful cleansing energy that the experience typically begins with, followed by the intense visionary current which arises, there are moments of utter stillness, the lucid openness of *Dharmakaya*.

While untrained participants may just drift in relaxation, the meditator can enjoy an easy familiarity with this open, limpid and lucent state. At times there may be an experience of our essential nature. In general we move from the coarse to the subtle, both in one session and over a series of sessions. First the purging and clearing, then visions, and then the open and still space of awareness reveals itself.

A Possible Approach

For Buddhists called to the jungle practice, a firm grounding in our Dharma practice is essential. Since the two experiences mirror each other so extensively, our practice helps in the preparation beforehand, the navigation during and in the integration afterwards. And again, integration is key. While certainly not the only one, perhaps the most useful perspective is that of Tantric practice. In fact there are scholars, such as R. C. Parker, who claim that visionary plants were once part of or even central to Vajrayana practice in India. It's easy to view Ayahuasca as an indigenous *yidam*. Seeing her that way, she may manifest in both wrathful and peaceful aspects.

There are two different approaches to working with ayahuasca. In one the dose is high and the emphasis is on emotional, energetic and karmic cleansing. The practitioner's capacity to stay grounded and centered is very important. Since the sessions can be very intense, the guide's role as a healer is quite important. In the other approach the dose is low, and the emphasis is on interaction with our higher-level structures of self and intentional meditative practice. In this style, the guide's role as teacher comes forward. Navigation is easier and there may be more self-reflection, life lessons and states of calm abiding in open presence.

Ayahuasca is a visionary path and the parallels with deity yoga are many. One interesting twist is that in an Ayahuasca ceremony the visions are usually self-arising and spontaneous. But a trained practitioner might find it easy to guide them and use the experience to deepen an ongoing sadhana practice.

Sometimes the visions that appear are the turbocharged manifestation of ordinary mind, what Trungpa Rinpoche called, "supersamsara." Other times people are graced with "pure visions," which actually do seem to reflect contact with one's ancestors, teachers, protectors, yidams or spirits of nature. These visions can open our awareness to the dreamlike appearance of the phenomenal world. The experience of having our own samsaric projections reflected back to ourselves can be just as valuable and far more humbling than those of a "higher" nature. The work of recognizing and releasing our own thoughts is equally, if not more, powerful at night in the jungle as when sitting on one's cushion after a morning cup of tea. The inescapability of having to deal with our projections is a powerful feature of this practice. For those with a yoga practice of winds and channels, many spontaneous openings of energies and chakras arise that can be engaged and may enhance one's ongoing practice.

In many ways, an Ayahuasca ceremony is like any practice or retreat, but its sudden, intense, and deep nature requires more attention to integration than other practices. It offers potent states of yogic and meditative experience, which are ordinarily available only to practitioners who devote years to retreat practice. Because of this quality, preparation and integration with our daily practice and daily life is clearly much more important than with an ordinary meditative practice. The purifications, insights and teachings must be put into practice in our life. The yogic openings must be exercised and extended. The experience of being embodied as a human here on our native Earth must be lived.

Preparing well and being in good company when drinking the Ayahuasca is the recipe for a powerfully beneficial experience. Respectful rituals of preparation with refuge, generation of Bodhicitta and calling on the protectors are all very supportive. Ideally a circle of yogis and yoginis would meet periodically to take their places in the medicine mandala of Mother Earth's self-arising net of healing, wisdom and love.

For an experienced Dharma practitioner, an Ayahuasca ceremony can be an excellent way to "test the depths" and conduct a kind of stress test of one's practice. Do you feel crushed by the oppressive weight of your karma? How does your ego respond to the feeling of supreme understanding and power? Are there obstructions you have missed in your practice? Since most of us living in the modern world are not able to leave our families, homes and jobs for a year or more of intense retreat, working with Ayahuasca is an opportunity to have an experience of the profound depth of our heart and mind.

For example, we have all received teachings on compassion and love. Many people engage in meditations which develop loving-kindness and Bodhicitta. But how deeply do we feel them? How deeply in our body is the experience occurring? How would it feel to have our heart bursting with compassion? It is a powerful experience indeed to have buried memories of our own losses and grief arise and be led through the subsequent opening of our heart chakra and thinking in a transcendent way; having a transpersonal experience of actually being some other sentient being is even more so. In that field of being, engaging in loving-kindness or Bodhicitta meditation can touch our heart at a depth that is extremely transformative. At that moment we embody the teachings: we are living them, breathing them, and being them.

A number of Buddhists are finding great benefit in the teachings of this jungle tradition as a complementary practice. It addresses the absence of a more fundamental relationship with the Earth and our own body that traditional Dharma assumes everyone has, but that our modern culture has forgotten. Unlike with some other substances, most Ayahuasca practitioners experience her as a wisdom being who is present with them and is guiding their experience. This can give rise to experiences of communion with the embodiment of the jungle or with all of nature herself.

In my own spiritual journey, I've struggled with how to integrate my Dharma practice with deep emotional healing. I've also had difficulty translating the teachings from traditional Asian teachers to my life experience, with its social environment of "de-natured," post-industrial, capitalist existence. The deepest benefit I have received from my relationship with ayahuasca has been to realize another "*kaya*" to go with the three traditional ones. And that is the "Gaia-kaya."

To have sloughed off the painful and distorted view of being some kind of disembodied object in a purposeless machine-like world is the kindest, most redeeming gift imaginable. To have some visceral sense of how it was for the Buddha living in the jungle—breathing Mother Earth's air, drinking her water and sitting on her body, gives me the courage and inspiration to take my own seat and practice. That sense of our own embodiment and of the Earth as a living, breathing being in whose embrace we live our lives is something that our

Asian teachers grew up with and that the traditions assume we already have. But many of us in the West lack it and without this seat, based in our bodies on this Earth, our Dharma seeds won't grow to their full potential. In some ways this meta-teaching is Ayahuasca's greatest offering.

All of this, for me, has been an amazingly powerful "*upaya,*" or skillful means. And the more powerful the means, the more skill required to use it correctly. So, careful preparation beforehand, clear and skillful guidance during the experience and integration afterwards are all of the utmost importance.

Those happily walking the traditional path of Dharma teachings, meditation and realization obviously have no need of something so strange as this bitter brew from the jungle. For them, practicing the teachings exactly in the way that they were received seems best. But for others of us there is much to learn by seeking out more ancient ways as well. It may turn out to be a sidetrack or dead end for some but it is worth exploring nonetheless, worth sending out scouts to report back. As a *Mahasangha*, we will all benefit.

I'm not suggesting changing the Dharma. The Dharma doesn't change but the skillful means certainly do—they have to grow and adapt as our lives change. Used wisely, the Ayahuasca experience is a safe and powerful tool that can lead us to fascinating edges of our practice. And the best learning happens at the edges, in the darkness out beyond those things we think we understand, in the great open jungle-like space of "not knowing."

As the great Zen Master Dizang once said, "Not knowing is most intimate."

BUDDHIST HARM REDUCTION AND CANNABIS ℮ Jana Drakka

I BEGAN OFFERING MEDITATION at a drop-in center for homeless folks, The Mission Neighborhood Resource Center, in 2004. We were trying a new kind of group—a combination of harm reduction, meditation and therapy for active drug users. Check-in had just finished when a man who was on speed came in shaking and sat down saying "I can't meditate . . . I just can't . . ." I told him it was fine to simply watch us. As I hit the bell to begin our *zazen* (just sitting) meditation, I could see that sitting still in his chair was impossible for him . . . and hoped he'd stay.

At the end of ten minutes I rang the bell again and looked over at him: he was sitting quietly! I asked if he had enjoyed watching the meditation. He looked up at me and said, "That was the first few minutes of peace I've had in years." This inspired my journey, and "Harm Reduction Meditation" became the foundation of my ministry. I left the temple and set up a street ministry supported by donations.

The therapist who co-hosted the group later wrote, "This combination of methodologies promotes non-judgmental reflection on the here and now, bringing group members into the present where they can get a clear understanding of themselves and how they interact with the world. Any harmful habit that the client wishes to change can then be worked on in the group setting—providing life skill tools for all involved. These groups have been described as a successful, popular, holistic, and low-cost way of increasing health and motivation among disenfranchised and 'hard to help' populations."

Harm Reduction is often seen as controversial as it involves the acceptance of the fact that some people use drugs and alcohol regularly even when doing so appears detrimental to their health. However, without that acceptance, how could one ever meet all the folks who want help? If I refuse to work with someone because he smokes cannabis to alleviate pain or perhaps she drinks too much in the evening, or perhaps they eat too many chocolate donuts to alleviate loneliness, is that right action? I have been criticized for many aspects of my harm reduction work: for my public support of medical cannabis, my ministry with active drug users, my support of legalization of sex work (another aspect of Harm Reduction) and much more. However, I really don't think the Buddha was teaching the way of liberation only for those living a "morally upright" life—probably quite the opposite. As a former Bible teacher, I really don't remember Jesus saying, "Come unto me and I will give you peace . . . but only if you're clean and sober!"

If you wear a seat belt in a car or a condom during sex, you're practicing Harm Reduction. It's a perfect fit with the Middle Way of Zen practice, allowing us to be true humans who don't always act in the most rational ways. We all know what a good diet and regular exercise look like, but how many of us actually eat well all the time and get the right amount of exercise? Harm Reduction could take the form of taking some vitamin supplements when you realize you've not been eating too well, or walking a few extra blocks. Powerful change doesn't have to be extreme. I always tell folks "there are enough people out there who will beat you up—no need to do it yourself." Forgiveness and loving-kindness for ourselves can take many forms. Harm Reduction Practice is a great vehicle for practicing gentle acceptance.

As a Zen Buddhist Priest and Dharma Ancestor in the Lineage of Suzuki Roshi, one of the great efforts of my practice is to stay open enough to meet what comes forward and present itself—without being in judgment. Complete acceptance is critical for working with others, particularly with those who have suffered from being judged and shamed for simply being who they are, or for the survival habits they employ. As a "monk at large" on the streets of San Francisco, I've found Harm Reduction techniques to be a vital tool in meeting people "where they are." These practices are a great tool in the spread of the Dharma. They present an opportunity to meet everyone just as they are, without (acting on) judgment or criticism, thus living out the teaching of Suzuki Roshi, "You're all perfect just the way you are."

The most effective ministry comes from a heart opened by experience and having met extraordinary challenge. In that case, you might say I have had a very full life. As a true child of the 60s, I tried every mind-expanding substance offered, mescaline, LSD, mushrooms, etc., looking for great spiritual insights. A difficult family life gradually led to developing a habit of escaping from troubles. Beginning to meditate in my adolescence was greatly helpful, as was my deep and growing interest in spirituality. Thus, at seven years old, I was sure that being a nun was my only salvation. My mother weighed in, "Don't be silly. We're not even Catholic!" But I loved church and became a Bible teacher at age 12. Shortly after that, it dawned on me that all ministers were men! I was 40 years old when I finally took monastic vows, and it's still a fascinating journey.

I moved to America from Amsterdam in the late 1980s and rapidly discovered how easy it is to become homeless. It only requires that you have a job with no health insurance benefits, become unwell, and then become unable to work! This gave me a greater understanding of what it really means to be homeless: the shame, the feeling of being treated like trash, and of having totally lost any place in life. I took refuge in Buddha. Fresh from the streets, I began formal training in Soto Zen Buddhism (not disclosing that I was homeless) and quickly became totally clear about how being still in the face of trouble was the key that unlocks for us the chance to respond skillfully to situations, instead of overreacting, or escaping through substance use.

The greatest breakthrough was accepting myself. Having grown up as so many of us do, with the idea that something was wrong with me (in my case apparently, nothing about me was right), the relief that came with realizing that we're all perfect—just as we are—was enormous! You can't offer complete acceptance to others without first accepting yourself. At peace with the self, I no longer feel a need to escape. I can't count the number of "Total Acceptance" workshops I've taught since then! The urge to share this great possibility for peace led me to leave the temple and go back to the streets—but this time offering services for homeless and low-income people, including meditation groups.

All the social workers and case managers that I encountered were trained in Harm Reduction, a client-centered modality developed in England in the 1950s as a response to the AIDS crisis. The initial focus was on clean needles to prevent the spread of HIV, which then developed into an essential skill in therapy and drug counseling. The key to Harm Reduction Counseling lies in the total non-judgmental acceptance of the person in front of you and support for their trajectory. Non-judgment does not mean we don't have any judgments—we're only human after all—but rather that we've learned how to resist being dragged around by them.

A majority of Americans use drugs and/or alcohol as people have done for centuries yet, until Harm Reduction practices arrived, many could not get treatment for various ailments if they told the doctor they used drugs, and the only mode offered in substance abuse programs was total recovery. In Harm Reduction (which includes recovery in its spectrum) the objective is to reduce the harm one does to oneself. The motto is, "Any small change is a success." If I'm working with someone who has a meth problem I will most certainly ask if they have considered using medical cannabis as, in Harm Reduction terms, medical cannabis is at the bottom of the scale for any damaging side effects. Top of the scale is alcohol, which has the least number of effective doses to be potentially fatal.

According to a recent scientific study of the effect of "Harm Reduction Meditation" on those with a meth problem, patients initially reported using two or three times a day, while at the end of eight one-hour sessions they reported using only two or three times a week! Along with the *zazen* games I've developed over the years to make "just sitting" more accessible, the study participants used medical cannabis to help lower their meth intake.

Substance abuse and dependence are complex issues, particularly with respect to treatment. Debates over treatment philosophies, along with the moral sanctions imposed by society for using illicit substances, stifle innovation and often demonize treatment programs that do not adhere to abstinence-only models. However, those engaged in treatment as patients are often left out of the conversation. Their desires regarding their substance use and its trajectory are not considered. Rather, authoritarian top-down style programs impose treatment upon patients, who can be released from the program for non-adherence.

One treatment philosophy that diverges from this model is Harm Reduction. In a Harm Reduction framework, patients drive the treatment program, making decisions about the trajectory of their substance use. Rather than focusing on the use itself, harms associated with use are the focus of the treatment. Patients may continue using substances while reducing the likelihood of other harms. For example, using clean needles every time one injects heroin reduces the likelihood of contracting HIV or Hepatitis C, even if the patient continues to use heroin. Similarly, setting use parameters around such things as days and times of use, geographic locations of use and using peers can assist the patient in reducing overall use and the harms associated with using at particular days and times, places or with certain people. Some patients practice harm reduction by substituting a less harmful substance for a more harmful one. For many patients, cannabis is a substance that poses little risk and leads to fewer harms than most other substances. Medical cannabis patients have been known to substitute cannabis for alcohol, prescription and illicit drugs.

This suggests that individuals wishing to reduce their use of harmful substances can use cannabis regularly without going back to the other substances. Contrary to the abstinence-only approach that frowns upon the use of all substances, this harm reduction approach might be more successful in preventing harmful drug use.

No temple or church currently supports my ministry; however, San Francisco Patient and Resource Center does support the Harm Reduction Meditation Groups: "Here at SPARC we pride ourselves on the services we provide to our patients. We have instructors whose goal is to help patients in need. One of our most admired providers is Jana Drakka who has done wonders for our patients in her Harm Reduction Meditation Groups."

SPARC has made impressive advances in the study of the medicinal uses of cannabis and, in particular, of CBD or Cannabidiol. THC in cannabis is what gets you high, whereas CBD has multiple healing effects without producing any high, making it much more practical and useable anywhere and anytime.

I have discovered that when I need to learn about something new, I ask my students. Mira Ingram, a medical cannabis patient and one of my lay-ordained students, gave me the latest info on CBD: "CBD has the widest-ranging array of medicinal effects, and is one of the most studied cannabinoids in medical research. There's a correlation between CBD and THC. Where there's more of one, there's less of the other. After a century of prohibition, underground breeding practices favored THC to produce the strongest high but at the cost of losing most of the CBD. Only within the past decade, with the emergence of medicinal cannabis labs that test cannabinoid content and levels, have plants containing higher levels of CBD been discovered, crossbred and propagated. Some contain negligible levels of THC. High CBD cannabis is still rare, and not often found outside of areas that allow medicinal cannabis and have organized communities." She went on to say that "the cannabis plant has so many healing properties that, if we discovered it today we'd think of it as a 'wonder drug!'"

A dear friend, meditator and cannabis patient, Sheree "Red" Bornand, gave me some great personal insights into the role of cannabis and CBD in lessening pain and helping with the everyday anxieties of life. "As a disabled person, I awake each day to varying levels of ability and challenge. Beyond the framework of somewhat predictable physical aches and pains lies a worn, torn landscape of reactionary thoughts." The complex dynamic between physical and mental discomfort creates difficulty when trying to find relief from suffering. "Finally, I found out that higher CBD strains are excellent for relieving pain, and lower THC avoids unwanted side effects." As a result, Sheree has been able to attend Harm Reduction Meditation groups with me regularly, which provide excellent community support and stress relief. "Each day," Sheree reports, "my life becomes stronger for I know the platform of practice I engage from is tried and tested by many who have successfully gone before me."

Prejudice around cannabis use is likely blinding some patients to the enormous range of its potential healing benefits.

I was sitting in a community garden recently, talking with some women dealing with substance abuse issues. Several of the women pointed to meditation as having helped them deal with their struggles. One woman said, "Well, I used it at 850 Bryant (the jail) yesterday! The cops were messing with me, and I was trying to get a felony expunged so I can get some decent housing." She went on to tell how she became completely enraged and felt like hitting someone, which would only send her straight back to prison when she remembered something. "I suddenly remembered what we do in group, I just watched the anger till it went down, and then I could handle myself just fine."

It's obvious that Harm Reduction Meditation techniques and the skillful use of medicinal cannabis can ease suffering. It's easy to see that research into potential lifesavers would serve us all far better than staying attached to prejudices. We can help improve so many people's lives not just here in America, but anywhere that substance abuse, mental illness and poverty exist. When we can completely accept ourselves and treat others with loving-kindness, just as they are, then we're truly living in Nirvana.

May All Beings Be Happy
May We Live In Peace

A TRIP NOT TAKEN ⊘ China Galland

"Since you're going to be in Brazil, why don't you think about taking ayahuasca?" a new acquaintance said to me. "There's a village in the Amazon that you can only get to by boat. I know someone there who would escort you and introduce you to the villagers. That's the way to do it." I was preparing to fly to Brazil and Argentina in the fall of 1995 to complete the research and interviews for my book, *The Bond Between Women, A Journey to Fierce Compassion*.

She assured me that she had taken ayahuasca several times, spending as much time in the jungle as she could. Being with people for whom sacred ceremonies with ayahuasca were a way of life had changed hers. It was not weekend recreation. It was "the real thing," she said emphatically.

She promised to send me some articles about the movement in Brazil. Two religions had grown out of using ayahuasca, distinct from traditional indigenous practices: the Santo Daime, founded roughly in 1940, and the União do Vegetal (UDV), which came about in 1961. As the use of ayahuasca made its way to the north, both to the US and to Canada, its context was changing again, she explained. That's why she was encouraging me to go into the Amazon, to the source. That was the proper environment for the experience, with the sounds of the rainforest and the smell of damp earth surrounding you.

I agreed to consider her offer. I was tempted. It sounded like a rare opportunity, to travel by boat up the Amazon to this tiny village. She explained that I could participate in a ceremony in Rio too, there was a church there, but it was a very different kind of ceremony than the kind they did in the jungle. She preferred the jungle.

More and more people I knew in the San Francisco Bay Area were trying ayahuasca—all Buddhists of one school or another—people in the Diamond Heart training, performers, writers. Another *ayahuascaero* encouraged me as well. A respected spiritual teacher, he had been to Brazil and connected with the grassroots movements that had grown from a rubber tapper's visions of a Green Virgin in the jungle in the 1930s. He vividly described to me his own passage through a terrifying night on ayahuasca and its subsequent remarkably positive resolution. His description was long on the spectacular and varied special effects produced by ayahuasca, a source of delight for him and a curiosity for me as listener.

His talk of a Green Virgin got my attention. I had been researching Dark and Black Madonnas and potential cross-cultural counterparts like Black Taras for years. The central Tara in the Tibetan Buddhist tradition is the Green Tara. Was this Green Virgin her counterpart? I was tempted to investigate.

Then I thought back to an afternoon in 1989 in the midst of a Kalachakra initiation with His Holiness the Dalai Lama, in Santa Monica. He was discussing the vows we were about to take as part of the initiation. He counseled us to consider them carefully and to only take those which we were prepared to keep. One of them was the vow to not use intoxicants. Not having had any alcohol or drugs for eight years at the time, I was delighted to take this vow. It showed me how Buddhist practice could undergird the practice of sobriety. Taking that vow in particular reinforced my commitment to the sangha of sobriety and its practices. I joined an ancient fellowship with that vow, and its recitation was deeply satisfying.

By 1995, I had fourteen years of sobriety. Could I take ayahuasca now? I knew that several teachers maintained that the vow not to use intoxicants actually means not to *abuse* intoxicants. Lots of Buddhists who had taken those vows used them with nary a thought. Others, like Thich Nhat Hanh, with whom I'd also taken vows, were quite strict and maintained that the vow not to use intoxicants was just that, a vow not to use alcohol or drugs, including psychedelics.

I knew that ayahuasca wasn't addictive; still, it was clearly outside the box I had drawn around sobriety. I had never been tempted to pick up a drug since I joined the "community of recovery." I could count the number of times that I wanted to drink or use drugs on my right hand, but this—ayahuasca—was a temptation. It didn't fall so neatly into the category of substances that drove people into recovery. I'd never heard or read about anyone who had become addicted to peyote or mescaline or mushrooms. Perhaps it happened. I didn't know. For me, it was a gray area. The few times in my life that I had taken psychotropic drugs had been very positive—one time in particular.

I was living in the mountains in Colorado in my twenties. A friend came over to take me out on the town that evening and brought mescaline to take beforehand. (I think it was mescaline, it might have even been peyote.) I got nauseated, the nausea passed and we went into town. I found myself walking down a familiar street, but in another dimension. I had no hallucinations, I saw nothing out of the ordinary, and yet I saw the extra-ordinariness of each and every person. I felt as though I was seeing into the heart of everyone I encountered, whether it was a person crossing a street, the waiter who brought us our dinner, or the friend who was with me. Each person, in his and her own way, was brimming with love. The curtain of samsara had been drawn back and I was in a state of bliss. I had the distinct sense that I was being shown something; I was being given a great gift, a profound teaching, a demonstration of the fact that all that goes on in the world is love. Nothing more, nothing less. Everything looked the same as it always had, only it wasn't. I was changed irrevocably, given insights and understanding that it would take me years to find my way back through to touch again.

I got sober in 1981 and fourteen years later, I was being encouraged to try another psychotropic. It was a deeply attractive offer. I spent weeks wrestling with the idea. An experience I'd had early in recovery weighed heavily on my mind.

Just after I stopped drinking I was invited to a no-alcohol party. I agreed to go, knowing that I needed to meet more people for whom alcohol and drugs were not an option. I needed to surround myself with them and I did. The only problem for me was that I knew no one at the party and I was overcome with loneliness, suffused with grief. I went out to my car and put my head down on the seat and wept inconsolably, not knowing what for. To say that "my skin didn't cover me" was a trite and nonetheless remarkably precise description of how I felt. I didn't know how to be with people without alcohol, especially people whom I didn't know. Alcohol hid my discomfort. Now it was visible, painfully. I didn't fit, inside or out.

One of the women from the party came out to my car and found me crying. After much talk, she convinced me that I needed to come back inside and marched me into the house, sat me down on the couch and brought me a cold drink. Before I knew it, everyone at the party, fifty people or so, had come into the room and sat down. The party turned into a twelve-step meeting and there it was again, right in front of me, only love happening, pouring into me, pouring in and out of each person.

I let go and simply sat before these people I had never met and wept. The love in the room held me like a fireman's blanket held a terrified child who had just leapt out of a burning building. The sorrow I felt became ecstasy and I found myself experiencing a depth of experience and a high that was greater than anything I had ever felt before. What was different was that I stayed in that highly exalted state. There was no diminishing of the experience, no coming down, no wearing off of a drug. Hours passed, the afternoon became evening, still I was in that altered state. When I went home, it was past midnight. Still I was ecstatic, as high as I was the first moment of the experience. I sat alone in the quiet of my living room, treasuring each moment, not knowing how much longer it could last. My three children were soundly asleep. I stayed up until probably three that morning, at least twelve hours later, the intensity undiminished in any way, though I was becoming physically tired. I knew that to go to sleep was to take a risk, but finally I was tired enough to realize that I had to let go, even of this bliss.

When I woke up the next morning, I was in a normal frame of mind. The altered state had disappeared. My head was clear. I had been given another gift, an immersion in a state of mind that was completely accessible without drugs or alcohol. I had only my Zen practice and my newfound sobriety. Whatever happened that afternoon came pouring out of the universe like warm golden honey, suffusing the world, even its daylight, with warmth and radiance. After twenty years of sobriety and to the day of this writing it has never happened again, and that is fine. The experience was so powerful that I remain grateful to have even had it once in my life.

After the suggestion to consider taking ayahuasca, I thought carefully about my choices. I imagined going to Brazil, changing from a jumbo jet to a smaller plane to the northeast, then taking a Piper Cub to a jungle airstrip, being met by this woman who invited me to join her, then stepping into a small outboard boat that would take us upriver to the village. There we would spend three to five days. It would be fascinating. Might I see a Green Virgin? Might I have another experience like the one I had in early sobriety if I took ayahuasca?

And I thought about the aftermath, about the inevitable comedown from the potent tea we would drink. After the ceremony, after the dancing, the singing, the insights, if I were to have any. What would I have?

I would have another exotic experience to write about—there was guaranteed drama in just getting there. But as I sat with the possibility, I realized that for myself, not for anyone else, but for me, given the vows I had taken, given my years of sobriety, to choose to use ayahuasca was a contradiction in terms. To take it meant that I could, at will, for a certain amount of money, produce a guaranteed high for myself. It would be consumer-oriented spirituality. I would be in control—the when, the where—I would buy the experience.

In contrast, my experience in early sobriety was so astonishing for the very reason that I had no control over it. I couldn't buy the access to it. That blessed state came from sources not my own and found its way to me through other people. The deep love that underlies all things came gratuitously, freely. It was what the mescaline had let me have a taste of so long ago; paradoxically, it took using nothing to experience fully.

It was humbling to realize that I might never in my life have that experience again and that I had no control over it. I decided that my task was to be faithful to my vulnerability, to my lack of power over this moment. If that love ever happened again, wonderful. If it didn't, that too was wonderful. I sensed that for myself—under the circumstances I was in, at the time I had to choose—my motives were not pure. There was ego attached, a desire to feel powerful, a kind of spiritual seduction going on, fueled by the potential of commanding a psychic experience to happen. The tea guaranteed a trip.

The more I thought about the jungle, the more I realized that I had been subtly uncomfortable when people who had used ayahuasca described their experiences. There was a focus on the display of awesome powers, on sensation. It reminded me of the warning against becoming attached to spiritual powers, to the fireworks. What wasn't as obvious as the drama of the experiences was whether or not these people had been transformed by it. Were they more concerned about others, more generous, more heartful, more active on behalf of others? I couldn't tell, nor did they report anything to me of this nature. I had no way to know nor had I known them enough beforehand to see a change.

Though I was enthralled by the stories people had told me, as I weighed these matters, the power of my own experience was undeniable. That golden afternoon at the party when I'd become high while sober was a high-water mark in my spiritual life. I could not deny it.

I did not go to the jungle.
That time.
Nor have I since.
One day at a time.

THE PAISLEY GATE ❧ Erik Davis

I FIRST VISITED GREEN GULCH FARM on a sunny Sunday in the fall of 1995. A group of students were sitting beneath the alien rows o' eucalyptus trees, talking casually with Tenshin Reb Anderson, then abbot of the San Francisco Zen Center. Jerry Garcia had recently died, and at one point in the conversation, a blond, fortysomething woman asked Anderson, in all seriousness, whether Garcia was a bodhisattva.

I would have failed this particular Marin County koan. But not Anderson, who answered the question promptly and without condescension. He first described the Buddhist idea of protectors: beings who encircle and guard the Dharma without being entirely within the fold. Presumably, Anderson was taking inspiration from the *dharmapalas* of Tibetan Buddhism, especially the *lokapalas*: ferocious local spirits who swore allegiance to the Buddha-way only after being magically subjugated by the tantric missionary and wizard Padmasambhava. Some of these shamanic entities are even said to not fully accept the Buddha's teaching, though integrated within Tibetan Buddhism, they retain an intense liminality, or "in-betweenness." And as the recent controversy over the protector spirit Dorje Shugden makes clear, one monk's manifestation of the bodhisattva Manjushri can be another monk's bloodthirsty demon.

In any case, Anderson's response was brilliant. Without castigating whatever visionary and communal ecstasy some Deadheads managed to extract from their loopy scene, Anderson established an open border between Garcia and the Dharma, at once separating the two while acknowledging their connection—a connection which, in the San Francisco Bay Area anyway, is as local as a *lokapala*. But while American Zen and the Grateful Dead have both served as major attractions in Northern California's spiritual carnival, the abbot also needed to draw the line. On the far side of this line lay drugs, because drugs, Anderson made clear, were definitely not the Buddha way.

Anderson did not name the drugs, which was just as well, as the day was growing short and the Dead's curriculum vitae is long. Garcia's appetite for heroin and freebase was at times prodigious, and few would make an argument for the enlightening nature of these substances. But in the larger context of the

Grateful Dead experience, "drugs" means psychedelics—the LSD, mescaline, peyote, mushrooms, and other compounds that transformed the Dead's cowboy jazz into the occasion for Dionysian romps in the electric bardo. In Anderson's analogy, then, psychedelics correspond to the unassimilable shamanic elements of Tibetan folk magic, to those pre-Buddhist beliefs and practices, *Bonpo* or not, that remain outside the circle of Dharma they nonetheless helped shape.

Leaving the Grateful Dead aside, I'd like to suggest that the overlap between American psychedelic culture and American Buddhism is roughly analogous to the liminal zone inhabited by the *dharmapalas*. The analogy works both historically and, if you will, institutionally. On top of providing an imaginative slant on the significant historical links between American Buddhism and psychedelics in the sixties and seventies, the tantric tension between local demons and Dharma protectors also helps us understand how some contemporary American Buddhists grapple with the controversial, even heretical specter of psychedelic spirituality. When Tibetan Buddhists engaged the fierce and sorcerous entities of the pre-Buddhist mindscape, they faced the same sort of problem that greets American Buddhists attempting to account for the convulsively magic molecules in their midst: how to simultaneously honor and vanquish, integrate and control.

The grizzled bearded visage of "Mahajerry" tells us something right off the bat: the question of psychedelics and American Buddhism remains intimately bound up with the collective spiritual narrative of one particular generation of Americans. Though American Buddhism sprouted from seeds planted long before the emergence of "the sixties," the Dharma rode to relative prominence on the same countercultural wave of mind-expansion that thrust Timothy Leary into the limelight. Indeed, if there had been no Pranksters, no acid tests, no "instant nirvana," it is hard to imagine that places like Green Gulch would exist at all. Buddhism in America first hit its stride in the context of countercultural spirituality, and it is simply impossible to understand countercultural spirituality without taking psychedelics into account. Indeed, such understanding is probably impossible without taking psychedelics, period.

The legitimacy of psychedelic spirituality is a vexed question, especially given the tricky ideas of authenticity and illusion that play such a pivotal role in the spiritual assessment of altered states of consciousness. Anthropologically speaking, though, it's hard not to see the question of legitimacy as anything other than a mechanism of cultural power through which religious institutions and lineages define and police their borders. (In this sense, religious discourse surrounding drugs is similar to that surrounding food and sex.) As we now know, psychedelic substances, not to mention other psychoactive drugs, have played a profound role in the history of the human spirit. We may never know what materials composed the soma praised in the Vedas or the punch that gave the Eleusinian Mysteries their mystical zap, but it's a pretty safe bet that something more than watery oatmeal was being quaffed. Psychoactive plants are even more fundamentally linked to those ancient indigenous practices we rather loosely describe as "shamanism." The religious culture of pre-Buddhist Tibet, for example, was part of a huge shamanic complex that stretched throughout Eurasia and included, in its more northern stretches at least, the ritual use of the psychedelic mushroom *Amanita muscaria*.

In any case, psychoactive drugs must be featured prominently in any catalog of what Mircea Eliade called humanity's "technologies of ecstasy"—a tool kit of altered states-production that includes dancing, drumming, fasting, fucking, and physical ordeal. But in the 1960s, in a culture that had swept its mystical and ecstatic traditions under the moldering carpet of mainline Christianity, there was little to no context for the experiences such technologies helped produce. While one can certainly explore psychedelic space as a "modernist," looking to art and science for models, many people found that only mystical language and occult images could frame their chemical illuminations. Many Westerners turned, in particular, to Eastern religion, partly because the Orient has long been an imaginal zone that beckons to Westerners who want to escape the prison of scientific materialism. The "Eastern turn" also makes phenomenological sense. LSD can send serpentine energy shooting up your spine, or thrust you into apocalyptic mandalas, or vibrate the world into an energetic void. At the same time, drugs can also unveil the simple, immanent "Zen" of the ordinary world: a leaf, a breeze, or, as in Huxley's famous mescaline tale in *Doors of Perception*, a fold in one's trousers.

Drugs and Dharma were themselves only a few of the ingredients in a heretical countercultural stew that included marijuana, free love, tarot cards, street protests, long hair, anarchism, the *I Ching*, electric guitars, the underground press, Carlos Castaneda, and Hindu iconography. From the perspective of serious Western Buddhists with Eastern teachers, not to mention the roshis and lamas who arrived in the 1960s and 1970s in order to found institutions, the freak scene must have seemed, in its eclectic mania, almost as wild and fierce as Tibet seemed to the Indian missionaries of the eighth century. In a sense, the counterculture was America's own fractured shamanism, seething with untamed energies and magical phantasms. By taking root within this intensely vibrant culture, the Dharma was able to make the transition from a marginal pursuit of intellectuals and cultural mavericks to the influential if constrained mass phenomenon it is today. While those roots may have been intoxicant-free, the soil they found was psychedelic, and its peculiar nutrients fundamentally shaped the blooms to come.

For one thing, Buddhism owed many of its recruits to the widespread fascination with altered states of consciousness—a fascination that was largely sparked, if not fueled, by drugs. Simply put, psychedelics gave people a taste for the excitement, power, anxiety, insight, and joy of altered states of consciousness. On an even more basic level, drugs also encouraged people to explore their own immediate experience, and to recognize that heaven and hell, like every other power structure, were functions of their own minds. Many Westerners were drawn to Buddhism because it too offered a "hands-on" dimension lacking in Christianity, one which also loosely accorded with the modern "scientific" temperament that drugs, in their molecular way, subtly reinforced. This democratic turn toward direct experience became one of the hallmarks of countercultural spirituality, just as it became a hallmark of American Buddhism. The notion that *samadhi* was available to all, that everyone possessed something like the Buddha-mind, was emphasized by the universal action of the Sandoz molecule. "Have you ever been experienced?" Hendrix asked. If not, why not?

Once blown, many Western minds were also far more likely to put up with alien rituals and grueling disciplines that promised even deeper and more subtle experiences. The notion of *practice*—perhaps the richest and most multivalent term in American Buddhism—is crucial here. One basic meaning of practice is technique: one does not believe, one acts (or, perhaps more accurately, "action happens"). In other words, one adopts a technique, an internalized technology or a psycho-behavioral recipe, and explores the results. Though the act of swallowing a sugar cube is a pretty rinky-dink operation compared to the rigor

THEOLOGUE Alex Grey, 1986

RADIANCE Sukhi Barber, 2012

EBB AND FLOW Sukhi Barber, 2014

JERRY'S FINGER (LSD Blotter Art) Anonymous, c. 1999

CONTEMPLATION Francesco Clemente, 1990

BUDDHAFIELD Michael Newhall, 1982

BOOM SHIVA Android Jones, 2012

THE BUDDHA Odilon Redon, c. 1905

and depth of zazen or hatha yoga, psychedelics did teach people that altered states, even refined ones, could be accessed through technologies of perception.

Indeed, LSD was only one device in the counterculture's ever-expanding occult tool kit, which included divination systems like tarot cards and the *I Ching*, biofeedback devices and flotation tanks, as well as a variety of internal and physical disciplines: breathwork, tai chi, massage, pranayama, veganism, Kriya yoga. Given the unprecedented technological experience of the baby boom generation, it's not surprising that they developed the conviction that technique, in some form, was integral to the process of transformation and insight. Whether the technology was external or internal was less important—was an acid test, with its feedback systems, light shows, and communal chemistry, inside or out? LSD helped ensure that the Eliadean metaphor of spiritual practices as "inner technologies" would find its way into the lexicon of countercultural spirituality, so much so that today it appears in the writings of a serious Buddhist scholar like Robert Thurman.

The problem with the metaphor of technology is that technologies generally encourage a dualistic viewpoint, while mature practice erodes the perception that there is a doer using a tool to pursue a goal. This was an important lesson for American Buddhists during the freak years, when the goals were cosmic. In those idealistic times, there was a veritable obsession with the achievement of enlightenment experiences—an obsession that may have owed much of its ferocity to expectations first laid down by drugs. Over the decades, the emphasis has shifted away from such fierce pursuits, and many teachers go out of their way to deflate the excitement surrounding powerful meditation experiences. Indeed, I suspect that the hostility that some contemporary Buddhists express toward psychedelics conceals an anxiety that their practice remains tainted, on some level, with the desire to merely get high. But this is an understandable desire—it's hard to say how many people would continue to practice over the years if they didn't occasionally "get the goods," whether on the pillow or on drugs.

But psychedelics don't just get people high. Like literal acid, they work to erode, on both individual and social levels, the apparently solid substance of conventional reality—so-called common sense. Regardless of the otherworldly visions drugs can bestow, the deeper psychedelic message concerned the relativity of thought and perception—a "philosophical" insight that drugs reveal directly through the operation of your own nervous system. Unfortunately, as Nietzsche saw with a prophet's eye, relativity is only a stone's throw away from nihilism. Strong psychedelics gave people a glimpse of emptiness, but while the void could be glittering at its peak, it could feel like a bottomless pit the morning after. The ease with which so many psychedelic users sank into cynicism, mental instability, and addiction to more insidious drugs shows that psychedelics themselves do nothing to build the contexts of meaning and spiritual aspiration necessary to prevent such ecstatic technologies from becoming hollow and even destructive mechanisms. Some of the new religious movements of the 1970s—like the Jesus Freaks—reacted against the druggy void with a new fundamentalism. But the Dharma—whose full-frontal embrace of *sunyata* is coupled with a compassionate rejection of nihilism—seemed unusually poised to answer the problems posed by a stark psychedelic confrontation with the ultimate relativity and provisional nature of all phenomenal experience.

So how do we express and characterize the relationship between psychedelics and Dharma practice? The conventional answer, offered by many once-tripping Buddhists, is that drugs can "open the door." Without much work or knowledge on the part of the user, psychedelics can crack open consensus reality, expand identity beyond the confines of the conventional self, induce ego-death, and unveil the connection between mind and the totality of the real. However "unauthentic" these experiences may be judged to be, many people respond to them by turning to Eastern practice in order to extend, comprehend, and deepen their insights. Once their practice has stabilized and opened up, many of these people abandon drugs as needless or even harmful distractions. In this view, spiritual practice becomes something like the liftoff of Apollo 11. Drugs point you toward the moon of enlightenment, and somewhat violently thrust you away from the gravity of consensus reality. Having done so, they can then be abandoned like the early stages of a rocket. Or as Alan Watts quipped, "Once you get the message, hang up the phone."

Here psychedelics, once again, play the role of a liminal technology. That is, like a doorway or a telephone, they stand in-betwixt and in-between, shuttling mind over a threshold. However, while the image of door-opener certainly jibes with many people's life experiences, it also serves to cordon off and subtly undermine the full force of psychedelic experiences—not to mention their ongoing potential for insight. In other words, once drugs become nothing but expendable tools, the experiences they help provide (with more than a little help from the mind) can be ignored without being wholeheartedly denied. In Zen terms, they can be dispensed with as nothing more than *makyo*.

But what happens when serious Dharma practitioners continue to follow what poet Dale Pendell calls "the poison path?" What happens when you open the door and don't shut it tightly behind you? Here is where the real controversy begins. No one's logging any numbers, but I suspect that a healthy chunk of self-identified practicing American Buddhists keep at least occasional dates with the writhing, world-rending void lurking in the heart of psychedelic hyperspace. But I also suspect that, if asked to render judgment on such activities, most Dharma teachers would deliver a fat thumbs down. Indeed, psychedelic spirituality may well be the only real heresy in American Buddhism (except for maybe voting Republican). Heresy, though, is a Western concept, the stuff of witch burnings and gnostic cults. And though serious psychedelic culture certainly has its gnostic aspects, in the context of American Buddhism, it is perhaps best described as a kind of tantra—a coarse and scandalous one perhaps, but homegrown at least, arising from our "native" tradition of countercultural craziness.

Given the generally cheesy spectacle of American neo-tantric sexology, I want to emphasize that I am not claiming that psychedelics have much of anything to do with authentic Asian tantra, an immensely rich and complex tradition about which I have only a scattering of book learning. Nonetheless, in the spirit of productive analogies rather than proclamations of metaphysical truth, I'd like to suggest a number of intriguing parallels. The most obvious one is secrecy. Despite their crucial role in the propagation of American Buddhism, psychedelics are basically not the stuff of Dharma talks, or Shambhala books, or *Tricycle* articles. Discussions can occur within the context of *sangha* and teacher-student relationships, but only selectively and probably not very frequently. One reason for this secrecy derives from another similarity: as with the *pañca-tattva* practices of "left-handed" tantric adepts, who, among other things, ritually consume booze, fish, and meat, the materials of psychedelic Buddhism are socially unsanctioned—literally, "against the law." In fact, the condemnation that surrounds psychedelics may actually lend them some of their esoteric power, just as the negative social mores surrounding meat, alcohol, and sexual congress in traditional India contributed a certain antinomian buzz to the feistier tantric practices.

The connection between psychedelics and tantra goes beyond social practices, into the heart of esoteric perception. This material is difficult to describe, but one could say for starters that psychedelics usher the bodymind into a magical, liminal realm that unfolds between the consensual sensory world and the transcendental worlds depicted in dream, art, and high-octane metaphysics. Within this "bardo zone," memories, ideas, and images multiply and pulse like hieroglyphic sigils, suggesting patterns of association and hidden resonances that voyagers often take—or mistake—for revelations. But the real object of revelation is the mind itself—not simply as a source of meaning, or linguistic categories, but as an organic machine of perception, a machine that can be tweaked. Simply put, psychedelics present the imagination. And by "imagination" I don't simply mean the source of our daydreams or visionary flights, but the synthetic power that Kant posited as the generally unconscious mechanism through which our basic conceptual faculties construct the world of space-time.

The status of the imagination in Buddhism is, to put it mildly, ambivalent. On the one hand, the imagination is often treated as a synonym for *avidya*—it is the imagination that mistakes the rope of reality for the frightening (or seductive) serpent. The very literary form of the earliest Buddhist texts—their dryness, repetition, and lack of flavor—argues that the desiccation of the imagination was a goal of practice. On the other hand, many Mahayana sutras are brimming with the materials of "fantasy:" galaxies of bodhisattvas, infinite garlands of wish-fulfilling gems, "clouds of spheres of light the color of the curl of hair between the Buddha's eyebrows." All this can sound very familiar to a seasoned tripper. Indeed, I have not come across a canonical religious text that can approach the psychedelic majesty of the *Avatamsaka Sutra*, whose infinite details and ceaseless lists capture both the adamantine excess and fractal multiplicity of deep psychedelia.

The literary function of such apparently "imaginative" materials is debatable. Are they glimpses of *Sambhogakaya*, crude folk material, depictions of literal powers, allegories of wisdom? Whatever its function in sutra, however, the work of the esoteric imagination in tantra is central, even on the most literal level of visualization. For the generation stages of tantra, during which deities and their associated mandalas are constructed with the inner eye, the merely individual imagination is used as a gateway, an engine to tame and train for the powerful perceptions of tantric reality. Through diligence, conduct, and ritual, the imagination itself is alchemically transformed, and the completion stages actualize, according to traditional accounts, what had only previously been imagined. Psychedelics are generally too chaotic and willful for this kind of controlled work; nonetheless, serious psychonauts will often encounter feelings, images, and pocket universes with an intensely tantric flavor. And why not? If one buys into tantric accounts of the subtle body, with its nadis and chakras and winds, then it is not too tough to imagine that, just as physical practices like hatha yoga, mantra, and *tummo* can stir up the energies of transformed perception, so might swarms of molecules swimming in the neural bath of the nervous system. Psychonauts who also practice yoga, tai chi, and visualization work regularly find these practices reshaping the phenomenology of their trips, sometimes in insightful ways.

Of course, even if drugs trigger actual changes in the esoteric bodymind, they may still be quite harmful, even demonic—a fear immortalized in the notorious claim that drugs somehow put "holes in your astral body." As the scholar and historian David Gordon White makes clear, however, medieval Indian tantrics were not above ingesting alchemical elixirs, even as renegade sadhus ingest hashish and even jimsonweed today (White, 1996). It is hard to imagine that if LSD, peyote, or DMT existed in ancient India, these substances would not have been used by at least some folks who conceived of their path as tantra. Despite the thoroughly integrated example of Vajrayana in Tibet, the religious temperament of tantra suggests that some of its practitioners will almost inevitably stray toward heterodoxy; its extreme wings will adapt extreme technologies, dangerous or not. Representatives of orthodoxy may argue that such activities represent degenerate tantra, and they may well be right. But technology is about nothing if it is not about speed, and tantra is the lightning path, appropriate for a time of waning Dharma. Perhaps psychedelics are the greased lightning appropriate for an even more degenerate West, when even the Vajrayana seems like a laborious grind.

One red herring in the psychedelic debate is the rejoinder that drugs are artificial and cannot provide "authentic" spiritual experiences. Leaving aside the reverse spiritual materialism of this argument (i.e., that there are some productions of mind that we can legitimately embrace as authentic spiritual experiences), there is the evident fact that psychedelics can produce *something* like spiritual or visionary experience. In other words, instead of worrying about authenticity, we can look at them as simulators of the mind. The use of the individual's imagination in the generation stages of tantra, during which images, colors, and processes are constructed which only later become actualized, alerts us to the productive work that can be done by staging "run-throughs" of later, more profound experiences.

The most profound experience that lies ahead for most of us, practitioners or not, is death. Given the scandalous liberties I've already taken, I don't want to draw too tight an analogy here, but the ultimate object of tantric simulation is the dying process: the loss of the elements, the experience of the clear light, and the bardo. Similarly, the most ferociously meaningful psychedelic experiences tend to be those in which something like dying seems to occur. These experiences can be so powerful that, even if some kernel of us knows that we are on drugs, they rip "us" down to the bones. (The nature of the witnessing consciousness that undergoes intense psychedelic experiences is one of the koans of drugs.) Even if psychedelic ego-death itself does not resemble the actual dying process—and given the dizzying range of psychedelic experiences across both substances and minds, I suspect it may often lie rather far from the mark—it may be the closest most of us come to having the world snatched away and replaced with an exhilarating, terrifying, and blissful realm of deep cosmic mind. From this perspective, drugs can be seen as flight simulators for the bardo; certain substances, including ketamine, ayahuasca, and 5MEO-DMT, seem to lend themselves particularly well to this kind of work.

And it is work. Psychedelics can be as grueling, frightening, and anxious as any *sesshin*. Moreover, they offer any number of yawning traps for the spiritually inclined experimenter, and part of the kind and grizzled wisdom radiated by some longtime heads arises from the deep work required to avoid those traps. One of these dangers is the temptation to cling to the visions, to interpret the images or narratives or self-models that arise as being messages from some being or deeper plane of reality. Besides literalizing the imagination—the sin of idolatry, if you will—this grasping overlooks the site of much of the real work. The visions are not the point. The point is how "you" change in relationship to your experience, both inside it and out—phenomenologically, ethically, aesthetically. There is no revelation but your own experience. And what is this experience? Submission to change, and the absolute truth of impermanence. After all, the altered states pass, obvious products of changing causes and conditions—in this case, eminently material ones.

Recognizing impermanence is a crucial ingredient for any spiritual path that involves altered states of consciousness, since the temptation to reify and cling to feelings, visions, and realizations is so overwhelming. This temptation leads to "religion" in the bad sense of the term, and it is one that Buddhism, at least some of the time, goes out of its way to undermine. One of the lessons dealt by psychedelics, at least for mature aficionados, is that they disenchant the very exalted states they introduce to the psyche. Not only do drugs demonstrate that such states can be generated by swallowing a pill or insufflating some noxious powder, but they invariably snatch those states away as they are metabolized and flushed from the body. Drugs are always and evidently *upaya*, or "means." In contrast, the material or contingent aspect of purely "spiritual" altered states of consciousness, such as those that, arise naturally in meditation, are not always so obvious, making the temptation to hold onto those states and experiences all the greater. Indeed, drugs may also have something to say to these apparently nontechnological states of consciousness that play such a profound role in deep meditation, reminding us that they too arise from causes and conditions that are material as well as karmic. In fact, drugs may encourage us to sap the illusion of "essence" from all states of consciousness—not only from this serotonin trance we take for ordinary reality, but from even the most "classic" mystical experiences. And yet the powerful phenomenology of drugs simultaneously argues that we would be foolish to take these material causes as the only reality. Their illuminations are paradoxical, not simply profane.

The dark side of drugs goes without saying (if only because it is said so much). One does not need to be a genius, or even a psychologist, to understand how easily drugs can amplify delusion, dissociation, and spiritual materialism, let alone feed into patterns of behavior and consumption that lead ever further away from the Dharma. Even if the real horrors are avoided, I suspect that anything more than occasional use of all but the most sacred medicines does not help much in the long run. From the perspective of an established meditation practice, with which even a mild drug like marijuana can interfere, drugs can come to seem quite crude, even ridiculous, their once awe-inspiring dynamics revealing ever more mechanical, repetitive, and confusing effects. Nonetheless, at this point in the history of the spirit, spiritual practice and the psychedelic path are perhaps most fruitfully considered as distinct paths. Just as therapy is perhaps best seen as a complement of Dharma, sharing elements but also diverging in both goals and results, so might psychedelics be seen as a kind of shadow practice, with its own peaks and pitfalls. For most of us, it will seem, like the *Bonpo* side of Tibetan Buddhism, always a little dodgy, a bit too earthy and intense for comfort.

And it is this discomfort that makes psychedelic Buddhism a marginal subject, buried beneath the far more established narrative of psychedelics as an historical door-opener. This latter narrative is simpler to accept, not only because it takes the heat off the present moment, but because it accords so well with the larger American Buddhist boomer narrative, a narrative that still dominates the American Dharma.

You know the basic tale: the sixties were a crazy time of collective and individual experiments, including the copious consumption of mind-bending drugs. The fascination with altered states of consciousness led some to the deeper rewards of Eastern practice, which many embraced with radical, even revolutionary, intensity. But the 1970s and 1980s brought various forms of disillusionment: cult-like scenes, sex, power, and money scandals, the erosion of naive expectations surrounding spiritual attainment. While continuing to refine their commitment to the Dharma, many practitioners embraced more conventional careers, married and spawned, and became increasingly integrated and identified with mainstream society. Meanwhile, previously uninterested, largely liberal boomers began to turn to pop Dharma as a path of healing rather than a means of probing the fringes of the mind. Today, as the gray hair thickens and bodies start to creak, American Buddhism has become a rather conventional affair, especially when compared to the days of Trungpa, early Tassajara, and *Be Here Now*. The popular focus has shifted from the great doubt to the gentle heart, from fierce aspiration to everyday integration. Jack Kornfield says it all in the title of his recent book: *After the Ecstasy, the Laundry*.

There is nothing wrong with this story, reflecting as it does the experience of a generation growing somewhat out of its unprecedented narcissism while simultaneously shaping a mass American vessel for the Dharma. But it inevitably marginalizes, if not denies, the crazy wisdom of psychedelia. In so doing, Buddhist boomers put themselves in a curious position, especially regarding generational transmission. Because even if psychedelic spirituality is a youthful folly, such folly may be necessary, at least for some of us. Are we to suppose that the doors of perception are somehow easier for younger generations to open than they were for children of the 1950s? If so, why? In rejecting (or more frequently, ignoring) psychedelia, Buddhist boomers find themselves in a similar position to middle-aged ex-hippies who pressure their children away from drugs, and justify their actions with the notion that "things were different then."

I can say this because I was born in the summer of love, and spent my teenage years tuning into Southern California's fading freak vibes. For me, The *I Ching*, psychedelics, Dead shows, anarcho-leftism, and meditation were all part of one countercultural package of hedonic pop mysticism. Though I make no claims for the lasting value of these teenage experiments, they certainly set me up for a more authentic contact with the Dharma in my mid-twenties, when I was ready to take on the more sobering kit-and-kaboodle of vows, retreats, and the four noble truths. In this way, psychedelic culture did serve to protect the Dharma for me, providing me with a host of superficial triggers that were only fired off later, when I encountered the "real deal." After all, years before an American Gelugpa monk slipped me a copy of Tsongkhapa in India, I had already seen the scary bodhisattva grin of Mahajerry beaming down from the stage, urging me to wake up and find out that I was the eyes of the world.

BUDDHA EMBRYO Alex Grey, 2000

LESSONS

PSYCHEDELICS ON THE PATH: Help or Hindrance? ◉ Charles T. Tart

IN THE EARLY 1950S, while still a teenager, I began struggling with a series of questions painfully familiar to many of us who were sincerely religious, but growing up in a secular and cynical society. Was there any place for religion and ideals in an intelligent life? Was the loving (and fearsome) God of my childhood just a primitive superstition, disproven by modern science? Were the feelings of connection with something higher just the imagination of my ignorant and frightened child self? How could I be sure of what was true and what was false?

Many of my peers followed two routes in trying to resolve this struggle. Some adopted a totally materialistic belief system, thinking themselves scientific and sophisticated in doing so, and in the process getting to express their anger at the pathological aspects of the organized religions we had been subjected to. Others managed to put their religion in a separate compartment of their minds, believing it for an hour or so on Saturday or Sunday, ignoring it the rest of the time. With decades of hindsight, I now know both these routes carried a high psychological price tag. Total denial cuts people off from their spiritual selves, and compartmentalization doesn't really resolve issues; it just lets them continue discord at an unconscious level. Being an avid reader, I was lucky to come upon a third route consisting of two new possibilities.

One I found in the writings of the founders of psychic research: educated and intelligent men and women of the late nineteenth century who also struggled with questions about the reality of religion when materialistic science seemed to be sweeping all aside before it. Clearly there was much superstition and pathology in religion, but was the baby being thrown out with the bath water? They recognized that the basic attitude of science—genuinely open-minded inquiry into everything—could be applied to all areas of life, including the religious; science did not have to be straitjacketed within a belief system that dogmatically assumed that only the material world is real. This line of thinking led to much of my own work in parapsychology, as psychic research is now called, where, using the most rigorous scientific methods, I and others have repeatedly shown that there is an aspect to the human mind that transcends the known material world, an aspect that provides a scientific foundation for taking some spiritual ideas as being about something real.

The second consideration developed from readings in religion, anthropology, Theosophy, yoga, and Buddhism. Swami Vivekenanda was especially important to me, for he claimed that yoga was not a belief system, and not a religion; yoga was (or at least could be) a science. If you practiced various meditation techniques you would be led to certain experiences, observations, and so could verify for yourself the realities underlying yoga. Buddhism makes similar claims, as in the well-known *Kalama Sutta* where the Buddha insists that people not accept his (or any) ideas on authority or faith, but rely on personal experience and "be a lamp unto yourselves."

Meditative practice also led me to a deeper spiritual life built on direct experience and not dogma. But there was a problem: meditation was far more difficult than I imagined, and a lot of "meditation" was spent daydreaming, rebuking myself for daydreaming, and generally getting nowhere. With the benefit of hindsight, it's clear that many of us Westerners have such hyperactive minds and complex psychological dynamics that it's very difficult to quiet and focus our minds enough to make any progress along the meditative path. So while I had a lot of intellectual "faith" that real spiritual experience was possible, this faith was shallow and fragile. Buddhism was touted as a science of the mind, but without being able to observe the basic nature of mind, it was just a set of ideas to me.

Life changed drastically one Saturday morning in 1961 while I was a graduate student. In J. B. Rhine's Parapsychology Laboratory at Duke University, a visiting European psychologist, Ivo Kohler, handed me a cup of lukewarm water in which four hundred milligrams of chemically pure mescaline sulphate had been dissolved. Professor Kohler had done some experiments in Europe in the 1930s with mescaline and wondered if Americans would react similarly to Europeans. No studies had been done in America, so I had volunteered to represent my country.

The mixture tasted like warm vomit, but for the sake of this scientific experiment (I believed and still believe in good science!), I drank it down. We waited two hours for something to happen: nothing did. I was told I could go home; it looked like mescaline didn't have the same effects on Americans as it did on Europeans—or I could try another hundred milligrams. Twenty minutes later I went from my normal state of consciousness to a full psychedelic high almost instantly; a lot of my ideas about the mind and the spirit became direct experiences.

For all my conscious openness to new ideas, I had unconsciously resisted the effects of the drug, in spite of the powerful dose, until it was increased enough to overwhelm my defenses. Then I saw incredible beauty. The plain, drab laboratory room in the old Parapsychology Laboratory at Duke University became the richest room I had ever seen, people became gods, and the flowers around the building became miracles of form.

I saw the mechanical, constricted nature of my mind. It could operate just like a machine: push the start button and mental tasks could be carried out with no real consciousness. I saw that this was the nature of my mind as I had known it. "I" saw that whatever my real nature was, it was "something" (though not really a "thing") immensely beyond my normal self and my ideas.

Although that mescaline experience is more than thirty years in my past, it influences me to this day. I have been meditating and doing other mindfulness work regularly for many years as a result of that inspiration. But when life is oppressive, and when meditation is unsuccessful or feels boring, I can sometimes reinspire myself by remembering the beauty, spaciousness, intelligence, and divinity that I experienced in that journey.

I know that my personal history parallels many, if not most, Euro-American practitioners of my generation: the aridity of conventional religion, the struggle to preserve something sacred against the powerful tide of materialism and cynicism, the frustration with spiritual practices that didn't seem to work, perhaps some jealousy of those for whom the practices did work, the sudden opening with psychedelics, then the renewed commitment to meditation and other practices because of an experience-based confidence that there is something real in the spiritual realm to strive for.

In 1990 I was able to study the prevalence of psychedelic experiences in some hundred Dharma practitioners' backgrounds. Through the cooperation of Sogyal Rinpoche, a well-known Tibetan Buddhist teacher and author of *The Tibetan Book of Living and Dying*, I was able to pass out questionnaires at one of the annual West Coast retreats of his Rigpa Fellowship. I didn't select this particular Buddhist group because I thought its members had an especially high familiarity with psychedelic experiences, but because I had been coming to these retreats for several years and was known to and trusted by many of the students.

How typical this group was of Buddhist students in general is a question for future researchers, but it was a dedicated group of nonmonastic practitioners of varying ages. Sixty-four of about one hundred retreatants returned completed anonymous questionnaires, a very high response rate for questionnaire studies. Of those who returned questionnaires, seventy-five percent were women, reflecting the typical predominance of women I have observed at most transpersonal and Buddhist functions in California. Eighty-three percent considered themselves members of the Rigpa Sangha, with length of membership ranging from a month to eleven years. They estimated an average of an hour a day in formal practice, ranging from thirty minutes to more than two hours per day.

Compared with many other, assorted groups surveyed over the years, these practitioners were extremely drug literate. Ninety-four percent of the respondents reported previous experience with marijuana, and seventy-seven percent reported previous experience with major psychedelics such as LSD or mescaline. I included questions on marijuana in the survey since it can produce psychedelic experiences in some people, especially in high doses (Tart, 1971).

These Buddhist students had largely given up psychedelics, with seventy-six percent no longer using marijuana and ninety percent no longer using major psychedelics. Although I didn't specifically ask about this in the questionnaire, Buddhism, with its emphasis on not being dependent on anything, was probably one reason for lessened drug use, as well as the opinion many users have given me that, having seen the possibilities through psychedelics, one then had to adopt a regular spiritual practice in life in order to manifest them. Options were left open, however, with a little over half of those who had previously used indicating they might want to use marijuana or psychedelics occasionally in the future.

Marijuana experiences were reported, on average, as moderately significant to the students' spiritual lives in general, less so for their Buddhist practice per se. As might be expected with the more powerful effects of the major psychedelics, three quarters of the users reported them as somewhat to very significant for their spiritual lives in general; about a fifth reported psychedelics as important in attracting them to Tibetan Buddhism in particular. In a somewhat complex series of questions on whether psychedelics had, on balance, helped or hindered these individuals' practice of Tibetan Buddhism, about four times as many reported they had been helped as hindered. Unless this group is quite atypical of Western Buddhist groups, then, psychedelic experiences have been quite important to Buddhist students in general and especially to students of Tibetan Buddhism, and so to the future of the Dharma in the West.

My questionnaire went on: "Please briefly describe two or three of the most important drug-associated experiences you have had that affected your spiritual perspective . . . and indicate what specific aspect of Buddhist or Tibetan Buddhist ideas you associate them with." Some of the major spiritual effects of psychedelics that affect the way these students hear and practice Buddhism (given in the students' own words as much as possible) can be assembled as follows:

A typical report, for example, was: "My whole narrow little perspective of myself and life as I perceived it was suddenly blown open. I became aware of the conscious energy of mind, which was not the same as the thoughts or thinking part of mind, and my sense of self and self-identity loosened up." According to the Buddha, a fundamental cause of suffering is ignorance. We can look at ignorance as consisting, in one important way, of a prejudiced and too-narrow mind-set, an active but automatized and habitual bias of perception, thinking, and action driven by conscious and unconscious attachments, desires, and aversions. Such constricted mind-sets have maximal power over us when we don't know we have them, so seeing that such limitations exist is an important step toward freedom. These limitations can be gradually seen through practice, but may also be seen more suddenly in a psychedelic experience.

But suddenness and intensity may be a mixed blessing. Several respondents reported that their psychedelic experiences had given them direct, sometimes painful knowledge of the "illusory," samsaric nature of phenomena. One woman reported: "The exposure of emptiness to the point of dissolution of all concrete phenomena was frightening rather than enlightening, and probably exists as a reason not to open rather than to open. The fear gets in the way." Another woman said, ". . . the way the mind influences everything so strongly on a trip helped me understand how we determine our reality by the attitude or view we have." An older woman, describing an experience with MDMA said, ". . . it became clear that one makes one's own life. It is all in our mind. It became clear that our parents and educators are just an excuse, although I had a heavy, turbulent, and suppressing youth."

Buddhism shows great respect for logic (but not for the rationalizations that commonly masquerade as logic), while going beyond intellectual processes to more fundamental experiences. One woman reported, "I totally went beyond intellect, couldn't communicate verbally . . ." Another woman said, ". . . I became aware of . . . an experience of heightened awareness which indicated a much vaster human capacity than was usually experienced."

One man, describing a peyote experience with American Indians, reports having had "a definite experience of clarity for about two hours. Saw every leaf, tree, plant, local animal, persons as exactly as they were—which was perfectly in harmony within their physical space, location, and relationship to all. The beauty of just the beingness of all things, . . . mind was clear, present and empty and completely aware." A woman offered: "I fully perceived all phenomena as transient and transparent, but beautiful and luminous." Just as understandings can go to a new depth and clarity beyond the ordinary, sensory perception can be experienced with a new clarity that seems to be a kind of knowledge in itself. Given the Buddhist idea that we live in samsara, a state of clouded perception and thinking, full of ignorance, attachment, and aversion, achieving a state of clarity is highly valued.

An especially common problem in Western culture, given our high valuation of rugged individualism, is a feeling of isolation. This includes feelings of isolation from other individuals and a feeling of lack of connection with the universe, often coupled with feelings of living a meaningless life in an inherently meaningless universe. Buddhism regards the feeling of separateness as an illusion, arising from the illusion of having a separate self. Psychedelics can sometimes change this feeling drastically and rapidly. One woman wrote that "the use of peyote allowed me to experience a deeper interconnectedness with all beings and all phenomena . . . thus some preparation for faith—the unquestioning faith in Tibetan Buddhism which can arise when you have experiential knowledge." A man wrote of his peyote experiences, "We're all in this together, part of each other." The development of compassion, in parallel with the development of wisdom and insight, is central in Buddhist thought. "I had a feeling of love for everyone and everything," wrote one woman of her psychedelic experience, and another reported, "I also had a deep heart experience which was more like a universal love experience than anything I can describe."

For students of Buddhism who are naturally talented at meditative and related practice and are moving along satisfactorily that way, the relation between psychedelics and Buddhism may be of passing intellectual interest, but not really vital. For those who feel frustrated with their practice and wonder if psychedelics would provide a boost, the subject is of much greater interest, but really solid knowledge and advice are lacking on this. It is dangerous to take psychedelics: they may change your whole orientation to reality in unpredictable (and sometimes pathological) ways. It is also dangerous not to take psychedelics: your life may remain stuck in the barrenness and suffering of everyday samsara. Yet I wish we had a broad and solid knowledge base to help us, such as detailed commentaries on various psychedelic experiences by enlightened Buddhas who had also taken psychedelics themselves—but we don't have them. So we are where students on the path have always been: starting and continuing from where we are, with our particular, unique, for better-or-worse personality and situation—and aspiring to observe and practice and learn, and to grow in wisdom and compassion.

BUDDHISM AND THE PSYCHEDELIC SOCIETY
Interview with Terence McKenna
Allan Badiner

ALLAN BADINER: You have emerged as the leading spokesperson for the use of psychedelics. What is the history of your encounter with Buddhism?

TERENCE MCKENNA: Like so many people in the sixties, I came up through D. T. Suzuki's books on Zen, which were very popular at a certain point. And then early on because of my art historical bent, I became interested in Tibetan Buddhism. But my interest was not exactly Buddhism. It was more the shamanic pre-Buddhist Tibet phenomenon of the Bön religion—which grew out of the shamanic culture of pre-Buddhist Tibet. I found among Tibetan Buddhists a lot of prejudice against the Bön. They were definitely second-class citizens inside theocratic Tibet, and they still are.

BADINER: Buddhist practice didn't attract you?

MCKENNA: Buddhist psychology was very interesting to me. I came to it through the works of Herbert Günther, who was a Heideggerian originally, and then found Mahayana thought parallel to his Heideggerianism. I was influenced by a book called *Tibetan Buddhism Without Mystification*, published later as *Treasures of the Tibetan Middle Way*, which contrasted paradoxically differing schools of Buddhist thought; Nagarjuna's writings on nothingness were also a big influence.

BADINER: What did you make of the *Abhidhamma*—the psychological component of Buddhist teaching?

MCKENNA: The Buddhist style of talking about the constructs of the mind is now a universalist style. The puzzle to me is how Buddhism achieves all of this without psychedelics; not only how but why, since these dimensions of experience seem fairly easily accessed, given hallucinogenic substances and plants, and excruciatingly rare and unusual by any other means.

BADINER: How would Buddhism fit into your notion of the psychedelic society that you often talk about?

MCKENNA: Well, compassion is the central moral teaching of Buddhism and, hopefully, the central moral intuition of the psychedelic experience. So at the ethical level I think these things are mutually reinforcing and very good for each other. Compassion is what we lack. Buddhism preaches compassion. Psychedelics give people the power to overcome habitual behaviors.

Compassion is a function of awareness. You cannot attain greater awareness without necessarily attaining greater compassion, whether you're attaining this awareness through Buddhist practice or through psychedelic experience.

BADINER: So compassion and awareness are the twin pillars of both Buddhism and the psychedelic society.

MCKENNA: Compassion and awareness. To my mind the real contrast between Buddhism and psychedelic shamanism is between a theory out of which experiences can be teased and an experience out of which theory can be teased.

BADINER: Well, this is a fundamental tenet of Buddhism, to abandon belief systems for direct experience.

MCKENNA: Yes, but like an onion, Buddhism has many layers. For instance, folk Buddhism is obsessed with reincarnation. Philosophical Buddhism knows there is no abiding self. How can these two things be reconciled? Logically they can't, but religions aren't logical. Religions are structures in the mass psyche that fulfill needs not dictated by reason alone. Any complex, philosophical system makes room for self-contradiction.

BADINER: One of the significant contributions Buddhism offers this culture is that it creates a context for the experience of death. You have said the awareness of death is one of the most important insights that the psychedelic experience offers. Are they similar perspectives?

MCKENNA: Well, they're similar in that I think the goal is the same. The goal, the view of both positions is that life is a preparation for death and that this preparation is a specific preparation. In other words, certain facts must be known, certain techniques must be mastered, and then the passage out of physicality and on to whatever lies beyond is more smoothly met. So in that sense they are very similar, and they seem to be talking about the same territory.

BADINER: You've said that the twin horrors or twin problems of Western society are ego and materialism, combining in a kind of naive monotheism. Why is Buddhism any less a remedy than psychedelics?

MCKENNA: Well, it's less a remedy only in the sense that it's an argument, not an experience.

BADINER: But it's a series of practices that enable experience.

MCKENNA: Yeah, but you have to do it. The thing about psychedelics is the inevitability of it once you simply commit to swallowing the pill. But Buddhism and psychedelics are together probably the best hope we have for an antidote to egotism and materialism, which are fatally destroying the planet. I mean, it's not an abstract thing. The most important thing Buddhism can do for us is to show us inner wealth and to de-emphasize object fetishism, which is a very primitive religious impulse. It's an aboriginal religious impulse to fetishize objects and Buddhism shows a way out of that.

BADINER: The way you describe ecstasy has kind of a Buddhist flavor . . . the edge or the depth of human feeling that includes suffering. This resonates with the Buddhist notion that nirvana encompasses samsara.

MCKENNA: True ecstasy is a union of opposites. It's the felt experience of paradox, so it is exalting and illuminating at the same time that it's terrifying and threatening. It dissolves all boundaries.

BADINER: Are you anticipating the emergence of a Buddhist psychedelic culture?

MCKENNA: No, it's a Buddhist, psychedelic, green, feminist culture! I've always felt that Buddhism, ecological thinking, psychedelic thinking, and feminism are the four parts of a solution. These things are somewhat fragmented from each other, but they are the obvious pieces of the puzzle. An honoring of the feminine, an honoring of the planet, a stress on dematerialism and compassion, and the tools to revivify and make coherent those three.

BADINER: The tools being psychedelic substances?

MCKENNA: Yes. It would be very interesting to find Buddhists who were open-minded enough to go back and start from scratch with psychedelics and not do the ordinary "We've got a better way" rap, but to say, "Maybe we do, maybe we don't. Let's go through these things with all our practice and all our understanding and all our technique and put it with botany, chemistry, and all this ethnography." And then what could you come up with? If, as Baker Roshi says, people advance quickly with psychedelics, then advance them quickly with psychedelics. And then when they reach a point where practice and method are primary, practice and method should move to the fore. And maybe there are several times when these things would switch position.

BADINER: You don't see any contradiction in being a Buddhist and exploring psychedelics?

MCKENNA: No, I would almost say, how can you be a serious Buddhist if you're not exploring psychedelics? Then you're sort of an armchair Buddhist, a Buddhist from theory, a Buddhist from practice, but it's sort of training wheels practice. I mean, the real thing is, take the old boat out and give it a spin.

BADINER: Maybe you should try taking out the old zafu for a spin!

MCKENNA: Or, try both!

LIBERTY AND LSD ⊚ John Perry Barlow

OVER THE LAST TWENTY-FIVE YEARS, I've watched a lot of Deadheads, Buddhists, and other freethinkers do acid. I've taken it myself. I still do occasionally, in a ritual sort of way. On the basis of their experience and my own, I know that the public terror of LSD is based more on media-propagated superstition than real world familiarity with its effects.

I know this, and, like most others who know it, I have kept quiet about it.

But I've finally realized that if I continue, out of fear, to conceal what I believe in this or any other area of public interest, I participate in a growing threat to the minds of America's young greater than any which acid presents. I mean by that the establishment of permissible truth in America. In a word, totalitarianism.

Shortly after the Bill of Rights was drafted, English philosopher John Stuart Mill said, "Liberty resides in the rights of that person whose views you find most odious." The Buddha was wise to point out that people must be free to work out for themselves what is true from actual experience and express it without censure.

I will go further and say that liberty resides in its exercise. It is preserved in the actual spouting of those odious views. It is maintained, and always has been, by brave and lonely cranks.

Lately, it seems our necessary cranks have been falling silent, struck dumb by a general assault on liberty in America. This is no right-wing plot from the top. Like most totalitarian impulses, it has arisen among the people themselves. Terrified of virtual bogeymen we know only from the evening news, we have asked the government for shorter chains and smaller cages. And, market-driven as ever, it has been obliging us.

This is what is still taking place in our conduct of the War On Some Drugs. In this futile jihad, Americans have largely suspended habeas corpus, have allowed government to permanently confiscate our goods without indictment or trial, have flat-out discarded the Fourth Amendment to the Constitution, and are voluntarily crippling the First, at least insofar as any expression might relate to drugs.

In my gloomier moments, I wonder if the elimination of freedom in America is not what the War On Some Drugs was actually designed to accomplish.

Certainly we haven't engaged this campaign because the psychoactive substances we are so determined to eliminate are inherently more dangerous than those we keep in plentiful and legal supply. Indeed, the most dangerous, antisocial, and addictive drugs I've ever taken—the ones I'm afraid to touch in any quantity today—are all legal.

Alcohol, nicotine, and prescription sedatives do more damage every day than LSD has done since its psychoactive properties were realized in 1943. Each year, alcohol kills hundreds of thousands of Americans, many of them violently. It is a factor in most murders and suicides in America. It is a rare case of domestic violence or abuse where alcohol plays no role.

Yet I don't hear people calling for its prohibition, nor would I support such an effort. I know it won't work.

It's not working for LSD either, and it's even less likely to. Lysergic acid diethylamide-25 is active in doses so small you can't see them. It's colorless, odorless, and it doesn't show up in drug tests. And you have to be pretty high on acid before anyone's going to notice you being anything but extremely alert.

Does this mean that I think LSD is safe or that I am recommending its use? Hardly. I consider LSD to be a serious medicine, strong enough to make some people see God or the Dharma. That's serious medicine. Two points need to be made: First, by diminishing the hazards inherent in our cultural drugs of choice and demonizing psychedelics, we head our children straight down the most dangerous path their youthful adventurism can take. Second, LSD is dangerous but not in the ways generally portrayed. By dressing it up in a Halloween costume of fictitious dangers, we encourage our kids to think we were also lying about its real ones. And LSD is dangerous.

It is dangerous because it promotes the idea that reality is something to be manipulated rather than accepted. This notion can seriously cripple one's coping abilities, although I would still argue that both alcohol and TV advertising do that more persuasively than LSD. And of course, if you're lightly sprung, it can leave you nuts.

But LSD is not illegal because it endangers your sanity. LSD is illegal because it endangers Control. Worse, it makes authority seem funny. But laugh at authority in America and you will know risk. LSD is illegal primarily because it threatens the dominant American culture, the culture of Control.

This is not a sound use of law. Just laws arise to support the ethics of a whole society and not as a means for one of its cultural factions to impose power on another.

There are probably twenty-five million Americans who have taken LSD, and who would, if hard pressed in private, also tell you that it profoundly changed their lives, and not necessarily for the worse.

I will readily grant that some of these are hopeless crystal worshippers or psychedelic derelicts creeping around the Oregon woods. But far more of them are successful members of society, CEOs, politicians, Buddhist meditation teachers, ministers, and community leaders.

This is true. Whether we want it to be or not.

But the fact that so few among these millions dare utter this truth is, in a supposedly free country, a symptom of collective mental illness.

I neither expect nor ask any young person to regard me as a role model. There are easier routes through this world than the one I've taken. But I do like to think of myself as someone who defends his convictions. And I hope to raise my three daughters to be brave enough to own their beliefs, no matter how unorthodox, and to own them in public, no matter how risky. I dream of a day when anyone's daughters will feel free to do that.

The most I can do toward a world in which their liberty is assured is to exercise mine in this one.

RICK DOBLIN INTERVIEW ⊘ Allan Badiner

ALLAN BADINER: Was there one moment in which you realized that your life's work was going to be about making psychedelic related medicines officially recognized as such and made available to those in need?

RICK DOBLIN: Yes. It was after I had started using LSD and mescaline. It was 1972, and I was eighteen years old and in my first year of college. I had quite a few difficult and challenging experiences, but also intimations of deeply personal emotional and spiritual issues coming to the surface that felt true and important. I went to the college guidance center to speak with a therapist about my struggles and had the incredible good fortune of speaking with a therapist who was familiar with the research and writings of Dr. Stanislav Grof, the leading LSD researcher of that era. I was handed a manuscript copy of *Realms of the Human Unconscious* by Grof that inspired me with its combination of science, spirituality and healing. I read that manuscript at a time when the entire field of psyche-delic research had been shut down all over the world for political reasons—just a few years before I woke up to its incredible potential. While reading Grof's book, I realized that devoting myself to the resumption of psychedelic research and the practice of psychedelic psychotherapy was going to be my life's work. Unlike many others, I was sure it would happen; I just didn't realize how long it would take. I'm turning sixty in November, 2013, and our current predic-tions at MAPS are for FDA-approval of MDMA-assisted psychotherapy to be in place in 2021!

BADINER: You know, for quite a few years I have viewed the work of MAPS, and its concern for reducing suffering and harm reduction as a kind of 'buddhism in action." What has been your relationship to Buddhist teachings? Do you have a spiritual practice?

DOBLIN: I have an affinity for the general philosophy of Buddhism and Zen, but I'm not a meditator. My spiritual practice has really been my work, raising three kids, and using marijuana in order to engage in brainstorming and reflection.

About five years ago, when the MAPS office was located on Love Creek near Santa Cruz in California, I spent about forty-five minutes digging out dirt from the bottom of the creek to make a little swimming hole. After I was finished digging, I had stirred up so much dirt that it was impossible for me to see what I had accomplished. I noticed that the flow of the stream, which was rather slow, was moving out the dirt along the edges of the banks and that it would take about twenty minutes to clear completely so that I could see straight to the bottom. I realized that this would be a perfect time for me to meditate and peacefully watch the creek flow by and clarify the water. I started meditating for about a minute and then felt that there was work I needed to do, so I stopped meditating and started working.

The only other time since then that I've come close to meditating was over the summer, when I was sitting for someone going through a difficult psychedelic experience. The person's eyes were closed and they were opening to the experience. I felt exceptionally peaceful and quiet, while remaining attentive to the person's body language and breathing. I wasn't actually meditating, but I imagined that there were elements of the meditative state that I was experiencing.

I had also tried to meditate as a freshman in college in 1971, but my story was rather classic. There was a girl who taught Transcendental Meditation and I wanted to get to know her better. I became initiated in TM and tried to meditate twice a day for a month or so. When it became clear that my approach to getting to know her more deeply wasn't actually working, my meditation practice came to an end.

BADINER: Have you been to India? What about the vast populations of China and India in relation to psychedelic medicines? Do they just miss out?

DOBLIN: I have not been to India. I wanted to go to the International Transpersonal Association conference in Mumbai in 1982 but I couldn't afford it. I've never gotten into guru worship and felt that much of the spirituality of India, that I was aware of, was too focused on individual enlightenment (*Hinayana*) rather than social justice (*Mahayana*), so I didn't feel the call on a spiritual level.

Regarding communicating to the masses of India about psychedelic medicines, they do have their own history of *Soma* that points toward the potential value of psychedelics, but that may not be sufficient.

Regarding psychedelic medicines in China, Albert Hofmann, shortly before he died, asked me to translate his book, *LSD: My Problem Child,* into Chinese and Russian, so that those large countries could hear about the therapeutic and spiritual potential of LSD. I eventually had the book translated into Chinese and found a publisher in China willing to publish several thousand copies. I found an existing Russian translation but there were no publishers in Russia willing to take the risk of violating a law that made it a crime to promote the use of illegal drugs.

BADINER: How is your family doing? How old are they? Have they shown any interest in your work? Have they had experience with or interest in psychedelics?

DOBLIN: My dad is eighty-seven and my mom is eighty-four. They will never try marijuana or psychedelics despite my raising the issue for over forty years. Still, they completely support my work, even when I was eighteen and told them that I wanted to drop out of college to study LSD-assisted psychotherapy and attend a workshop by Stan Grof. My parents' attitudes changed fundamentally in 1986, when I spent a day with my grandmother who was in the midst of a treatment-resistant unipolar depression, eventually causing her to stop eating as a relatively painless way to commit suicide. Without telling her, I took MDMA and thought I might be able to lighten her mood through a contact high. I was able to listen more deeply, and she ended up telling me that while she was ready to die, she wondered how her life might have turned out if a romance that she had before meeting my grandfather (married for forty-nine years until he died) hadn't been broken up by her father. She then showed me a wedding present she received from her earlier romance, an illuminated copy of the *Song of Songs*, a dried rose and a note, all of which she had saved for over sixty years! Nobody in the family knew about this prior romance, and my parents were astonished that MDMA played a role in bringing to the surface this unknown part of our family history. I think they valued my work even more at that point. Getting my PhD from Harvard in 2001 also helped them to see that I wasn't brain damaged from my use of psychedelics.

My wife and I first met in a class at the Kennedy School. She learned about my interests and wanted to speak with me about a profound mushroom experience she had in college which, after nine years, she was still processing. She previously worked in Washington DC as a lobbyist for the Quakers during the Reagan era with the unmet goal of reducing military spending, but never prevailed. She said she developed an appreciation for lost causes, which at the time was what she thought about my effort to obtain FDA approval for the medical use of psychedelics.

Our three kids, ages eighteen, seventeen, and fifteen, are also supportive of my work and of my absences when I travel. They haven't developed similar interests, at least not yet. Ironically, my two daughters both won the DARE essay contest when they were in fifth grade—not because they believed that illegal drugs were always harmful, but because they wanted to get good grades in school.

BADINER: What is the history of the Zendo Project? Why the Buddhist name and aesthetic?

DOBLIN: In 1984, the Assistant Secretary General of the United Nations, Robert Muller, introduced me to Vanja Palmers, one of the leaders of the Zen community in Switzerland. Vanja was willing to try MDMA, which was legal at the time, in combination with meditation. Over the years, Vanja struggled to balance his position in the Zen community with his growing interest in using psychedelic experience to deepen Zen meditation.

Starting in 2003, MAPS began working at Burning Man to provide psychedelic harm reduction services for people having difficult psychedelic experiences. We wanted to demonstrate how the risks of psychedelics taken in recreational/celebratory experiences could be addressed through compassionate care, as a way both to avoid tragedies that could lead to a backlash against psychedelic research as well as to help people feel more comfortable about moving to a post-prohibition world.

In 2006, I decided to celebrate MAPS' twentieth anniversary at Burning Man. I teamed up with artists Alex and Allyson Grey and with Matt Atwood and others to create Entheon Village. Our vision was to offer the fruits of psychedelic experiences to the Burning Man community, in science, art, medicine, and spirituality. The Zendo structure was donated to MAPS by Vanja Palmers for one-time use at our twentieth anniversary. It was named Open Mind Zendo by Vanja, who brought over a group of Zen meditators so that there was always at least one meditator in the Zendo throughout the week of Burning Man. Vanja wanted to combine sitting meditation with dance. At the end of Burning Man, we decided to save the structure rather than burn it. We have used it every year since as a place for people to meditate, rest, and reflect.

In 2012, we decided to offer psychedelic harm reduction services out of our Burning Man village inside the Zendo structure. We searched for a name for our work and felt that the Zendo Project would be ideal since it conveyed a spiritual element as well as peaceful reflection and the attitude of open awareness and would help people connect the structure with the services that we were offering.

BADINER: Who designed the Zendo? What interesting details are there in relation to its creation?

DOBLIN: The well-known Zen architect, Paul Discoe, designed the Zendo. There is a one hour and fifteen minute long video about him here: http://fora.tv/2009/03/21/Paul_Discoe_Talks_Zen_Architecture And an article here: http://www.sfgate.com/homeandgarden/article/BURNING-MAN-Designers-eager-to-try-Zen-and-the-2489149.php

WAKING YOURSELF ⊚ Brad Warner

AFTER THE FIRST EDITION of *Zig Zag Zen* came out, I wrote some unkind things about it in my book *Hardcore Zen* (Wisdom Publications, 2003). But I have a confession to make. While I am not a fan of taking drugs to supposedly attain states of heightened spirituality, I have to admit that I am a great fan of all things psychedelic. I had my own psychedelic band in the 1980s called "Dimentia 13" who released five albums of trippy stuff. So I didn't hate *Zig Zag Zen* quite as much as it seemed in my book. I thought the graphics looked damn cool and I agree that it's important to discuss the relationship between drugs and spiritual practice since so many people are so deeply confused about the matter. I'm honored to be asked to contribute to this new edition.

The problem for me was that so many of the contributors to *Zig Zag Zen* who ought to have known better didn't seem to be able to see the fundamental flaw in the logic of thinking that drugs could enhance spiritual practice.

LSD, mescaline, MDMA and all of the rest of the drugs promoted as tools for spiritual enhancement do nothing in and of themselves to give a person access to states of higher consciousness. Rather, they induce a highly confused mental state that traumatizes the mind and body. Any kind of trauma can have the side effect of inducing what are often called "spiritual experiences." People have had great awakenings after being involved in car crashes or wars. But nobody believes car crashes and war are intrinsically spiritual.

I don't doubt that drugs often act as a kind of catalyst to further exploration of meditation and other related practices. Car crashes, wars and other such traumatic experiences often have the same effect. Nobody would keep crashing their car again and again hoping to have another spiritual awakening. Yet some people believe they can deepen their spiritual experiences by taking more and more drugs.

Western society is obsessed with medication. Because medical science has advanced so far so quickly, we are prone to imagine that drugs could cure any illness if only we could find just the right combination of chemicals. So naturally, when we hear representatives of Eastern religions describe our normal condition as diseased, we wonder what we can take to fix that. The notion that there might be a pill to make us Enlightened seems like it makes perfect sense.

The idea that psychedelic drugs might be able to do in minutes what used to take years of deep introspection and hard practice has recently made a major comeback. As if the Sixties and Seventies taught us nothing, there is a whole new generation promoting hallucination as a substitute for meditation. The first edition of *Zig Zag Zen* provided these folks with numerous supposed experts to support this view, and I'm sure this new edition will do the same.

I don't doubt that these formerly vilified medications can have therapeutic uses and I'm glad that research is being done in that area. But the question of whether or not they can be used as a shortcut to the goals of Buddhist practice is one that I think the Buddha might have answered with his characteristic phrase: "The question does not fit the case."

James Hughes, PhD, Executive Director of the Institute for Ethics and Emerging Technologies, a bioethicist and sociologist at Trinity College, recently published his views in an article titled "Using Neurotechnologies to Develop Virtues: A Buddhist Approach to Cognitive Enhancement" on the Institute for Ethics and Emerging Technologies website (ieet.org), available as a pdf at: http://digitalrepository.trincoll.edu/cgi/viewcontent.cgi?article=1093& context=facpub.

In the article Dr. Hughes postulates ways in which various psychoactive drugs might help those who are not genetically predisposed to do so follow various Buddhist *paramitas* (perfections) of generosity, proper conduct, renunciation, transcendental wisdom, diligence, patience, truthfulness, determination, loving-kindness and serenity. For example, he speculates that MDMA (which those who came of age during the 1990s rave scene will know as "Ecstasy") could be used to chemically stimulate the Buddhist virtue of loving-kindness. Drugs being developed to treat Alzheimer's and Down syndrome might, he hypothesizes, be used to bring about the transcendental wisdom spoken of in the sutras.

He goes even further, envisioning a future wherein, "we will have the capacity to change genes that affect the brain permanently, and install neuro-devices that constantly monitor and direct our thoughts and behavior" in order that we all might follow the Buddhist perfections.

But I have to wonder who is going to program these neurodevices or decide which of my genes need changing. Based on what criteria? Who decides what is and is not enlightened thought and behavior? Do we really want devices

RAINBOW BODY PADMASAMBHAVA / *Guru Rinpoche* Gana Lama, 1992

PADMAPANI AVALOKITESHVARA Robert Beer, 1976

FOUR-ARMED AVALOKITESHVARA Robert Beer, 1975

NATURE OF MIND (Panel 4) Alex Grey, 1996

TETRAGRAMMATON Carey Thompson, 2011

REGENERATION Amanda Sage, 2012

THE ENLIGHTENMENT Robert Venosa, 1977

GREEN TARA Anonymous, 17th century

of any kind directing our thoughts and behavior even if it means we'll behave in ways that someone has designated as "Enlightened?" Do we really want someone's ideal of a perfect society enforced upon us by genetic manipulation and machines in our brains even if that perfect society is labeled as "Buddhist?" And even if we do, what happens when the devices break down?

Once during a *sesshin,* a participant waxed lyrically about the benefits of the *kiyosaku,* the "staff of instruction" used in many Zen temples to stimulate effort in sleepy meditators with a sharp whack across the shoulders. My teacher, Gudo Nishijima, who never used the *kiyosaku* listened patiently and finally said, "Maybe that's true. But I think it's better to learn to wake up by yourself."

The basic problem with Dr. Hughes' speculations and the opinions of the many supposed experts who think drugs can enhance or initiate spiritual experiences is that a crucial element of Buddhist practice is learning to wake up by oneself. Even if drugs and genetic manipulation could be used to create real compassion, loving-kindness and so forth—and I don't believe they can—this would not be at all the same as learning how to have these qualities by oneself. What happens when your prescription runs out or your insurance gets canceled? How much does loving-kindness cost at your local pharmacy?

Dr. Hughes, and the many others who find his line of thinking reasonable, imagine that Buddhist practice is all about goals. They imagine that we strive to have transcendental wisdom and use meditation as a means to reach this goal. Since they seem to believe that reaching our goal is the point of the exercise, wouldn't it make more sense to get there as quickly as possible by taking a pill?

But Buddhist practice is never about creating goals and trying to achieve them. It's about learning to see our own real state in each and every moment clearly for ourselves. As we come to see what life really is, we begin to behave more logically and ethically because that's what makes sense. Drugs can't help us with that. Buddhist practice is a journey to be enjoyed and savored, not a race to be won quickly and efficiently.

Supporters of drug use as a way to gain spiritual insight often fall back on the cliché that drugs are like taking a helicopter to the top of a mountain rather than climbing it, to which they liken long-term meditation practice. A guy in a helicopter gets the same breathtaking view as someone who has climbed the mountain, but he gets there much quicker and more easily. "You can't deny it's exactly the same view," a supporter of this idea told me once. But, in fact, I would unequivocally deny that it's the same view. It's not.

Let's say you meet a veteran mountaineer with over a quarter century of climbing experience, a person who has written books on mountain climbing and given personal instruction to others in the art of climbing. And let's imagine what would happen if you tried to convince this guy that people who take helicopters to the tops of mountains get everything that mountain climbers get and get it a whole lot easier. The mountain climber would certainly tell you that the breathtaking view a guy who takes a helicopter to the top of a mountain gets is not in any way, shape or form the same view experienced by a person who climbs the mountain unassisted.

To the mountain climber, the guy in the helicopter is just a hyperactive thrill seeker who wants nothing more than to experience a pretty view without putting any effort into it. The helicopter guy thinks the goal of mountain climbing is to be on top of the mountain and that climbing is an inefficient way to accomplish this goal. He just doesn't get it.

The helicopter guy misses out on the amazing sights to be seen on the way up. He doesn't know the thrill of mastering the mountain through his own efforts or the hardships and dangers involved in making the climb. And he'll never know the awesome wonder of descending the mountain back into familiar territory. All he's done is paid some money to a person who owns a helicopter. He probably couldn't even find the mountain himself, let alone make it to the top. When there are no helicopters around, the poor guy is helplessly grounded.

To a mountain climber, the goal is not the moment of sitting on top enjoying the view. That's just one small part of the experience. It may not even be the best part. To a mountain climber, every view, from every point on the mountain is significant and wonderful.

People who think that the pinnacle of the experience is that moment of being right on the tippy-top, don't understand the experience at all. The poor attention-addled persons probably never will.

What I am working on in meditation involves every single moment of life. So-called "peak experiences" can be fun. But they no more define what life is about than so-called "mundane experiences." When you start making such separations, you have already lost the most precious thing in life, the ability to fully immerse yourself in every experience.

Whenever someone puts forth ideas like this, they generally bring up the Buddhist prohibition against the use of intoxicants and then use clever wordplay to pretend it doesn't really matter. The usual tactic is to claim that this prohibition is only against certain "bad" drugs, not the "good" drugs they recommend. "While alcohol, opiates and cannabis certainly could not create a permanent state chemical happiness, much less facilitate spiritual insight," Dr. Hughes says, "the neurotechnologies of this century might create permanent changes of mood."

But the Buddhist prohibition against intoxicants isn't about bad drugs versus good ones. It's about learning to wake up by oneself. A thousand years after the Buddha, Dogen Zenji amplified the precept saying his students should not try to augment their practice by taking "medications prescribed for mental diseases." The notion that Buddhist virtues could be stimulated chemically has been with us a long time. And so has the knowledge that this goes against the very core of what Buddhism is about.

I also enjoy the way some people want to have it both ways. They laud the use of peyote and psilocybin mushrooms in ancient and indigenous religious rituals while ignoring, and in doing so, denigrating religions and cultures that regard cannabis, opiates, alcohol, and even tobacco as sacraments capable of creating deep spiritual insights.

The Buddhist way is to do without drugs or enhancements of any kind. This is an intrinsic aspect of the path. The use of drugs, gene manipulation or brain implants to enhance our mental states runs counter to the very core of what Buddhist practice is all about: Learning to wake up by yourself.

THE ZEN COMMANDMENTS ☙ Lama Surya Das

I'VE SCALED THE HEIGHTS, and also fallen into crevasses. I've stumbled through the dark night of the soul, experimenting with drugs. I have seen friends go off the deep end, never to return. Now I understand the Biblical notion that no one can look upon the burning bush and live. There are risks if we try to ascend the spiritual peaks and plumb their depths. Yes, I have been to the top of the mount—and carved in stone there are the Zig Zag Zen Commandments.

The First Commandment is: "Take care. Watch your step. Be careful," But don't take these commandments too seriously—even stone is nothing but light, energy.

Zig zag reminds me of "roll your own," as in cigarettes. But there are perils as well as opportunities on a zig zag/roll your own spiritual path. I have experienced some of them myself. That is why I prefer to walk an integrated, well-rounded, tried-and-true path of spiritual transformation—the Buddha's Middle Way.

Whenever Western Dharma teachers get together, there is a White Rabbit in the room, an unmentioned subject of which we all are aware. This is our generation's unexpected gateway to Dharma, or Buddhist wisdom, through opening the doors of perception with consciousness-altering drugs. For many of us, they facilitated our first experience of transcendence, about which we had only heard rumors from scriptures and mystics. Drug experience helped us discover that things are not what they seem, nor are we just who we thought we were. That is why the ancient Buddhist scripture, the *Lankavatara Sutra*, says: "Things are not what they seem to be; nor are they otherwise." This is a mind-breaking conundrum we learned to chew over and reflect upon, until not only our teeth and jaws grew tired but also our heads came off. Then life began anew.

I don't want to be a cheerleader for drugs. Drugs, both legal and illegal, can be addictive. I think the first question to ask ourselves is whether they are abused, or used well. Drugs can be dangerous. They can place your freedom and even your life in jeopardy. As a meditation teacher, I feel that on a more subtle level, the instant access to extraordinary mind states that mind-altering drugs can provide—with the surprisingly swift onset of expanded consciousness, and the equally quick comedown—can addict us to thrill-seeking and make us greedy for, and more attached to, mere phenomenal appearances and temporary mind states. This creates a karmic conditioning that limits our infinite conscious potential.

The intensity of drug-enhanced experiences can also stunt our ability to appreciate everyday spirituality, causing us to overlook the subtle luminosity amidst the less vivid, yet equally sacred and significant, nitty-gritty details of daily life. Intense drug-induced openings can, in certain cases, help temporarily crack open the ego-shell and break through a heavily guarded, stiff persona, providing nonconceptual mystical, sensual, emotional, visionary, heart-opening, and mind-expanding experience otherwise unavailable to ordinary consciousness. However, after being blown wide open so quickly, the ego's defensive reaction is often to contract even more tightly in order to protect its domain. Thus the experience can become a hindrance rather than a boon.

Spirituality, which at its best combines truth and love, wisdom and compassion, is the best medicine. LSD is strong yogi medicine; an almost infinitesimal amount can deliver you to other worlds. It can propel deep self-inquiry and gnostic experience. It can also precipitate psychosis. Youthful curiosity definitely played a part, but my main purpose in taking it in the sixties and early seventies was a sacred vision quest: to free the mind and heart, not further entrap or obscure them. This is the true purpose of spirituality. Psychedelic experience provided me a glimpse of other realms of existence; other ways of perceiving; other lives and lifetimes—and a preview of the dream state and the passageways after death and before rebirth, known in Tibetan Buddhism as the *bardo*. This has helped me prepare for conscious dying as well as more conscious living. It has also expanded my sense of humor by unveiling the cosmic absurdity of life; and humor, as we all know, is a crucial spiritual quality. For if you don't get the joke this time around, you will have to be reborn again and again until you do!

I have been concerned in recent decades about drugs in our culture. Drugs are a means, not an end in themselves. Consciousness-altering drugs are not a religion. Just as the Buddha said we need to let go of the raft once we have reached the other shore, we need to be able to relinquish the means and freely enjoy the end, or the next stage, of the journey. We don't want to become stuck along the way, nor become chemical burnouts or psychedelic relics.

I find that the entire societal context of drug-taking is more complicated today than it was in the sixties and seventies. The increasingly young age of drug-takers, combined with the war on drugs' severe sentencing, the involvement of criminal elements and other insalubrious strands of the underculture, as well as the unreliable quality of street drugs, all coincide to lend, for some, an atmosphere of risk, guilt, and paranoia that we did not suffer to such an extent at college campuses in the sixties. In that experimental age of innocence, we thought we were going to change the world. The social activism and spiritual consciousness of the peace movement and the counterculture helped support or bring about, if not a revolution, then at least significant societal and political changes—activism for civil rights and human rights, the environmental movement, and the women's movement. This consciousness remains alive, at least to some degree, today. Mind-altering substances and Eastern spiritual practices were part of this evolving social change. But now when I am asked about the use of drugs for spiritual purposes, especially by young people in public, I usually just say no, or just say maybe. Meanwhile I'm thinking: read between the lines. Just notice my initials, Lama Surya Das. What can I say? I "just said no" for decades. Yet there remains within me an inner smile, like the Cheshire cat's shit-eating grin.

So the Second Zig Zag Zen Commandment is: "Just say maybe."

While I didn't have these initials in the sixties, I certainly had that experience. Drugs were an unexpected gateway to spirituality for me. But I found that it is far easier to have a genuine theophany, a breakthrough spiritual experience, than to develop an authentic spiritual life.

When I was growing up in suburbia in the fifties, the religious atmosphere was quite stifling. There was not much room for questioning. When I asked about God, the answer was usually "Be quiet," or "No one knows." Spirituality was not spoken of at my synagogue or home, although we heard plenty about religion. So naturally enough, the best and brightest of my generation sought spiritual experience elsewhere.

By the time I was bar mitzvahed at thirteen, I no longer believed in God, Judaism, or any organized religions. However, by the time I was sixteen or seventeen, I came under the influence of Bob Dylan, the Beatles, the Stones, the writings of Joseph Campbell and Teilhard de Chardin, Schopenhauer's philosophy, and Timothy Leary and Richard Alpert's experimental psychedelic research at Harvard. Many of us were reading books that bridged East and West, including those by Aldous Huxley, Alan Watts, Jack Kerouac, Allen Ginsberg, Hermann Hesse, Ken Kesey, and Carlos Castaneda. Be-Ins were in. I went to Woodstock in 1969, and the following winter drove to Esalen in Big Sur in my first car, an old Mercury Comet convertible. I was nineteen, and well into my own psychedelic experiments. I wonder now how many brain cells it may have cost me!

My first teenage trip on mescaline was reality-shattering, and totally shook me out of my complacency. I realized things were not just what they seemed to be, nor was I who I thought I was. A year later at college came my first LSD trip. One fine spring day, I had my first glimpse of God, of what Meister Eckhart calls "the Great Emptiness," the via negativa. I knew what the Christian mystic had meant when he said: "The eye through which I see God is the eye with which He sees me." This epiphany, this spiritual breakthrough, was overwhelmingly moving. For a few hours I felt totally connected and loved, and at the same time as if dissolved. I disappeared, and yet I was connected to everything and everyone, graciously blessed with a profound sense of meaning, belonging, acceptance, and unconditional compassion for all living things. There was nothing more to do or undo, and all of reality seemed perfectly radiant, stainless, whole, and complete, just as it was.

My close friends and I tried to ingest psychedelics in a sacred manner, but like explorers—a half-baked combination of holy mystics and intrepid psychonauts. We tripped mostly in wilderness areas with best friends and lovers, rather than frivolously at rock concerts and movies. I found that the organic psychedelics, such as organic mescaline, peyote, and mushrooms, were softer and smoother than LSD, and thus more conducive to exploring the spiritual domain.

Peak experiences don't happen with every drug trip. I had some hellish experiences too, including one in which I thought I was dying as I unexpectedly began to black out, and another in which I experienced firsthand what many religions call hell. Some of my friends dropped off along the zig zag highway, and I mean literally. I still miss them.

To say drug experience is unreal, and thus cannot provide an experience of reality, is nonsense. Mind-altering substances have been used throughout history by holy men and women, shamans, and spiritual seekers. In rites and rituals harking back thousands of years, India knew *soma*, the magic god-medicine, and *amrita*, the elixir of deathlessness. South American shamans still drink ayahuasca for their sacred rituals, gaining over millennia profound knowledge of plant medicines and more, while the Native American Church uses peyote in a legal as well as a sacred manner in the United States.

For me psychedelic experience opened an unexpected glimpse of the Ultimate. I had previously thought religion and God were just a matter of faith not experience. Then suddenly I had my own experience—I knew there was a "there" there. We may feel far from it, but it's never far from us. "It," by whatever name we call it, is still as sweet, and as near. As we say in Dzogchen, "Buddhahood in the palm of your hand."

The question is: How can we access it? Paul Tillich said at Harvard: "The question our century puts before us is: Is it possible to regain the lost dimension, the encounter with the Holy, the dimension that cuts through the world of subjectivity and objectivity and goes down to that which is not world but is the mystery of the Ground of Being?"

How to bring about spiritual insights, and sustain them, was the subject of many conversations that I would have with my gurus and friends along the path, including Ram Dass, Bhagavan Das, Dan Goleman, Krishna Das, Werner Erhard, Charles Berner, Joan Halifax, Allen Ginsberg, Gary Snyder, Abbie Hoffman, Ken Kesey, Acharya Munindra, Joseph Goldstein and Sharon Salzberg, and with saints, Muktananda, Ananadamayi-ma, and Sathya Sai Baba. Many of us wondered how to bring Eastern teachings back to America, and how they would fit into our culture.

The Third Zig Zag Zen Commandment: "**Find a way to have your own spiritual practice and experience.**" **Find a way to live in the sacred zone—not just visit.**

Spirituality of all kinds requires honesty and sincerity, combined with curiosity, exploration, perseverance, questioning, and self-inquiry. Spirituality is a heroic journey, a grail quest.

After graduating from college I went to India, seeking just this kind of personal spiritual connection. I found it through meditation, yoga, fasting, chanting, ritual. I was amazed to find that my gurus regularly experienced what I had been seeking through drugs. Through their skillful means, I learned to access the same states more intentionally, more consciously, more reliably—and without the "accidental tourist" aspect of drugs, when you never know what you're going to get—chemically, as well as experientially.

Having glimpsed the true nature of things—as it's described in Dzogchen—or the true nature of heart and mind, the whole practice of continuing along the path is a matter of getting used to it, or experiencing it through and through, continuously, amidst ordinary reality, not just now and then through extraordinary drug-induced experiences. This is the secret of everyday mysticism or Dharma in daily life.

The Fourth Zig Zag Zen Commandment is: "Awaken your mind, open your heart; learn to see clearly and to love."

One problem with glimpses from drug trips is that it's easier to get enlightened than to stay enlightened. What you experience is not ultimate, final, unshakable, and irreversible. It's not *anuttara-samyak-sambodhi*, perfect complete awakened enlightenment. It's just a breakthrough, a *satori*, a single enlightenment experience. People may have glimpsed the completeness, but they don't continue to feel complete. It's like glimpsing the golden sun when it momentarily breaks through the clouds. Forever after, you know what "sun" means. You've seen it, yet you don't see it all the time because it's hidden behind the clouds of your own karmic obscurations. One downside of psychedelic experiences is that you may think you're there when you're not really there. I diagnose this as "premature immaculation," a condition that can paralyze the further impetus of your spiritual journey. We have to keep going on the path, not just stop at the first beautiful view. Drug use generally decreases with the deepening of spiritual practice; moreover, chemically induced experiences produce more personal change and inner growth if done in the context of some form of spiritual practice.

It is a Buddhist precept to refrain from intoxicants that cause heedlessness. If we are heedless we may cause harm to others and to ourselves. However, I think taking certain drugs in a conscious, mindful manner—as a spiritual experiment, in a safe container, with a guide or a loved one—can be an important part of spiritual experience.

So the Fifth Zig Zag Zen Commandment is: "Go on this journey with a friend, even a guide, if possible." Otherwise, we may be blown away, rather than just blow our minds and experience our true self, which is closer to the true goal.

I stopped taking drugs decades ago. Being a Buddhist monk with vows made that part easier. I had continual access to extraordinary states of consciousness, for some hours a day and I had guidance, with training, through the months and years of meditation practice.

I fondly remember my first guru, Neem Karoli Baba, taking three tabs of Ram Dass's Sandoz Laboratory acid in the late sixties and then throughout the day asking Ram Dass if and when it was going to have some effect. It's really Ram Dass who went on a trip that day. It didn't seem to change Neem Karoli Baba's consciousness much. Drugs opened up my cosmic sense of absurdity! I could see from another angle, like in the "Far Side" cartoons, and not get stuck thinking things are merely what they seem. My world turned upside-down and I could see the emptiness of things, the funny side of things, and open up to what we call in Dzogchen, The Twelve Laughs of the Primordial Buddha.

The Sixth Zig Zag Zen Commandment is: "Lighten up while enlightening up. Cultivate joy. Don't take yourself too seriously, or it won't be much fun."

Once in 1971, I was with Lama Thubten Yeshe, the first lama in India to teach Westerners, at his hilltop monastery outside Kathmandu. I decided to leave the monastery to go trekking in the Himalayas. Those were my halcyon days; I was twenty-one years old, footloose, and feckless, with nary a care in the world—or even a ticket home. After several days of walking I sat down to meditate, with my T-shirt wrapped around my head for shade from the intense Himalayan sun. I took my last tab of mescaline.

I experienced my consciousness begin to radiate outward, dissolving, and then manifesting as infinite realms of light like Buddha-fields. All kinds of blessings, divinations, prognostications, Buddhas, *dakinis*, guardian angels, and Himalayan spirits came to life in my mind as I sat for hours under the shade of a tree. Upon my return to the monastery I was excited to tell Lama Yeshe what I had seen. He just said, "American boy's dream! You too much. Have some tea." He laughed, and we had tea.

So the Seventh Zig Zag Zen Commandment is: "See everything as impermanent and like a dream."

Later that week I discussed my mescaline Buddha-fields experience with a friend, and she suggested I ask Lama Yeshe for refuge vows and tantric empowerment, so I could practice self-empowerment, rather than just waiting for some epiphany to break through the clouds of my obscuring mind once in a decade, or when I take some purple pills.

But my first winter in Bodh Gaya, in 1972, an American Dharma friend gave me half a purple tab of mescaline. I sat beneath the Bodhi Tree where the Buddha had become enlightened, and experienced an incredible vision of him still sitting there in meditation, radiant and comforting. This was similar to my previous experience in college, which I called my first glimpse of God. Although the iconography was different, the feeling of oneness and noneness, of infinity and luminous presence combined with compassion was the same.

My own last Dzogchen master, Nyoshul Khen Rinpoche (who died in 2000) was amazed how many Westerners seem to have had visions of Buddhas and bodhisattvas, mandalas and Buddha-fields. He felt they could develop all this good karma by practicing more meditation. Khenpo was part of the Crazy Wisdom Lineage. I was fortunate to be his main Western disciple, and spent several years with him as his attendant and close disciple. I invited him to America and hosted him, and we taught together many times in the early nineties. Students were starting to ask him about psychedelics and to recount the bardo experiences similar to those described in the *Tibetan Book of the Dead*, and visions similar to the *togal* visions of Dzogchen practice. Being a really open-minded lama and a truth-seeker, he asked if I could get him some. I'm not sure why, but it never happened.

Surely the attitude that most lamas and teachers have toward psychedelics is culturally based. I remember a lama in Darjeeling saying that drugs clog your psychic channels, energy paths, chakras, and *nadis*. On one occasion, he had everyone at his meditation center bring their stash and toss it into the campfire as an offering up of illusion. Yet, Chogyam Trungpa Rinpoche didn't mind alcohol. High-mountain Tibetans need their lung capacity, and smoking was not a good thing for them, so perhaps alcohol was more acceptable. Whatever substance is being used, it should be used consciously and intentionally, and not mindlessly.

So the Eighth Zig Zag Zen Commandment is: "Be mindful. Be vigilant and intelligent about your experiments." For if the wind changes, the altered state might stick, and you might never get home to Kansas again!

Allen Ginsberg once asked my late master Dudjom Rinpoche about his psychedelic visions and experiences, especially the terrifying ones. Dudjom Rinpoche said: "Whatever you see, good or bad, don't cling to it." Enlightened advice for all seasons!

So this is the Ninth Zig Zag Zen Commandment: "Don't cling to anything."

Some poets, including Rimbaud, Coleridge, Burroughs, Ginsberg, and Kerouac, have written extensively while using drugs. I personally find it difficult to read and write clearly, or meditate under their influence. In the seventies, once I got into monastic training, I stopped using drugs and remember feeling a great clearing-out of my energy channels. Breathing exercises, in particular, clear out the cobwebs, psychic pollution, and spiritual sludge. Pranayama and other yogic breathing techniques are, like regular physical exercise, extraordinarily energizing, restorative, and healing. If you are concerned about the amount of drugs you have taken, and the aftereffects, the practice of Tibetan energy yoga can do a lot to restore the natural state of pristine clarity.

The unexpected psychedelic gateway to spirituality turned my heart and mind toward seeking my transpersonal aspect of being on a more consistent basis. When I began to meditate, I found that I was again being reconnected to my non-self. Through practice, I could get ever more continuous access to that underlying continuity that is like a string holding together all the bead-like experiences of our life in one beautiful rosary. Words are just like mere finger-painting. All language is a weak translation of this ineffable experience. As the Buddha said, according to Zen tradition: "I never uttered a word; yet everybody heard what they needed to hear."

The Tenth Zig Zag Zen Commandment is: "Don't rely on mere words and concepts."

After having a psychedelic opening, you have to come back and live in the here and now. Otherwise, psychedelic revelations might paralyze the impetus toward deepening that glimpse. I try to integrate the Absolute and the Relative in my body, my feelings, my work, and in my own relations by making authentic connection in every contact in daily life. One of the best ways to abide in the non-dual is by practicing the Six Paramitas of the Bodhisattva Path, or principles of enlightened living: generosity, virtue, patience, diligence, concentration, and transcendental wisdom. The Middle Way means not falling into the ditch on either side. But the Middle Way is not like a narrow yellow line down the center of the road. It has plenty of lanes on either side for us to enjoy at our different speeds and in our different ways.

So an extra commandment, for good measure, is: "Be good and do good. There are no enlightened individuals; there is only enlightened activity."

For some people, a psychedelic experience might be too much to handle, or out of the question. It might shake up an unstable ego structure too much, and therefore be unhelpful. You must develop a healthy, autonomous adult ego before you can genuinely transcend the ego. Or in Buddhist parlance, you must become somebody before you become nobody. It is not a commandment, but one would do well to realize one's true self.

LAMA SAYS: Spiritual practice is perfect. Just do it.

To sum up my lighthearted Zig Zag Zen Commandments:

1. Take care. Watch your step. Be careful.
2. Just say maybe.
3. Find a way to have your own spiritual practice and experience.
4. Awaken your mind, open your heart; learn to see clearly and to love.
5. Go on this journey with a friend, even a guide, if possible.
6. Lighten up while enlightening up. Cultivate joy. Don't take yourself too seriously, or it won't be much fun.
7. See everything as impermanent and like a dream.
8. Be mindful. Be vigilant and intelligent about your experiments.
9. Don't cling to anything.
10. Don't rely on mere words and concepts.

And—the extra one—for good measure: Be good and do good.
There are no enlightened individuals; there is only enlightened activity.

ON THE FRONT LINES—Interview with Michele McDonald
Allan Badiner

ALLAN BADINER: You have many young people attending your meditation retreats. Do you find yourself having to address the issue of psychedelic use?

MICHELE MCDONALD: Yes. The drug issue is right on the front lines. As a meditation teacher, it takes a lot of reflection to present something that's helpful and relevant in the face of how many choices students have around drugs. From my experience, no matter what kind of deep opening one might have on a drug, it isn't going to develop one's ability to have those experiences naturally. Other people might say that drugs are a doorway, but I don't see it develop anything. It doesn't develop equanimity, it doesn't develop investigation, it doesn't develop any of the factors of enlightenment.

BADINER: What do you see drugs doing?

MCDONALD: Drugs take a considerable toll on the body and the mind. They bring all this energy into the system so that it catapults you into a different state of consciousness at the same time that it taxes your body, mind, and heart. You get a sort of beatific view, but actually you're further down the mountain.

BADINER: Do you think that applies across the board to all psychedelic experiences? Some people use MDMA, or Ecstasy, in conjunction with their meditation, such as *metta* meditation, and claim the openings that they get from this material translate into real change in their daily lives. Are they deluded?

MCDONALD: The initial experience with the drug might help one to experience intention to develop loving-kindness, but the ability to access that on a regular basis takes practice. A drug can't help you create or develop your ability to practice loving-kindness.

BADINER: So the drug can't get you there, but can it show you that there's somewhere to go?

MCDONALD: No. I don't think that a drug experience from five years ago, or three hours ago, is going to make metta accessible for me. It's the willingness to put in the time through ordinary consciousness and develop your ability to practice deeply that allows you to access the mind of loving-kindness when you're in traffic, or at the grocery store, or talking to your kids. To depend on a drug to develop that quality is antithetical to what we would call the development of mind. So while drugs may spark an interest in those states of mind, one always has to assess the toll it takes on the body and the mind.

BADINER: What has been your experience on retreat with people who use?

MCDONALD: I've had people who have come to retreats who've done a lot of drugs, and it seems like they don't have the energy to go deep. They've blown it off with drugs. You pay a price for any drug experience. There's no price that your body or mind has to pay to be in retreat and deepen those states naturally.

BADINER: So you feel that it's not only that drugs don't help one along the path, they are actually a hindrance?

MCDONALD: On a really deep level of letting go, drugs get in the way. This is especially true for those who are heavily armored.

BADINER: What I hear you saying is the opposite from what some conservative Buddhists might say; that if you're heavily armored and you desperately need an opening, well then, and only then, maybe it would be OK to use a psychedelic. But what you are saying is to avoid drugs particularly then, because they will increase your already strong resistance to doing the hard work.

MCDONALD: Right. I'm talking about a deep level of attachment in the mind, where if one is needing to repeat an experience, it is reinforcing that attachment. When a person feels that they need drugs to deepen in their spiritual journey they're just reinforcing the attachment to those particular states of consciousness.

BADINER: How is that different from attachment to the state that one reaches in meditation?

MCDONALD: In a retreat you're going through sleepiness, you're going through restlessness, you're not aiming for a certain state. At least in vipassana practice, which is what I teach, it's not state-oriented. The idea is that freedom isn't based on any experience, so you're developing an awareness that isn't imprisoned by being attached to certain experiences. When you take a drug you're definitely attached to an experience, or you wouldn't be taking the drug.

BADINER: Have you had personal experience with psychedelics?

MCDONALD: I can very happily say that I've had some very deep experiences, even spiritual experiences on drugs.

BADINER: But you don't recommend them?

MCDONALD: I don't. While I did have some very powerful experiences on drugs, I've had much deeper and more powerful experiences in meditation. I wasn't looking for any particular experience when I took the drugs, I took them because my friends thought it would be great if I finally dropped acid or if I finally tried the marijuana brownie. But when you put in the work of going into retreat, you're going to open up and it doesn't take such a toll, and it's much more dependable in the long run. I recommend doing the work.

BADINER: So you didn't get attached?

MCDONALD: No. I feel that drugs promote attachment to experience. In terms of my idea of what liberation is, they make that deeper letting go of experience itself harder. I really saw this in my own work.

BADINER: I wonder if you could say more about the distinction between the psychedelic high and the meditation high?

MCDONALD: Meditation strengthens your ability to cope with the ups and downs of life so that you're coping with being depressed, you're coping with being tired, and you're developing an equanimity and an awareness that helps you cope with the downs as well as the ups. In taking the meditative path, you will come out stronger and win in all ways. You learn that you can feel "high" and how to access that when you create the right conditions. Then you can cope with the downs without needing drugs. But what you actually get from drug experience is the desire to take the drugs again. The basic urge is to be free; but true freedom is awareness that isn't tied to experience. The underlying urge is healthy. I really try to support that urge. But drugs don't make it easier in the long karmic trip we are on.

BADINER: Why do you think so many people feel like psychedelics help?

MCDONALD: There are two aspects to our spiritual journey: one is transformation, the other is transcendence. It can feel like drugs are helping. But each breath that we're really aware of, day by day, in ordinary life, each step we take with awareness will in some ways feel very ordinary initially, but we are cultivating true freedom. You can develop great awareness without drugs. We have twenty-four hours in the day, and there are a lot of moments while we're washing the dishes, while we're driving the car, that we can practice being aware. When we're on retreat we intensify the practice, while we're watching the breath, while we're watching our steps. And we learn through this sometimes incredibly tedious repetition how to have an awareness that's free of any one experience. Any attempt to escape that, or avoid putting in that time just sets you back. In the long run the very attempt to escape itself makes it harder to escape.

DO WE STILL NEED PSYCHEDELICS? ☉ Myron Stolaroff

THE DEBATE AMONG FOLLOWERS of the Buddha's path regarding the efficacy of psychedelics on Buddhist practice ranges from a high degree of support to outright opposition. Those who are interested in the possible application of psychedelics in meditative practice might well be puzzled by such a diversity of viewpoints. Yet, the answer is simple.

Psychedelics can be used in a great variety of ways for an enormous array of purposes. The results depend greatly on the experience, knowledge, skill, and level of development of the practitioner. Thus, the person presenting his or her own particular point of view may or may not be aware of numerous other considerations involved.

Widespread unfavorable public bias toward psychedelics has been created by very selective reporting by the media, as observed by researcher Roger Walsh. As Walsh reports, this bias is so unfavorable that a reputable journal refused to accept an article that indicated some beneficial outcomes from the use of psychedelics unless the reference to positive effects was removed (Walsh, 1982). I hope to shed some light on the diversity of viewpoints by first laying out what I consider to be important factors to take into account in effectively employing psychedelics. From this perspective, we can examine some of the more relevant positions held within the Western Buddhist community.

Psychedelic agents, when properly understood, are probably one of the most valuable, useful, and powerful tools available to humanity. Yet, their use is extremely complex, which means that they are widely misunderstood and very often abused. Let me be clear: It is not psychedelics that are complex. In their most useful application, they play a rather straightforward role. After forty years of careful study, it is my observation that one of the outstanding actions of psychedelics is permitting the dissolving of habitual patterns within the mind. One of the most powerful mental habits that humans employ is the hiding of undesirable material from consciousness. Thus, a very important function of psychedelic substances is to permit access to the unconscious mind.

The unconscious mind is enormously complex and possesses an extremely wide range of attributes, from repressed, painful material to the sublime realization of universal love. We probably shall never cease to discover new aspects and dimensions of the mind, as it appears endless; I am convinced that continual searching will reveal new discoveries. Probably every hypothesis that any scientist, therapist, or mystic has conceived ultimately can be observed to fit some set of conditions, from psychological dynamics to the ultimate nature of the universe. Always remarkable to the experienced psychedelic user is discovering how the boundaries of perception dissolve to permit viewing ever new images, perceptions, concepts, and realizations. The biggest problem lies in incorporating discoveries into meaningful, enhanced functioning in life.

Humans love structure, and at the same time, the ego loves certainty, so a great variety of claims often are made about what psychedelics can or cannot do. With integrity, commitment, and courage, vast aspects of the mind can be explored. It is important to realize that what one experiences depends a great deal on his or her value-belief system, motivation, conditioning, and accumulated unconscious content, which includes the rigidity with which the mind functions.

I am an early stage novice in my practice of Buddhism, so there is a great deal about the subject of which I am ignorant. However, I have had considerable experience with psychedelics; my major concern is that there will be attempts to categorize these potent aids and contain them within the walls of narrow, judgmental decisions, thereby cutting off much potential usefulness.

I personally have found that appropriately understood and used, psychedelics can play a significant role in deepening and accelerating the progress of one's meditative practice. This is not true for everyone. Psychedelics are of little use for advanced practitioners who have learned to achieve results without the benefit of such aids or for those who can free themselves from worldly obligations for extensive daily practice. Also, encountering heavily defended areas in the psyche with psychedelics may produce intense, uncomfortable feelings that many may prefer to work through more gradually.

My concern is mostly for the large number of people who could benefit from meditation practice but must still be occupied in the world by earning a living and perhaps raising a family. Such persons lead busy lives and may not have the time to devote to perfecting a practice that will lead to significant freedom (in the sense of liberation from greed, hatred, and delusion, and thus from suffering—the aim of Buddhist practice). For these individuals, informed use of psychedelics can be quite helpful in more rapidly reaching the level of accomplishment at which practice becomes self-sustaining. The ultimate achievement of liberation must occur through interior development that does not depend on the use of a plant or a chemical, although these may help in discovering the way.

There are several key factors to consider regarding the use of psychedelics in relation to spiritual practice and meditation:

1. **LEGAL STATUS.** In a sense, this discussion is hypothetical because now most psychedelics are illegal to possess in the United States. Westerners for several centuries have focused primarily on the outer world, with the resulting neglect of developing inner resources. This neglect, coupled with a heavy emphasis on materialism and reductionism, has created a painful schism between adopted conscious values and the deep interests of the Self. For individuals and society, it has become so potentially dangerous or painful to unmask this powerful conflict that those substances that might accomplish this have been made illegal to possess. This has not stopped many dedicated therapists and seekers who find that the value of such substances exceeds the risk of incarceration. The illegal status also creates the problem of finding pure substances in reliably known dose levels. I am not advocating that anyone break the law, but I am pointing out the importance of developing sound, rational policies that will permit appropriate scientific evaluation of these substances and, ultimately, the realization of their potential.

2. **METHODOLOGY.** It is important that those who wish to work with psychedelics be fully informed of appropriate procedures. Unfortunately, the illegal status of psychedelics has prevented the publication and sharing of results and effective practices. However, a great deal of information is available to guide the serious seeker if one has the diligence to seek it out. Some excellent examples of appropriate procedures can be found in the following references:

   Stanislav Grof's *LSD Psychotherapy* (1980) is a treasure house of good information, particularly the sections "Psychedelic Therapy with LSD," "Personality of the Subject," "Personality of the Therapist or

Guide," and "Set and Setting of the Sessions." A pamphlet, *Code of Ethics for Spiritual Guides*, was prepared by the Council on Spiritual Practices.

3. **LOW DOSES.** Many who have experimented with psychedelics have used high doses of substance to assure penetration into the very rewarding transpersonal levels of experience. Such experiences can be awesome, compelling, and extremely rewarding. Yet, it is often the case that these experiences fade away in time unless there are diligent efforts to make the changes indicated. In profound experiences, the layers of conditioning that, in ordinary states, hold one away from liberation are transcended, and from the lofty view of the transcendental state, personal conditioning seems unimportant and often unrecognized. Yet after the experience, old habits and patterns reestablish themselves and often there is no alteration in behavior.

The use of low doses often can be much more effective in dealing with our "psychic garbage." Low doses can stir up uncomfortable feelings; many individuals prefer to transcend them by pushing on into higher states, but it is precisely these feelings that must be resolved to achieve true freedom. With low doses, by focusing directly on the difficult feelings and staying with them without aversion and without grasping, they will in time dissipate. This permits the deepening of one's meditation practice. The surfacing of buried feelings can often bring new understanding of one's personality dynamics. Resolving one's repressed feelings clears the inner being, permitting the True Self to manifest more steadily; such a result provides greater energy, deeper peace, keener intuition and perceptive awareness, and greater clarity and compassion.

4. **FREEING DEEPLY OCCLUDED AREAS.** The practice of Buddhism in general, as I understand it, is not necessarily therapeutically oriented. There is much advice in older texts to resolve personal problems with focused attention and application of intention to change behavior, but much unconscious material may remain unresolved despite the ability of the mind to achieve high levels of awareness. Ken Wilber has written of the difference between meditative realization and the uncovering

process achieved through psychotherapy. Psychedelics facilitate reaching these deeper, often highly defended levels and clearing them out, thus permitting greater liberation and dropping of undesirable personality and behavior patterns.

5. **DIFFERENT COMPOUNDS.** Some compounds may be more suitable for enhancing meditation practice than are others. I personally have had substantial experience with the phenethylamines, outstanding examples of which are 2C-T-2, 2C-T-7, and 2C-B [code names for 2,5-dimethoxy-4-(ethylthio) phenethylamine, 2,5-dimethoxy-4-(n-propylthio) phenethylamine, and 4-bromo-2,5-dimethoxyphenethylamine, respectively]; the synthetic procedures and physical characteristics of all of these were published by Alexander Shulgin. These compounds have the characteristic of having some of the centering qualities of MDMA, yet being more LSD-like than is MDMA without the powerful push of LSD. This lowers the likelihood of the user being trapped in deep pools of repressed material.

Not being as pushy as LSD, these compounds require developing volition to achieve similar levels of experience. This is the same kind of volition that develops the attributes for good meditation practice. Consequently, it is easier to focus attention under their influence; as one develops proficiency in entering the desired state, it is found that the advantage of one compound over another diminishes. The appropriate dose (found by experiment—generally equivalent to 25-50 micrograms of LSD) of most any long-acting psychedelic is helpful.

6. **JUDICIOUS SPACING OF PSYCHEDELIC EXPERIENCES.** The psychedelic experience provides extremely effective clearing and a quantum jump improvement in well-being and meditative proficiency. At the same time, it is important not simply to rely on another experience to overcome difficulties. Mustering a deeper degree of intent can resolve important restrictions through properly focused meditation practice, with the advantage of a more permanent and satisfying state of well-being.

7. **HONORING THE EXPERIENCE.** A very important aspect of employing psychedelics is to acknowledge fully the graces that have been received. This is done through appreciation and gratitude, which are

best expressed by determinedly putting into effect in one's life the changes that have been indicated. In fact, failure to do so can contribute to subsequent depression. Thoroughly honoring the experience and postponing further psychedelic exploration until a real need is determined that cannot be resolved in straightforward meditation practice ensures that the next experience will be fruitful.

8. **HISTORICAL PRECEDENCE.** Psychedelics have had extensive use in spiritual practices in numerous cultures around the world, encompassing thousands of years of history. Current legally sanctioned spiritual practices with psychedelics include the Native American Church in North America, based on the use of peyote, and the Santo Daime and União do Vegetal churches in Brazil employing ayahuasca.

Using Psychedelics in Meditation Practice

i. ETHICAL FRAMEWORK. Committing oneself to a suitable ethical framework, such as the Buddhist Eightfold Path, is essential. This is an important part of the mental set and also provides help in integrating psychedelic experiences.

ii. PREPARATION. The participant should have a thorough understanding of psychedelics including the types of experience that may be expected, factors affecting experience, the importance of set and setting, how to handle various kinds of experiences and how to follow them up. It is important to have first undergone a high-dose experience with a qualified guide that has resulted in reaching transpersonal levels. This will put the entire process into perspective.

iii. EMPLOYING AN APPROPRIATE AND PURE SUBSTANCE AT THE APPROPRIATE DOSE LEVEL.

iv. DEVELOPING MENTAL FOCUS. A practice focusing on the breath is particularly appropriate. Distractions may be more intense than in ordinary meditation practice because the action of the chemical releases more material from the unconscious. At the same time, the enhanced awareness resulting from the action of the psychedelic allows one to notice in greater detail how various attitudes, thoughts, and actions affect the ability to hold one's focus steady.

From this, one learns to hold the mind in the position of maximum effectiveness for becoming free of distractions. One then experiences the deepening of the practice, moving into areas of peace, calm, and growing euphoria.

With continuing practice, it is easier to enter the numinous levels that one ultimately is seeking. The volition gained in developing this practice under the influence of a psychedelic carries on into day-to-day practice during which the same level of achievement becomes accessible. The outcome that I have found most satisfying is the ability to hold the mind perfectly still, giving access to previously unrevealed realms, including direct contact with one's essence or divinity.

v. Deepening the Meditation Practice. When experiences are spaced judiciously—working to obtain maximum benefit from one psychedelic experience before proceeding with another— one learns under the influence to go deeper into contact with the numinous. As the ability to hold the mind steady grows, it becomes possible to focus more directly on the contact with the inner teacher—our deepest Self, our Buddha nature, or however one chooses to call the wise, guiding entity within us. Eventually, use of the psychedelic substance is no longer required to achieve similar results in ordinary practice. I like to call this "developing a Buddha muscle."

Psychedelics alone will not necessarily develop the ability to have unassisted transpersonal experiences. Nevertheless, it is of enormous benefit and inspiration if one can glimpse and experience firsthand the territory to which we aspire. I maintain that psychedelics can show the way; we then must work independently with serious intent to attain the states that are shown to be possible.

Psychedelics and deepened meditation practice have the potential to help us develop greater wisdom; heighten our perceptions, self-understanding, energy, and freedom; release habitual blocks that interfere with the total response of our senses; facilitate the flow of ideas; release intuition and creativity by the removal of unconscious blocks; and put us more in touch with our inherent faculties.

in this way? So if we do use psychedelics, this would be the bottom line: Is it harmful to others or harmful to ourselves?

I think that's a good context to look at the use of different substances. Do we think that it would be beneficial to our self and—from a Bodhisattva perspective, being beneficial to our self is not the foremost thing—is it beneficial to our deeper unfolding of realization so that we can help others more fully?

JIM: The serious question seems to be: Does having psychedelic experiences improve or degrade my practice? This isn't yet looking at the inner framework, or the life situation of the person. This question, "What does it do to my practice?" is still internal. I'd like to share some stories that have helped my understanding.

Near the end of his life Alan Watts was asked by a young man, "Is it worthwhile to take LSD?" After pondering a bit, Alan replied, "That's like asking me if life is worthwhile."

Next is a quote from the website DMT-Nexus: "I can say this after a lifetime of meditating and only two trips on psychedelics, that they are not just a trip. The lasting effects are huge. The changes in me have been profound and seem substantially permanent. I agree; it is best to work on yourself using all available methods." And finally this from a professor, speaking of a high dose experience: "After the collective purification ended, I was spun into the radiance of what, using Buddhist vocabulary, I perceived to be the domain of diamond luminosity. I've known light many times before, but this was an exceptionally pure light. Its clarity was so overwhelming, its energy so pure, that returning to it quickly became my deepest agenda for future sessions. After my first initiation into this reality, it took five sessions of intense purification and surrender before the doors were opened again and I was returned to the diamond light, now experienced at a slightly deeper and even purer form."

For me, these reports bring up very practical questions: Are psychedelics beneficial in the sense of moving you towards living a life more like a Bodhisattva? Are they good for you right now?

KOKYO: One place we can go is to talk about what qualities of psychedelic experience could be in accord with Buddhism—because there are lots of things that happen in a psychedelic experience that have nothing to do with Buddhism.

A basic Buddhist teaching is that the root of all our problems is the belief that things are separate, outside us, and things substantially exist in and of themselves. So the profound insight that those are actually illusions can release one from all kinds of suffering, if it's deeply realized and integrated into one's life. But going beyond this, in Mahayana Buddhism the purpose of that very insight is not even for our own liberation from suffering; it's so that we can really help others, and really meet others with complete openness and a sense of non-separation. That's the Bodhisattva path. So, there can be realization of non-duality, of non-separation, that people aren't who we think they are. And to realize that people aren't who we think they are is very beneficial to those people who we meet.

There may be—lastly, and maybe most importantly—persisting positive changes in attitude and behavior after a psychedelic experience is over: Changes in attitude towards oneself, towards others, towards life and towards spiritual experiences. Deep meditation practice and psychedelics can both bring up unconscious problems or issues, karmic patterns, and enable us to really look at them in a caring and therapeutic way. More sensitivity, tolerance, openness and love of others, with lasting change, can occur through a psychedelic experience. Vocational commitment and appreciation of all life can be strengthened.

AUDIENCE: Either with psychedelics or practice, how do we get past the problem that, once we've seen something, we want to get back there, and we're grasping, and we're looking for it, and it's hard to get there because it's a state of innocence?

KOKYO: That's a great question. We have a wonderful experience that we feel is really beneficial, and then we wonder how do we get back there? It's a state of innocence, so any movement or wish to get back to that state of innocence is already not innocent. This is a major issue in Buddhist practice, maybe not talked about so much in psychedelic practice but I think should be. That's what we call grasping or attachment, saying, "I gotta get that again." That is the definition of discontent in Buddhism.

JIM: It's not talked about in psychedelics enough. It is that wonderful paradox of, "I just did this and then this incredible wonderful thing happened. And, I want it again." The question all too often is: "What drug should I take, and do you have any?" instead of the questions we are asking.

In an early chapter of my book, *The Psychedelic Explorer's Guide,* I say that after you have a major experience, if within the first six weeks after it you feel you have the need to get back there, what you are doing is avoiding working with something in yourself that has come up. (sigh from the audience) The advice is wait another six weeks.

We know from the meditative traditions, if you get out of the way, the universe brightens. Here is what interests me: if "I," Jim Fadiman, want that experience, and the "I" that wants it is going to be diminished, then if I get it, "I" can't get it. The me that needs to get out of the way can never get it. But maybe, of course, if I had the right psychedelic (laughter) or the new ones maybe (laughter), it would be different. You see the problem.

KOKYO: A quote comes to mind from Dogen Zenji, "Buddha-Dharma cannot be realized by a person . . . Only a Buddha can realize Buddha-Dharma."

JIM: Let me ask a question: Whatever that highest and most amazing experience is, let's call it unity, where there is no division between you and the universe, and that you understand that there's no distinctions of time and space, and that while your personality and body are mortal, you're not. How many people have actually experienced that? (looking around, many raised hands) So, here we are, everybody came back. Many of the people I have guided have this question when they come back. "Why did I come back into this body, with all of its neurotic problems? When I was out there, it was clear that I was not necessarily attached to it."

KOKYO: In ultimate truth there is no division, just complete unity; there's no self and no other. Emptiness. The conventional truth is where there is the appearance of self and other; those two truths are not separate: the conventional and the ultimate truth. Of course, most of us live in the conventional truth, the conventional world, almost all the time. We need to realize the ultimate truth, but as Nagarjuna, one of the great Indian ancestors, says, "in order to realize the ultimate truth you must be completely grounded in the conventional truth," which means the precepts of ethical conduct, and so on. If we neglect how we are taking care of ourselves and other people, then it is actually impossible to realize the ultimate truth, at least in the Buddhist view. Now, in the psychedelic world, some of us might say, "Let's bypass the conventional and go straight to the ultimate." This can be a problem.

AUDIENCE: I wanted to ask about the practice. In your experience and the experience of people in the room, how can psychedelics be used as a practice, as an ongoing process of spiritual maturation?

KOKYO: Maybe part of that question is implying that there are two different types of psychedelic use, especially in relation to Buddhism. I think we could look at a psychedelic experience as an initial opening, like you have an insight into non-separation for example, and then you pick up a meditation practice or some other method to sustain and develop that insight. Another use would be to use psychedelics as an ongoing path of practice. One problem with an initial experience is that you "see" a certain realm of reality—you "see" it; just that very language implies there may be a subtle duality there, that you're seeing "something." It might be very, very subtle, but the emphasis is on seeing a realm. In my tradition of Soto Zen, Dogen Zenji criticized the term "*kensho*," which means seeing the nature of reality, seeing nature, seeing Buddha Nature. This is usually said to be the goal in Rinzai Zen, seeing your nature. Dogen, with his emphasis on nonduality, was critical of that term because it's putting something out there. Dogen is always talking about manifestation or becoming. So you might say that it is not a matter of seeing your true nature. It's about becoming that, manifesting your true nature, which you might not even realize is happening as some objective thing. It's easy to make enlightenment into some thing and then try to get it.

JIM: You mean it's not a thing? It's not a destination? It's not a realization that colors the rest of your life? It's not a sense of awareness that pervades more and more of your life? We're asking what's the purpose of psychedelic experience? When is it appropriate? When is the correct time in one's life to do such and such? Those questions must occur in Buddhism. There is something about timing, what the Sufis call, "a sense of occasion" and what therapists call, "a teachable moment." Kokyo, you have devoted your life not to just work on yourself, but to working on yourself in the service of others. Most people who take psychedelics don't say that. They do say that they are working on themselves, and want to make the world a better place. But there is still a lot of self that is primary, and that may be a difference.

KOKYO: Myron Stolaroff in his essay, "Are Psychedelics Useful in Buddhism?" said that another thing they both do is dissolve mindsets. Any kind of fixed mind set, cultural and societal assumptions—a lot of things we just take for granted—one can see through, with both of these technologies. And that's part of the reason, some people have theorized, why most of these substances are illegal, because they threaten the very fabric of society as we know it.

JIM: Kathy Speeth, a gifted teacher, had a wonderful saying: "Enlightenment is always a crime." What she was saying is that every culture wants to remain stable and wants its institutions to be supported and believed in. Enlightenment, from any tradition, cuts through that. What she was pointing out that it is culturally correct to define enlightenment as a crime.

KOKYO: To add to the discussion about ritual settings for psychedelics, and to bring Buddhism and psychedelics together, you might be surprised that there's an experiment scheduled to begin this year by a friend of mine. Vanja Palmers is the senior Dharma heir of Kobun Chino [Otagawa] Roshi, who taught at Santa Cruz Zen Center many years ago. Vanja is a longtime, very serious Zen practitioner and priest. He lives in Switzerland most of the time, and he got permission from the Swiss government to do an experiment during a *sesshin*. "*Sesshin*" means to collect the mind, to gather the mind. It's the Zen name for an intensive meditation retreat. In a five-day *sesshin*, you're meditating basically all day, completely in silence; from four or five am until nine pm there is sitting meditation, interspersed with walking meditation. The experiment will be that on the fourth day of *sesshin*, twenty people will take a medium dose of psilocybin, and twenty won't, in a double-blind experiment, and basically see what happens—particularly around mystical experience. Vanja is hand selecting the people, inviting particular longtime experienced meditators, who ideally also have some experience with psychedelics. He's doing interviews with them beforehand and following up afterwards for at least six months, and maybe longer. In the "Good Friday Experiment" in the Christian tradition that I mentioned earlier, they followed up with the subjects six months later, to see how many of the changes had lasted. And they admitted that six months is not very long. So in this case they may check after six months, maybe longer, to interview people regarding the lasting effects of the experience.

This may be the furthest that this kind of experiment has gone, integrating serious intensive Buddhist meditation with psychedelics. Part of this particular experiment is a medium dose. People often have mystical non-dual experiences with a high dose but without meditation. So part of the proposal of the experiment is to see if after four days of all-day meditation, can a similar thing happen with a smaller dose?

AUDIENCE: I have a question about Buddhism. Could you compare something like the *jhana* states with the psychedelic experience?

KOKYO: The *jhanas* are different levels of concentration, or states of absorption, particularly emphasized in Theravada Buddhism. They are deepening levels of withdrawal from the external world, or more simply, becoming more and more absorbed in non-dual concentration. These *jhanic* states were taught by the Buddha, not as enlightenment itself, not as insight, but actually as concentration practices to develop a stable body and mind in order for insight to arrive. The *jhanas* are not the main point. They are part of the path, and many traditions don't practice them methodically. The practice of withdrawal from the external sensory world is one way to develop these *jhanas*.

That's often the case with psychedelics as well. Part of the setting, with psychedelics, is whether the eyes are opened or closed. With eyes closed, there can be an internal unity experience, a whole internal world going on, where one is not really relating to objects. With eyes open, one is still visually relating to the apparently external world. Then there's the unity of self and sensory objects, an experience that happens in a so-called mystical experience. *Jhana* is maybe more related to the inner unity as opposed to the external unity.

AUDIENCE: Can you talk about the role of *satsang* in Buddhism and how community can be used in the integration process in the psychedelic experience?

KOKYO: In Buddhism, sangha is the spiritual community and it's very important, one of the refuges to rely on. We rely on the spiritual community to help sustain our practice and encourage us. So practice is not just an individual thing; we do it together. Especially in the Zen tradition, meditation practice and retreats are very much a group thing. We're in silence, but in very close quarters, sitting right together, and it's very interactive, with lots of rituals. We serve food to each other in very particular ways in the silence.

The spiritual community in Buddhism is very important, because part of what we're realizing through practice is non-separation and intimacy. The realization is that we're all completely intimate beyond our imagination. Psychedelic work tends to be more individual, even if people are tripping together. On the other hand, I have had experiences with psychedelics that were excruciatingly intimate; for example, at a Grateful Dead Concert. (laughter) We are one being! (laughter) That is one example of a communal ritual that has been commonly used in the tradition.

JIM: There are communities that help their members with integration. The one that is most developed is the Burner community. Burning Man is one of the closest replacements we have to Grateful Dead concerts, and it lasts for a week, not an evening. If you look at this stage of development, and compare it to Buddhism in the first fifty years after Buddha's death, which is where we are with psychedelics in this country, we may be doing all right. Buddhists have had a lot more time to work out some of the problems.

KOKYO: May we all stay connected and realize our intimacy. As we often do at the end of Dharma events, let's dedicate the merit, any positive energy that was generated by this discussion, to the benefit of all beings, to the awakening and freedom of all beings.

I'd like to finish with a classic quote from Dogen Zenji, the Japanese founder of Soto Zen:

To study the Buddha Way is to study the self. To study the self is to forget the self. To forget the self is to be actualized by myriad things. When actualized by myriad things, your body and mind, as well as the body and minds of others, drop away. No trace of realization remains, and this no trace continues endlessly.

This chapter is an edited version of a public event;
the full evening was video recorded and is available in three parts on YouTube:
Part 1 http://www.youtube.com/watch?v=RYnheKnpmGs
Part 2 http://www.youtube.com/watch?v=ZyeYH4xKoaY
Part 3 http://www.youtube.com/watch?v=pcmwZdHA-iE

A ROUNDTABLE with Ram Dass, Robert Aitken Roshi, Richard Baker Roshi, and Joan Halifax Roshi

Allan Badiner

ALLAN BADINER: Ram Dass, some people say you're a Buddhist, studying Tibetan Dzogchen and doing long retreats in Burma, but others claim you are really a bhakti Hindu.

RAM DASS: I was in Israel last year, and I did a Hebrew retreat. I guess I'm a "hin-boojew!" Seriously, I feel enriched by all the traditions I work with, and I just don't feel a label is necessary.

BADINER: Psychedelics comprise a huge category. We are focusing mostly on materials that are derived from plants, that when ingested in appropriate doses and in appropriate conditions may contribute to an expanded state of consciousness.

JOAN HALIFAX: In the earlier days, we defined *psychedelic* as "mind-manifesting" The way it was seen, particularly by LSD researcher Stan Grof and others, is that domains of the mind are evoked when certain substances are taken. Different plant teachers are like keys that unlock different doors within the mind. For example, mescaline produces a different kind of vision than psilocybin does, or yagé, and so on.

DASS: From my point of view, Buddhism is the closest to the psychedelic experience, at least in terms of LSD. LSD catapults you beyond your conceptual structures. It extricates you. It overrides your habits of identification with thought and puts you into a nonconceptual mode very fast.

BADINER: What about MDMA, or Ecstasy, what they call "the Buddhist pill"?

DASS: I don't find it to be a Buddhist pill. I find that MDMA is wonderful for relational therapy. It enhances the quality of compassion, of loving, of seeing the beauty in people and all that, but not the experience of formlessness or emptiness.

I don't like the speed component in it, the jaw-clenching and all that stuff. I took about fifty trips of MDMA and decided that was enough. My guru, Neem Karoli Baba, commented on psychedelics once. "It's useful," he said, "but it's not the true *samadhi*. It allows you to come in and have the *darshan* of Christ, but you can only stay two hours and then you have to leave." And he said, "You can't become Christ through your medicine." The distinction between seeing and becoming is where Buddhism comes in.

BADINER: Two hours of Christ doesn't sound so bad!

DASS: It's not bad! But it can also trap you in a certain kind of experience. And *experience* isn't non-experience. It's an analog of the thing but it's not the thing itself. It's like the *experience* of emptiness rather than emptiness.

BADINER: Ram Dass, you mentioned the habit-override potential of psychedelics, But this is short lived, isn't it?

DASS: Everybody's a little greedy for being enlightened immediately. What I've noticed in my own life over the thirty-five years since my first ingestion, is that when I reenter, the habits come back in. But what I have in addition to the habits is the memory of the experience, the sense of knowing that it's possible. Knowing that it's possible changes the meaning of all spiritual practice that follows because you go in with a perspective that's not just from here, but from there as well.

ROBERT AITKEN: I think that there are both negative and positive experiences possible under psychedelics, but I think you must leave them behind if you want to take up Buddhist practice seriously. Old-timers at the Honolulu Diamond Sanga recall that for a decade, between '64 and '74, many-people came to Zen Buddhist practice through their experience with psychedelics. I don't meet many newcomers that have that experience now.

BADINER: How did the refugees from psychedelica do?

AITKEN: Drugs gave them a sense of religious possibility, but then they felt they had exhausted the potential and wanted to take up a practice that would lead them to religious insight. There were people during that period who tried to do zazen and take drugs at the same time. This really didn't work at all because there was a quality of self-absorption in the experience of the people taking drugs that was quite out of keeping with the goal of practice.

RICHARD BAKER: We were in San Francisco right in the middle of the whole scene from '61 on. What Suzuki Roshi and I noticed was that people who used LSD, and a large percentage of the students did, got into practice faster than other people. Not always, but usually it opened them up to practice faster. But what we also noticed is that for the most part, those people leveled off after a couple years and didn't advance much in Zen practice, particularly those people who used it a lot. My feeling is that psychedelics create a taste for a certain kind of experience. It seems that because of the way their mental space was so strongly opened and conditioned by LSD, that Zen practice was only fruitful when it related to this mental space. People who used it a lot, i.e., fifty trips, two hundred trips, didn't advance much past what a good practitioner would after two years. Also in part because of a familiarity with such strong inner mind language, it was harder for these students to recognize the more subtle inner mind language that one learns to recognize in Zen practice.

BADINER: Zen didn't get them high enough?

BAKER: They got a taste for a certain kind of mental, spiritual excitement, and when it wasn't present, and the mind was more in the neutral category, their interest in practice diminished. Much of Buddhist experience occurs in the territory where you neither like nor dislike—so-called neutral territory. Neutral, as in nongrasping, is the deepest kind of feeling, but you can't call it either good or bad. Psychedelic experience tends to have such a strong and exciting quality that it can block the more subtle internal language.

BADINER: So it was easy to distinguish those who used psychedelics from those who didn't?

AITKEN: Absolutely. There were people who would be training in our zendo during the week, and then smoke and drop or whatever on their days off. When they came back I would definitely notice the difference in their manner and in the quality of their practice. They would be quite scattered and unsettled instead of returning refreshed. We would have these fierce arguments and, although I wasn't a teacher in those days, I was certainly an elder brother in the Dharma, but they were not open to any kind of guidance.

HALIFAX: It's almost like a smell: you can pretty much tell who does and who doesn't. Those who use are not as tightly knit as those who don't, in terms of the way the mind is woven. It took me quite a while to settle down on the cushion. After I stopped taking psychedelics, my tendency toward dispersion definitely ceased, and my reactivity definitely diminished. I am relieved to have committed myself to the path of meditation.

BADINER: Although for some time you must have found much relief in psychedelics.

HALIFAX: There is no doubt about that. Psychedelics are an extraordinarily powerful tool for opening the mind field. I look at psychedelics as a phase through which we pass when we're trying to become more truly who we are, more authentic, and more genuine. I feel like I graduated from psychedelics, but that they were definitely part of the evolution of my own psychological or developmental maturation. But it's really a different kind of mind that is cultivated in meditation, where the qualities of stability, and loving-kindness, and clarity, and humbleness, are the primary qualities. Psychedelics don't necessarily cultivate those qualities.

BADINER: Did you ever mix media?

HALIFAX: Of course I have. This was during the seventies and in the late sixties when I first took LSD. But after a while I didn't find it was too successful an experiment, frankly. At least for me.

BAKER: There were a small number of students at Zen Center who tried to smoke marijuana and practice. One student became upset and stopped practicing because I told him he couldn't be my student if he was smoking marijuana.

DASS: A lot of people say that smoking grass helps their meditation, but I don't find that it does.

HALIFAX: I think everyone has their own response to psychedelics. I didn't find that it really worked, for the kind of mind that I found emerging in meditation free of psychedelics, to do both. As time went on, I became less and less interested in the qualities of mind evoked by psychedelics. I don't know many people who have managed to actually keep a psychedelic practice and a mature Buddhist practice going at the same time . . . except maybe Ram Dass.

DASS: I don't see psychedelics as an enlightening vehicle, but I do see it as an awakening vehicle. I see them beginning a process that awakens you to the possibility. That's the way I'm using the word "awaken." It breaks you out, in the same way that trauma can do it, near-death experiences, and perhaps years of intensive meditation.

BADINER: Once you have the memory and you start using methods that are perhaps more satisfying in the long run, your work then becomes collapsing the gap between that memory of freedom and your current experience of reality. Is that right?

DASS: Yeah.

BADINER: So do you still take drugs?

DASS: I have.

BADINER: And have you found it useful?

DASS: Yes, and I'll tell you why. I saw that I could socialize any method. I could make any method work to keep my ego going . . .

BADINER: This is sounding familiar . . .

DASS: You know? The first hit or the first retreat is, "Oh, my God! It's going to do it." And then you figure out the little corners of the mind, to play with it, to protect yourself. So I use one method against another continually as a check and balance to see where I'm conning myself.

BADINER: But you can't always control or direct the experience to be what you want it to be, or can you?

DASS: I'm part of the psychedelic explorers club from back in the sixties, and I understand that the nature of the experience you have with psychedelics is a function of your set as well as your setting, and that as I do my spiritual practices my set changes. So I will go for two years of deep practices, and then I'll be interested to see where I am in relation to psychedelics. I'm at the point now where, if I never had them again, it would be fine, and if I have them again, it'll be wonderful. I may take mushrooms next week, and I may not. I don't know and I don't care. That's a different set from which to do them, instead of "I need them to find reality."

AITKEN: All you have to do is pick up a good Buddhist text, and there's reality. You don't have to take drugs to wake up to it. Most people that come to me now are awakened by reading. They just realize, "Oh, there's something more to my life." But it's correct to say that the acquisitive society is very seductive and draws us in. The average couple work very hard and they come home and, naturally, they want to unwind. So they want to have a drink, or look at TV. It's a kind of vicious circle. Zen Buddhism has its work cut out for it, you know. We need to find ways that people can leave home without leaving home.

BAKER: I also think it's true that the job of a culture is to be totally seductive and to offer no other alternative. And that's what Buddhism is always facing in every culture, how to break through this very convincing cultural, societal thought-sheath.

BADINER: Many Buddhist teachers appear to be saying "do what I say, not what I've done." Young people today seem very sincere about the quest and unwilling to take it on trust that certain methods are helpful or not helpful, particularly when they are controversial.

AITKEN: I don't think drugs have particularly helped anybody arrive where they are. It's just that by the cultural circumstances of the time, in the sixties and early seventies, it so happened that people came to Zen through their experience with drugs. Before that they came to Zen by their experience in theosophy and other occult paths. And after that they came to Zen practice through their reading and their experiences with yoga or aikido or Theravadin practice or whatever. It was just a peculiarity that at that particular time LSD was discovered and made widespread. It coincided with a lot of disillusionment with the Vietnam War and frustration around the civil rights movement. People were in despair of standard forms. They were ready to experiment. But that was then. When I hear this talk I feel transported back about thirty years. It seems like kicking a dead horse to me.

DASS: It's a great gift, a profound sacrament. You can't put it down. We just don't know how to use it, for the most part. Look at all the people who are teaching Buddhism. You see more than some temporary correlation, and you can't interpret it away as karmic. Knowing the human life experiences of all those people, to say that this was some kind of historical accident is absolute nonsense. One needs only to take a big trip and . . .

AITKEN: I have experimented with LSD, and several times with marijuana.

BADINER: What did you learn?

AITKEN: None of them were really satisfactory experiences. The marijuana experiences left me with a false impression of solidarity with peers. In fact they weren't my peers—they were a lot younger than I. Shall I tell the story?

BADINER: Yes, please.

AITKEN: Anne Aitken and I had purchased a little house on Maui that later became the first Maui Zendo. But before we moved, we rented it to a group of young people and would go over and visit them. All of them smoked marijuana. On one occasion I was sitting in a circle with a group of young men, and we were passing the marijuana cigarette around. I had this wonderful feeling of solidarity with the circle. The women were in the kitchen cooking, and one of the women had a little baby that was very fussy. Anne came out and asked me if I would look after the baby while the women did their cooking. I refused. But then I thought to myself, what's the matter with me? I love little kids, and I can pacify any baby. What sort of delusion of solidarity am I under when I'm excluding the rest of the world, so to speak? So that was my awakening to the limitations of marijuana.

BADINER: But you had that realization as you were sitting there stoned?

AITKEN: Yes.

BADINER: Did you act on it?

AITKEN: Oh, sure. I got up, left the group, and picked up the baby.

BADINER: A reasonably short-lived delusion. What about the LSD trip?

AITKEN: The one LSD experience was an experience of illusion. I was lying on my back in the tall grass, looking at the clouds and finding Roman legions in the clouds and so on.

BADINER: Did you enjoy it?

AITKEN: Well, I kind of enjoyed it at the moment, but then afterwards there was this terrible comedown where everything looked ugly and I could see very clearly how wrinkled people's faces were and how disagreeable everything was. I suppose it's that type of experience that takes people back to the kinds of delusions that they experience on LSD. It was only one experience so I can't really judge on that narrow base.

BADINER: Richard Baker, any notable experience here?

BAKER: I do not use psychedelics. I would not recommend that my two daughters use psychedelics. And although in the sixties, I organized a conference on LSD in Berkeley, I have never taken LSD. In the late fifties, I took some peyote buttons and mescaline a few times, and maybe some psilocybin. I didn't like the lack of fluidity, and the way it kind of pushed my mental states around. I preferred the fluidity that I could develop in meditative concentration. One time I was in Chile with two native shamans and a friend who teaches shamanism. I was part of the group, so I drank all the brews that they did. I think they wanted to test the Zen teacher, so they loaded me up. I ended up having to stay up all night and take care of everybody. No big deal.

BADINER: Joan, what was it like to immerse yourself in older, indigenous cultures and take psychedelics with them, and do it by their rules?

HALIFAX: In so-called psychedelic cultures, cultures where hallucinogens are used by indigenous peoples and where the psychological technology is highly developed, I observed that the religious set is so utterly well-articulated and elaborated, and of course it's culturally acceptable and not on the fringe like it is here. In the case of the Huichols or the Mazatecs in Mexico or the Kayapos in Ecuador, you saw a world that was really harmonized to the use of hallucinogens and the visions that were given by these plants.

BADINER: What about ayahuasca, or yagé? I recall Allen Ginsberg's letters about this native South American psychedelic in *The Yage Letters*. Ayahuasca in particular has taken the Buddhist world for a spin lately.

HALIFAX: Ayahuasca is just an amazing plant teacher.

DASS: It's the current ritual of choice. But I think the rituals tend to keep you in dualism. Shamanic journeys are, for the most part, boring to me because they are usually concerned with good and evil and power.

BADINER: I understand there are Buddhist groups that meet in Mill Valley, California, and take ayahuasca regularly.

HALIFAX: Well, I wasn't aware of this, but it doesn't surprise me.

BADINER: Is this all a hindrance, Joan?

HALIFAX: Even asking that question is a hindrance. You know what I'm saying? Even Buddhism is a hindrance. What I ask is: What kind of mind do you want to bring forward? What qualities do you think would serve you and really serve other beings in this world? What do you think would really help you? What's the most healing thing to do? I try to ask those questions in a way that is noncondemning of any choice they would make, but is also an invitation to make a choice that is deeply wise. On the other hand, many of us wouldn't be comfortable on a cushion had we not taken psychedelics.

AITKEN: When I look back on my first introduction to Zen, which was R. H. Blyth's *Zen in English Literature*, I can see lots of mistakes in that book. But it was very important for me at the time. That doesn't mean that I'm now going to tell people to read *Zen in English Literature* first, you see. It just happened that that was my experience back in 1943.

BADINER: The late Venerable Dr. Ratanasara, a Sri Lankan monk who chaired the American Buddhist Congress, was fond of pointing out that when you act unskillfully, the worst damage is not external to you, not divine displeasure, karmic effects, or even the logical consequences, but rather the uneasy feeling or disequilibrium that lingers in the mind. Would not using psychedelic drugs, on some level, create a hindrance just by virtue of the fact that they are illegal, or that studies find them harmful physically?

DASS: Most of the data critical of psychedelics, claiming brain damage, or that they lead to harder drugs, and all of that, come from politically motivated research that does not stand up under independent study. As far as breaking the law is concerned, what we are really talking about is the politics of consciousness and control. Those vested with power fear the destabilization of society by forces that they can't control. The desire for drugs cannot be controlled. It's disrupting all the structures of society, it's overwhelming the judges and the jails. Drug policy has been a total failure.

BADINER: What about bad trips?

DASS: For the most part, bad trips can be prevented by care in the set and setting, and of course, the illegality of the material is itself part of the setting. But those that do occur usually consist of what I call the "outs" (on the way out), and the "ins" (on the way back in). On the way out, what may happen is that the person reaches a point where even the minimal structure needed for holding onto a sense of self is perceived to be in jeopardy. Some people who are not prepared for that push against it, and when you push against it, the whole paranoid process starts; energy is taken from the psychedelics, and a user-generated hell realm is created for you.

BADINER: And on the way back in?

DASS: You're resting formlessly in peace, and equanimity, and awareness, and bliss. As the chemical wears off, you see what you're going back into and it seems like such a prison, such a corruption, that you just don't want to go back, and you push against reentry. It's a bad trip when you come back and everything's "yick." You don't like the people, and they all look plastic and false.

BADINER: It isn't always pretty.

HALIFAX: To have the feeling that you're doing something against the social grain that could actually bring harm to yourself, or others, in terms even of prison, is not a very comfortable position to be in when you're trying to become more vulnerable and peaceful. I'm really glad that I've had those experiences in other cultures, because no matter how authentic we try to be in our own culture, vis-à-vis creating a beautiful setting for psychedelics, whether it's in nature or whether it's having icons, music, incense, and candles around, there's something about an integrated vision—a spiritual vision that's part of a continuum of a culture—that is irreplaceable.

BADINER: Can Westerners ever escape their conditioning? Can they legitimately partake in and fully benefit from these rituals?

HALIFAX: If I go to Japan, or Korea, or Vietnam, and sit in a temple and have an authentic experience of *samadhi* while doing zazen in these environments, is that any different, for example, than somebody going to South America or staying in middle America and having a psychedelic epiphany in a particular cultural setting? I think it's fairly comparable. I think we can cross those boundaries. Meditation and this medicine are both powerful contexts for shifting our assemblage point out of the habitual mind of culture and into a new frame of reference.

BADINER: Unlike our own psychedelic unfolding, we are now seeing a generation blur the distinctions between so-called psychedelics and hard drugs, and we see lots of crossover. A little LSD, a little heroin, a lot of pot, some pills . . .

DASS: But the distinctions are there. I think they can tell the distinctions among them. I think what we are generally dealing with is the attraction to altered states, to the intensity of the experience, and the excitement that comes from taking a risk.

BADINER: Ram Dass, you have some responsibility for this, don't you? We all recall a wild enthusiasm that you brought to the use of drugs.

DASS: There's really a contrast between escape drugs and sacramental drugs. There's clearly a great deal of drug taking now that no one would want to endorse. Children and drugs just don't mix, for example. I've always said, "Become somebody before you become nobody." But drug use is like these pseudopods that shoot out from the culture, and, in the case of crack and coke, represent clear statements of the failure of cultural mythology. Crack is used in reaction to the ceiling of opportunity for people in the inner cities. And in the middle class, it's coke which is used in reaction to the failure of the myth that success brings happiness. I mean, you win and you're still not winning. People with millions of dollars feel cheated somehow. The philosophical materialism that undercuts the society, and the zeal to keep it stable, result in an oppressive atmosphere. I'm not upset about being part of something that shakes that system up.

BADINER: What about marijuana? Do you still smoke it?

DASS: I'm a light user of marijuana. I see it as an elevator to shift my planes of consciousness. That's kind of the technical way I would say that I'm using it. I like to watch the way my mind works—in all the planes, and not in them at the same moment—on marijuana.

BADINER: Does a new student of Buddhism need psychedelics to make real and rapid progress on the path?

DASS: No. I don't see any reason why. Psychedelics are now just another method. They are even kind of an anachronism because of the politics of drugs in this culture. The paranoia connected with them renders them much less useful.

BADINER: Do you have to have a spiritual context to make progress on the psychedelic path?

DASS: You need some context in your life outside of drugs to create the proper setting. Buddhism is a good context for the psychedelic experience.

BADINER: Is there something that psychedelics can teach us about death? Is there an advantage to using psychedelics to overcome the fear of death and promote one's acceptance of it?

DASS: Yes, absolutely. Starting with Eric Kast's work back in the sixties at the University of Chicago. One quote from his work stands out in my mind. It was from a nurse who was dying of cancer and had just taken LSD. She said, "I know I'm dying of this deadly disease, but look at the beauty of the universe."

BADINER: Joan, you have done, and are still doing, a lot of work around death and dying. Would you use psychedelics in this work again, or encourage others to?

HALIFAX: Not anymore. What I have found is that one's inner attitude, a quality of presence that one can bring to a dying person, or that one can bring to oneself, is sufficient and itself a profound comfort and relief. I've had some extraordinary experiences with dying people without drugs having to mediate them. In the latter phases of dying, people are frequently in such altered states of consciousness that gilding the lily further doesn't seem necessary. What really works is a kind of a transmission of the heart, a flooding of love, a quality of absolute love and patience in the presence of dying. This magic of being both empty and full of compassion at the same time produces an incredible effect for both the caregiver and the dying person.

BADINER: Richard Baker, so there are no herbs or plants in the bowl of the Medicine Buddha, only sutras?

BAKER: Buddhism is a religion and not a philosophy because you only take refuge in Buddha, Dharma, and Sanga and nothing else. And there's an alchemy to that which cannot be duplicated by sometimes taking refuge in Buddha Dharma Sanga, and sometimes taking refuge in something else. For me, the chemistry or alchemy of Buddhism, of serious practice, really functions when you give yourself no other alternative.

One definition of an enlightened person is one who always has everything she or he needs. At every moment what they need is there. They're not seeking anything. If you really are seriously practicing to be free and to simultaneously realize enlightenment, you enact that state of being. In other words, you practice "Just now is enough." You never seek out of the immediate situation, no matter how bad it is. You transform the immediate situation into what you need. You imagine that feeling that you need something as being exactly what you need. For instance, if I missed zazen one morning, I might think later in the day, "God, I wish I'd been able to do zazen this morning." At that moment, I take that statement to mean not only that I didn't do zazen, but also that what I need from zazen at this instant is the idea that I didn't do zazen. You don't try to change your state of mind, you always try to find exactly what you need in your present state of mind. So for me this is a kind of alchemy that has a psychedelic quality to it, but the pill is made from the ingredients of your immediate situation—not from attempting to change your state of mind, but changing through not changing.

AITKEN: I would add that there is a qualitative difference between the ecstasy that some people report from their drug experiences and the understanding, the realization that comes with Zen practice. We seek understanding, not ecstasy.

DASS: I feel sad when society rejects something that can help it understand itself and deepen its values and its wisdom. Just like the church ruling out the mystical experience. It's not a purification of Buddhism. It's trying to hold on to what you've got rather than growing.

"G" IS FOR GRATEFUL Frank Olinsky, 1991

CONTRIBUTORS

Robert Aitken Roshi (1917-2010) was master of the Diamond Sangha, a Zen Buddhist society he founded in Honolulu in 1959. He was a graduate of the University of Hawaii where he studied literature and Japanese. Interned during World War II in Japan, he met British scholar R. H. Blyth, who introduced him to Zen Buddhism. He practiced Zen with Senzaki Nyogen Sensei and was given approval to teach by the Yamada Roshi. Aitken authored eight books on Zen Buddhism, was a social activist, and cofounder of the Buddhist Peace Fellowship. His books include *The Mind of Clover: Essays in Zen Buddhist Ethics*; *The Gateless Barrier: The Wu-men kuan*; *The Dragon Who Never Sleeps: Verses for Zen Buddhist Practice*, and many others.

Allan Badiner is a student of Buddhism, a contributing editor at *Tricycle* magazine, and an ecological activist. He edited the books, *Dharma Gaia: A Harvest in Buddhism and Ecology* and *Mindfulness in the Marketplace* (Parallax Press), and his written work appears in several other books including *Dharma Family Treasures*, *Meeting the Buddha*, and *Ecological Responsibility: A Dialogue with Buddhism,* and *The Buddha and the Terrorist*. Allan holds a master's degree in Buddhist Studies from the College of Buddhist Studies in Los Angeles and serves on the boards of Rainforest Action Network, the Threshold Foundation, and Project CBD.

Richard Baker (Zentatsu Baker Roshi) is Harvard educated and one of only three Dharma heirs to Shunryu Suzuki Roshi. In 1966, he cofounded the internationally renowned Tassajara Zen Monastery. He also conceived and designed the world-famous Greens Restaurant in San Francisco, as well as Green Gulch Farm in Marin County, California. Baker Roshi was the second abbot of the San Francisco Zen Center for twelve years. He is founder and director of Dharma Sangha in the United States and Europe, serving as abbot of Crestone Mountain Zen Center in Colorado and the Buddhist Study Center in the Black Forest in Germany. He is the author of *Original Mind: The Practice of Zen in the West*.

Sukhi Barber, British-born sculptor, received her classical training at City and Guilds of London Art School. Simultaneously having her eyes opened, and her third eye squeegeed by various psychedelic experiences, Sukhi then traveled to India and Nepal, where she met her Tibetan Buddhist teacher and settled for the next fifteen years, studying Buddhism and bronze casting. Sukhi seeks to build a bridge between East and West by presenting images of meditation that are free of cultural and traditional symbolism, choosing rather to abstract the figures through the experience itself, thus inviting an intuitive response, representing complex philosophical ideas in simplicity and balance.

John Perry Barlow is a retired Wyoming cattle rancher, a lyricist for the Grateful Dead, and cofounder of the Electronic Frontier Foundation. He has also been a director of the online community known as The WELL. Born in Wyoming, Barlow graduated from Wesleyan University with an honors degree in comparative religion. He is a poet, essayist, and lecturer on subjects relating to the virtualization of society and is a contributing editor for *Wired*.

Stephen Batchelor was born in Scotland and educated in Buddhist monasteries in India, Switzerland, and South Korea. He was a monk for ten years in both the Tibetan and the Zen traditions. He now lives in France with his wife Martine and teaches Buddhist meditation and philosophy worldwide. His many books include: *Buddhism without Beliefs*; *Living with the Devil*; and *Confession of a Buddhist Atheist*.

Robert Beer is a British artist who has studied and practiced Tibetan thangka painting for the last thirty years. One of the first Westerners to become actively involved in this art form, he initially studied in India and Nepal with several of the finest Tibetan artists living at that time. His work has appeared in numerous publications, including *Buddhist Masters of Enchantment* (with Keith Dowman). He has written and illustrated both *The Encyclopedia of Tibetan Symbols and Motifs* and *The Handbook of Tibetan Buddhist Symbols*.

Luke Brown is a Canadian-born multimedia artist who currently resides in Bali, Indonesia. His art materializes sacred liturgy in the third dimension, an alchemical ritual in which consciousness explicates itself in form and time. His visionary images simultaneously reflect and catalytically effect an expansion of consciousness throughout the underlying field of the collective unconscious. In being informed by and creatively translating the deeper transpersonal energies that are pulsing through him into a communicable language, Luke taps into forms that exist in the formless, synchronic, archetypal dimension of consciousness itself.

David Chadwick grew up in Texas and moved to California to study Zen. He began practicing with Shunryu Suzuki Roshi in 1966 and was ordained by him in 1971. He is the author of *Thank You and OK!: An American Zen Failure in Japan*; *Crooked Cucumber: The Life and Teachings of Shunryu Suzuki*; and *Zen Is Right Here: Teaching Stories and Anecdotes of Shunryu Suzuki*. He maintains an archival site: www.cuke.com

Dean Chamberlain has traveled the world making unusually glowing portraits of significant psychedelic chemists and cultural heroes, including Albert Hofmann, Timothy Leary, and Terence McKenna. He is often called the "Father of Light Painting Photography." The illumination in Chamberlain's work is a result of his photographic process, in which he leaves open the shutter of a camera as he shines a series of lanterns and high-powered flashlights in the environment, thereby painting light directly onto the film. His subjects take on symbolic importance because of their unusual illumination. He currently lives in Los Angeles.

Francesco Clemente was born in Naples, Italy. His hallucinatory style expresses an internal imaginary world ranging from tragic scenes to ironic self-portraits. Subtle and unpredictable, his figures have a primitivism reminiscent of symbolists such as Paul Gauguin and Odilon Redon. Self-taught, Clemente came to prominence world-wide in the 1980s and has since had major retrospectives at the Philadelphia Museum (1990), the Sezon Museum of Modern Art in Tokyo (1994), and the Guggenheim Museum in New York (2000). He divides his time between Italy, New York, and Madras. In 2014, the Rubin Museum mounted an exhibition of his work devoted to the Indian influences in Clemente's work and how they relate to artistic practices and traditions of various regions in India.

David Coyote has been a Buddhist and shamanic practitioner for the past thirty-five years. He has lived and studied throughout Asia and North and South America. He currently resides in a hermitage in the Sierra Nevada Mountains of California.

Lama Surya Das is a Buddhist meditation teacher, scholar, and director of the Dzogchen Foundation in Massachusetts. Born Jeffrey Miller, he grew up on New York's Long Island, and was active in the antiwar movement in his college years. Surya Das has spent thirty years studying Buddhism, and now teaches, lectures, and conducts retreats and workshops worldwide. Surya Das is the author of *Awakening the Buddha Within: Eight Steps to Enlightenment; Awakening to the Sacred: Building a Spiritual Life from Scratch;* and *Awakening the Buddhist Heart: Integrating Love, Meaning and Connection into Every Part of Your Life*. www.dzogchen.org

Ram Dass has been a professor at Harvard and Stanford Universities and a well-known leader at the forefront of change. He led the baby boomers to psychedelic drugs, Eastern spirituality, and social activism. Now he leads the graying boomers toward aging and sickness, using his experience of a stroke to proclaim old age a spiritual opportunity. He is the author of many books, including *Be Here Now; The Psychedelic Experience (*with Ralph Metzner and Timothy Leary*); The Only Dance There*

Is; Grist for the Mill (with Steven Levine); *How Can I Help: Stories and Reflections on Service* (with Paul Gorman); *Still Here: Embracing Aging, Changing, and Dying;* and most recently, *Polishing the Mirror: How to Live from Your Spiritual Heart* (with Rameshwar Das).

Erik Davis is a writer, podcaster, teacher, and award-winning journalist. His books include *TechGnosis: Myth, Magic and Mysticism in the Age of Information; The Visionary State: A Journey through California's Spiritual Landscape;* and *Nomad Codes: Adventures in Modern Esoterica.* He hosts the podcast *Expanding Mind,* and is currently earning his PhD in Religious Studies from Rice University. www.techgnosis.com

Rick Doblin, PhD, is founder and executive director of the Multidisciplinary Association for Psychedelic Studies (MAPS). His undergraduate thesis at New College of Florida was a twenty-five-year follow-up to the classic Good Friday Experiment. He wrote his doctoral dissertation (in Public Policy from Harvard's Kennedy School of Government) on the regulation of the medical uses of psychedelics. His professional goal is to help develop legal contexts for the beneficial uses of psychedelics and marijuana and eventually to become a legally licensed psychedelic therapist.

Jana Drakka is a Zen Priest and Dharma Ancestor in the lineage of Shunryu Suzuki Roshi. Jana was born in Scotland and moved to America in 1989 where she soon discovered how easy it is to become homeless in San Francisco. After ordination in 2001, she began a very successful "street ministry" bringing peace of mind to those living in poverty and on the streets. www.janadrakka.com

Eun (1598-1679) was the 184th abbot of Daitokuji Monastery. The *enso* is the circle of infinity, completion, and oneness, the Zen satori experience embodied in a symbol.

James Fadiman, PhD, is a Senior Research Fellow at Sophia University. He is the author of *The Psychedelic Explorer's Guide: Safe, Therapeutic, and Sacred Journeys* and many other books. He has been involved in psychedelic research since the 1960s.

Rick Fields (1948-1999) was editor-in-chief of *Yoga Journal,* author of *The Code of the Warrior* and *How the Swans Came to the Lake: A Narrative History of Buddhism in America,* and coauthor of *Chop Wood, Carry Water* and *The Turquoise Bee.*

Robert Forte, AMRS, is an independent scholar, writer, and editor, who studied the history and psychology of religion at the University of Chicago Divinity School. He is the editor of *Entheogens and the Future of Religion; Timothy Leary: Outside Looking In: Appreciations, Castigations, and Reminiscences,* and the twentieth anniversary edition of *The Road to Eleusis,* by R. G. Wasson, Albert Hofmann, and Carl A. P. Ruck. He taught at the University of California, Santa Cruz, and is currently a faculty member of the California Institute of Integral Studies, Transformative Studies. He served on the board of directors of the Albert Hofmann Foundation and has been president of the Church of the Awakening since 1985.

China Galland, MA, is a scholar, lecturer, filmmaker and writer whose nonfiction books include *Love Cemetery: Unburying the Secret History of Slaves* and *Longing for Darkness: Tara and the Black Madonna.* She was an early writer about Buddhism and Recovery in *Tricycle* magazine. She founded the Images of Divinity Project at the Graduate Theological Union in Berkeley, has lectured at Harvard, Prescott, Columbia, and other colleges, and has led retreats and pilgrimages nationally and internationally. www.resurrectinglovemovie.org & www.chinagalland.com

Alex Grey, artist, poet, author, minister, is best loved for his paintings portraying multiple dimensions of reality, interweaving biological anatomy with psychic and spiritual energies. His books, *Sacred Mirrors, The Mission of Art, Transfigurations, Art Psalms* and *Net of Being,* trace the visions and mystical experiences that shaped his spiritual creative life and address how art can evolve the cultural body through icons of interconnectedness. Co-founded with his wife, the artist Allyson Grey, Chapel of Sacred Mirrors (CoSM) is an interfaith church celebrating creativity as a spiritual path. Alex has long been a practitioner of Buddhism and a stand for cognitive liberty. alexgrey.com

Allyson Grey was born in Baltimore and studied at the Museum School of Boston. Her watercolor and oil paintings are filled with a mystical unpronounceable alphabet and vivid spectral geometries of order and chaos. Grey's abstract works employ densely measured grids coalescing into crystalline mandalaic imagery or shattering into fields of lush impasto color. The labor-intensive and spiritual quality of her paintings relates them to tantric art, Jain cosmological diagrams, and the science of chaos dynamics. Her work has been exhibited at Stux Gallery in New York City and the Museum of Fine Arts in Boston. www.allysongrey.com

Joan Halifax Roshi, PhD, is a Buddhist teacher and anthropologist. She has been a member of the faculty of Columbia University, the University of Miami School of Medicine, the New School for Social Research, the Naropa Institute, the California Institute for Integral Studies, and is a founder of The Ojai Foundation. Her books include: *The Human Encounter with Death* (with Stanislav Grof); *Shamanic Voices; Shaman: The Wounded Healer; The Fruitful Darkness; Simplicity in the Complex: A Buddhist Life in America;* and *Being with Dying.* She was ordained as a Buddhist roshi by Zen master Seung Sahn, Thich Nhat Hanh, and Roshi Bernie Glassman.

Joan is Founder, Abbot, and Head Teacher of Upaya Zen Center in Santa Fe, New Mexico, where she also trains people to work with prisoners and with the dying. www.upaya.org

Kokyo Henkel has been practicing Zen Buddhism since 1990 at San Francisco Zen Center in the lineage of Shunryu Suzuki Roshi, and at Bukkokuji Monastery in Japan. He was ordained as a priest in 1994 by Tenshin Anderson Roshi and received Dharma Transmission from him in 2010. Kokyo is currently the Head Teacher at Santa Cruz Zen Center.

Robert Jesse, trained as an engineer, once served as vice president for Oracle Corporation, a leader in software. He is a founder and director of the Council on Spiritual Practices in San Francisco, a collaboration of spiritual guides, experts in behavioral and biomedical sciences, and scholars of religion, dedicated to studying primary religious experience, with special interest in entheogens. Through CSP, Robert has sponsored the drafting of a Code of Ethics for Spiritual Guides. www.csp.org

Android (Andrew) Jones is an American born visual artist who creates what has been described as "Electromineralism" with a dash of Pop-Shamanism. He has created live art around the world, including digital visual art projections from the Sydney Opera House in Australia to the Ghats in Varanasi in India and events such as Boom and Burning Man. Android has worked with animators in the film and gaming industries, is a founder and creative director for the entertainment development company Massive Black Inc. In 2002, he helped found a non-profit online art community, conceptart. org. His innovative work has been featured in many magazines and on album covers of several electronic and rock music artists such as Papa Roach, Bluetech, Beats Antique, Sporeganic, Phutureprimitive, and Tipper.

Mati Klarwein (1932-2002) was born in Germany. His family immigrated to Israel in 1934. He studied with Fernand Léger in Paris, then met Ernst Fuchs who taught him the mixed tempera and oil technique of the Flemish masters. Klarwein's paintings meticulously reproduce his magnificent and outrageous imagination, including vibrant, colored landscapes and scenes richly populated with every race and nationality. Klarwein painted the cover to Carlos Santana's most popular album, *Abraxas*, and was a well-known exponent of psychedelic art. Klarwein's many books include *Milk and Honey*, *A Thousand Windows,* and *Improved Paintings*.

Jack Kornfield trained as a Buddhist monk in the monasteries of Thailand, India, and Burma, studying under Ajahn Chan and Mahasi Sayadaw. He is a founder of the Insight Meditation Society and Spirit Rock Center and has taught meditation internationally since 1974. He also holds a PhD in clinical psychology, and is a husband and father. His books include *A Path with Heart; Buddha's Little Instruction Book; Teachings of the Buddha; Seeking the Heart of Wisdom; Living Dharma; A Still Forest Pool; Stories of the Spirit, Stories of the Heart;* and *After the Ecstasy, the Laundry.* www.spiritrock.org

Paul Laffoley was born in Cambridge, Massachusetts in 1940 and studied at Brown University, Harvard School of Design, and in New York City with visionary architect Frederick Kiesler. In Boston he founded a one-man think tank called the Boston Visionary Cell. His ingenious inventions and fantastic architectural plans include time machines, levitating gyroscopes, and Klein bottle houses. A postmodern Leonardo da Vinci, his work integrates extensive and diverse scientific, philosophical, and spiritual references and he is a prolific writer and lecturer as well as an artist. He is represented by Kent Galleries in New York City, and has had numerous one-man exhibitions throughout the country.

George Leonard (1923–2010) was president of Esalen Institute and a pioneer in the field of human potential. He authored twelve books, including *The Transformation; Education and Ecstasy; The Ultimate Athlete;* and *Mastery.* He was a senior editor for *Look Magazine*, and wrote numerous articles in such magazines as *Esquire; Harper's; Atlantic; New York; Saturday Review;* and *The Nation.* Leonard held a fifth-degree black belt in aikido, and co-owned a martial arts school in Mill Valley, California.

Bernard Maisner was born in Patterson, New Jersey, in 1954 and received his BFA from the Cooper Union College of Art in 1977. He has been lecturer and instructor of medieval manuscript illumination at the Cloisters Museum of the Metropolitan Museum of Art, and at the Morgan Library in New York City, and at the Getty Museum in Los Angeles. His subtly nuanced abstractions intricately weave together text and image. A twenty-five-year retrospective of paintings and modern illuminated manuscripts entitled *Entrance to the Scriptorium* toured nationally in 2001. His calligraphy has appeared in numerous magazines and motion pictures. He lives in Bay Head, New Jersey, and New York City.

Peter Matthiessen (1927–2014) was born in New York City. He was a graduate of Yale University, and founder of the *Paris Review.* Peter worked as a commercial fisherman and was ordained as a Zen priest. Besides *At Play in the Fields of the Lord*, which was nominated for the National Book Award, he published many novels, most notably *Far Tortuga* and *Killing Mr. Watson.* His parallel career as a naturalist and explorer resulted in numerous and widely acclaimed books of nonfiction, among them *The Tree Where Man Was Born* and *The Snow Leopard.*

Michele McDonald has taught Insight meditation around the world for thirty-two years. She co-founded Vipassana Hawaii in 1984 with Steven Smith. Michele is most inspired by her practice with Dipa Ma and Sayadaw U Pandita and more recently in Burma with the Mya Taung Sayadaw. She encourages an understanding of the path of insight and a gentle strengthening of mindfulness and concentration so that, ultimately, people can access the peaceful depths of their experience in every moment.

Terence McKenna (1946-2000) was a scholar of the ontological foundations of shamanism and the ethnopharmacology of spiritual transformation. An innovative theoretician and spellbinding orator, McKenna was a powerful voice for the emergent societal tendency he called The Archaic Revival. Poetically dispensing enlightened social criticism and new theories of the fractal dynamics of time, Terence was the author of *The Invisible Landscape*, *The Archaic Revival*, *Food of the Gods*, *Trialogues at the Edge of the West* (with Rupert Sheldrake and Ralph Abraham), and *True Hallucinations*.

Brigid Meier writes and paints and tends to bees and goats at Tierra Drala Farm in Taos, New Mexico.

Ralph Metzner, PhD, is a recognized pioneer in psychological and cross-cultural studies of consciousness and its transformations. He is a psychotherapist and Professor Emeritus at the California Institute of Integral Studies. His books include *The Unfolding Self*; *The Well of Remembrance*; *Green Psychology*; *The Expansion of Consciousness*; *Worlds Within and Worlds Beyond*; and *Mind Space and Time Stream*. He is the editor of two collections of essays on ayahuasca and of psilocybin mushrooms and is coauthor with Ram Dass of *Birth of a Psychedelic Culture: Conversations about Leary, the Harvard Experiments, Millbrook and the Sixties*.

John F. B. Miles (1944-1997) was little known in his lifetime, but is possibly one of the greatest visionary painters and colorists of the twentieth century. A flamboyant British character who seemed to encompass a dozen different personalities, John was a single parent; a prolific sportsman; a great lover of beauty, women, and nature; and a champion of the rebel and outcast. He died of heart failure at the age of 52, leaving behind a legacy of several hundred visionary-impressionist paintings. The most potent of these artworks are around twenty intricate mandala paintings—each of which took around a year to paint.

Mariko Mori was born in Tokyo, studied fashion design in Japan, and worked as a fashion model during the late 1980s. She attended art schools in London and New York, and her work reflects the influences of Eastern and Western pop culture and ancient shamanic ritual. Mori is known for her large photographs and video performance installations that present elaborately costumed self-portraits in futuristic and spiritual scenes. She has had several major museum shows, including at the Serpentine Gallery in London, the Warhol Museum in Pittsburgh, the Brooklyn Museum of Art, and the Chicago Museum of Contemporary Art.

Claudia Müller-Ebeling, PhD, was born in 1956 and lives in Hamburg, Germany. She is an art historian and anthropologist who wrote her doctoral thesis on visionary art in nineteenth century France. Müller-Ebeling is coauthor (with Christian Rätsch) of *Shamanism and Tantra in the Himalayas* (trans. Annabel Lee); *Witchcraft Medicine: Healing Arts, Shamanic Practices, and Forbidden Plants;* and *Pagan Christmas: The Plants, Spirits, and Rituals at the Origin of Yuletide.* Her most recent book is *Ayahuasca,* coauthored with Rätsch and Arno Adelaars.

Michael Murphy is the cofounder and Chairman Emeritus of the Board of the Esalen Institute; he directs the Institute's think tank operations through its Center for Theory & Research (CTR). He is the author of *Golf in the Kingdom*; *The Future of the Body*; and *The Life We Are Given: A Long Term Program for Realizing the Potential of Body, Mind, Heart, and Soul.* A graduate of Stanford University, he lived at the Sri Aurobindo Ashram in Pondicherry, India, in the early 1950s. In the 1980s, Murphy helped organize Esalen's pioneering Soviet-American Exchange Program, a vehicle for citizen-to-citizen relations between Russians and Americans and he later initiated Boris Yeltsin's first visit to America. www.itp-life.com

Michael Newhall was invited to lecture and teach as a visiting artist at Osaka Institute of Arts in Japan in 1978. Newhall's *Buddhafields* series began in 1979 and has taken many forms, including ceramic works, oil paintings, and many drawings. The series is influenced by the Chicago imagist movement and comics, but primarily referenced to historical Buddhas and bodhisattvas. Newhall is Resident Teacher of the Jikoji Zen Retreat Center in Los Gatos, California. Shoho Michael Newhall was ordained and transmitted by Kobun Chino Otogawa Roshi. He leads sesshins and meditation workshops at Zen centers in the US and Europe.

Frank Olinsky is a graphic designer, art director and illustrator. He was instrumental in the creation of the chameleon-like logo and original look of MTV, and has created album packages for the Smashing Pumpkins, Sonic Youth, Philip Glass, and many others. He is also the founding art director of *Tricycle* magazine and the author of *What the Songs Look Like: Contemporary Artists Interpret Talking Heads Songs* and *Buddha Book: A Meeting of Images.* He is also an Associate Teaching Professor at Parsons School of Design in New York City.

Ed Paschke is widely regarded as one of the greatest of the Chicago imagist painters and has long been represented by Phyllis Kind Gallery. He learned to paint based on the principles of abstraction and expressionism, but in the late 1960s began surrealistically appropriating images from popular culture. His early violent themes have transitioned to imagery influenced by electronic media, carefully modeled in aggressive and brilliant colors. In his most recent work, Paschke paints enlarged and unnaturally colored portraits of well-known figures including Elvis, the Mona Lisa, or the Buddha. www.edpaschke.com

Christian Rätsch, PhD, was born in 1957 and lives in Hamburg, Germany with his wife Claudia Müller-Ebeling. Rätsch is an anthropologist and ethnopharmacologist who wrote his doctoral thesis on the magical spells used by the Lacandon Indians of Chiapas, Mexico. He is an authority on the subject of shamanic plants and their use in healing and rituals, and has authored several books, including *Plants of Love, Marihuana as Medicine,* and *Encyclopedia of Psychoactive Plants.* He is much in demand as a speaker and scientific director of expeditions to explore indigenous healing traditions (such as GEO) and an expert in state institutions for drug counseling.

Odilon Redon (1840-1916) was a primarily self-taught painter who lived in Bordeaux and Paris. He is considered the greatest of the French symbolists. Until Redon was in his fifties, he worked exclusively in black and white, exhibiting charcoal drawings, lithographs, etchings, and engravings. In the 1890s, Redon revealed his amazing powers as a colorist as he began his dream works using oil paint and pastels. His flower pieces, in particular, were much admired by Matisse, and the surrealists regarded Redon as one of their precursors. www.artmagick.com/pictures/artist.aspx?artist=odilon-redon

Randal Roberts is an internationally recognized self-taught painter. Having identified as an artist his whole life, at the age of 30, Randal met Alex and Allyson Grey and at last quit a factory job to dedicate himself to art full time. He has lived in the beautiful Hudson Valley in New York, the beloved San Francisco Bay, and currently resides in Boulder, Colorado.

Ethel Le Rossignol (1885-1970) was a British artist who began receiving painting instructions from spiritual beings in 1920. Ten years of drawings and gilded gouaches followed, showing symbol-laden and intertwined rainbow-hued spirits representing the hereafter's great companionship of shared unity. A selection of her psychic artworks and writings were published as a book entitled *A Goodly Company.* Her paintings are on permanent display at the College of Psychic Studies in London.

Mark Rothko (1903-1970) was born in Russia and immigrated to the United States in 1913. Rothko is considered one of the preeminent artists of the abstract expressionist movement. His timeless abstract paintings are characterized by subtly toned rectangles of color, huge in scale, and capture a fundamentally religious feeling without any identifiable object or symbol of worship. Public installations of his work include a mural in the Seagram's Building in New York City and the Rothko Chapel in Houston owned by the Menil Collection. www.menil.org/rothko.html and www.nga.gov/exhibitions/rothwel.htm

Amanda Sage is a visionary artist using her painting as a tool for spiritual and planetary growth and transformation. Originally from Colorado, her interest in understanding the world in its complexity and beauty has driven a nomadic lifestyle as she shares her holistic approach to art as a way of living worldwide. Bridging cultures and concepts, her paintings represent multidimensional aspects of humanness in harmonious balance.

Robert Schrei is the co-founder of SourcePoint Therapy®, an energetic healing modality, with his partner Donna Thomson. This work has arisen from the confluence of his activities and interests in healing, Zen, and art. He currently lives in the mountains outside of Santa Fe, New Mexico and teaches SourcePoint therapy internationally. www.sourcepointtherapy.com

Ang Tsherin Sherpa was born in 1968 in Kathmandu, Nepal. Tsherin Sherpa trained from a young age in the art of traditional Tibetan thangka painting. In recent years, he has shifted away from traditional subjects to depict more contemporary concerns. His precise and immaculate paintings of Tibetan spirits and deities are explorations of the detachment experienced by the Tibetan Diaspora in relation to their homeland. Sherpa's work has been exhibited in numerous exhibitions around the world including *The Scorching Sun of Tibet* (2010) in Beijing, *Tradition Transformed: Tibetan Artists Respond* (2010) at the Rubin Museum of Art in New York and *Anonymous* (2013) at the Dorsky Museum at SUNY, New Paltz. In 2012 Sherpa had his first solo show, *Tibetan Spirit*, at Rossi & Rossi, London.

Huston Smith lives in Berkeley, California. He is the holder of eleven honorary degrees, and an internationally recognized philosopher and scholar of religion. His book, *The World's Religions*, is the most widely used textbook on its subject. Smith has taught at Washington University, MIT Cambridge, Massachusetts, Syracuse University, and the University of California at Berkeley. He has authored over eighty articles in professional and popular journals and twelve books including, most recently, *Cleansing the Doors of Perception*.

Myron (J.) Stolaroff (1920-2013) held a master's degree in electrical engineering from Stanford University, and left an executive position in business to conduct psychedelic research. He was the founder of the International Foundation for Advanced Study in Menlo Park, California.

Rick J. Strassman, MD, lives in Gallup, New Mexico and is clinical associate professor of psychiatry at the University of New Mexico School of Medicine. Strassman conducted US government-approved and funded clinical research at the University of New Mexico in which he injected nearly sixty volunteers with DMT, one of the most powerful psychedelics known. His book, *DMT: The Spirit Molecule*, is an account of those sessions and an inquiry into the nature of the human mind. His latest book, *DMT and the Soul of Prophecy* relates Hebrew Biblical prophetic states and the DMT effect.

Charles T. Tart was born in New Jersey and studied at MIT in Cambridge, Massachusetts, at the University of North Carolina at Chapel Hill, and Stanford University. He is a Professor Emeritus of psychology at the University of California at Davis, a member of the core faculty of the Institute of Transpersonal Psychology, and one of the founders of the field of transpersonal psychology. He is the author of twelve books including *Altered States of Consciousness*, *Transpersonal Psychologies*, *On Being Stoned*, and *Body Mind Spirit: Exploring the Parapsychology of Spirituality*. psychology.ucdavis.edu/tart/

Carey Thompson is a sculptor, painter, and installation designer based in the Bay Area of California. Both his paintings and installation work have been exhibited all over the world mainly in the growing festival scene promoting visionary culture. Regardless of medium, Carey pushes the levels of his art to ignite the world with inspiration, understanding that change begins with that internal spark that catalyzes transformation from within.

Fred Tomaselli was born in Santa Monica, California, in 1956. He credits the influence of psychedelics as one of the inspirations for his retinally enthralling art. His work incorporates arrangements of thousands of actual hemp leaves and pills, suggesting the visual pleasures of looking at art and ingesting psychopharmaceuticals are parallel experiences of transport into another reality. Beneath a veneer of resin are collaged biological illustrations, actual plants, paint, and drugs in web patterns and imagery that refer to both Eastern and Western art history. His works have been shown throughout the US and Europe with exhibitions at the Whitney Museum and James Cohan Gallery in New York City.

Robert Venosa (1936-2011) was internationally recognized as one of the outstanding masters of fantastic realism in art. Associated with such artists as Salvador Dali, Ernst

Fuchs, Mati Klarwein, and H. R. Giger, Venosa's work has been exhibited worldwide as well as being the subject of three books: *Manas Manna*, *Noospheres*, and *Illuminatus*. His work also graced the CD covers for such artists as Santana and Kitaro, and he created conceptual design for the films *Fire in the Sky*, *Race for Atlantis*, and *Dune*. www.venosa.com

Dokushô Villalba Sensei is a Soto Zen master, founder and spiritual director of the Spanish Soto Zen Buddhist Community and of the Luz Serena (Serene Light) Zen Monastery in Valencia, Spain. He has written and translated several books on Zen in the Spanish language.

Roger Walsh MD, PhD is a long-term meditation practitioner, and is professor of psychiatry, philosophy, and anthropology at the University of California at Irvine. His publications include *Essential Spirituality: The Seven Central Practices*; *The World of Shamanism; Paths Beyond Ego*, and he recently edited *The World's Great Wisdom*. www.essentialspirituality.com

Trudy Walter was born in 1958 and lives in Boulder, Colorado. She is a practicing Jungian psychotherapist and wrote her master's thesis for Antioch University on the archetype of the Crone. Walter has practiced Buddhism for twenty-five years.

Brad Warner is author of *There Is No God and He Is Always With You: A Search for God in Odd Places; Hardcore Zen Strikes Again; Sit Down and Shut Up: Punk Rock Commentaries on Buddha, God, Truth, Sex; Death, and Dogen's Treasury of the Right Dharma Eye; Zen Wrapped in Karma Dipped in Chocolate: A Trip Through Death, Sex, Divorce, and Spiritual Celebrity in Search of the True Dharma; and Sex, Sin and Zen: A Buddhist Exploration of Sex from Celibacy to Polyamory and Everything in Between*. He is an ordained Zen teacher in the Soto lineage. He has practiced Zen for over thirty years, and once worked for the company founded by the man who created Godzilla.

ARTWORK CREDITS

Anonymous, *Jerry's Finger*, c. 1999, undipped LSD blotter art, courtesy of Mark McCloud

Sukhi Barber, *Radiance*, 2014, bronze, courtesy of the artist

_____, *Ebb and Flow*, 2014, bronze, courtesy of the artist

Robert Beer, *Four-Armed Avalokiteshvara*, 1975, gouache with crystal, gold, and silver on paper, 9" x 9", courtesy of the artist

_____, *Padmapani Avalokiteshvara*, 1976; gouache and gold on artboard, 18 1/4" x 14 1/2", courtesy of the artist

Luke Brown, *Lightspeak*, 2013.

Dean Chamberlain, *The Trail*, 2000, photograph, courtesy of the artist

Francesco Clemente, *Contemplation*, 1990; gouache on twelve sheets of handmade Pondicherry paper, joined with handwoven cotton strips, 96" x 98", collection Sezon Museum of Art, Tokyo. Copyright © 2000 by Francesco Clemente

Eun, 184th Abbot of Daitokuji (1598-1679), *Untitled Enso*, from Sacred Calligraphy of the East, 3rd Edition, Revised and Expanded by John Stevens. © 1981, 1988, 1995 by John Stevens. Reproduced by arrangement with Shambhala Publications, Inc., Boston, www.shambhala.com

Alex Grey, *Tears of Joy*, 2014, acrylic on linen, 24" x 30", courtesy of the artist

_____, *Nature of Mind*, Panel 4, 1996, oil on wood, 32" x 48", courtesy of the artist

_____, *Theologue* (detail), 1986, acrylic on linen, 60" x 180" (overall), courtesy of the artist

_____, *Buddha Embryo*, 2000, multimedia, courtesy of the artist

Allyson Grey, *Order with Chaos Letters*, 2000, oil on wood, 30" x 30", courtesy of the artist

Android Jones, *Harmony of the Dragons*, 2012, digital art, courtesy of the artist

_____, *Dharma Dragon*, 2012, digital art, courtesy of the artist

_____, *Boom Shiva*, 2012, digital art, courtesy of the artist

Mati Klarwein, *Grain of Sand*, 1962-1968, oil and tempera on canvas; 78 3/4" x 78 3/4", collection of Juan Sanahuja, Barcelona, courtesy of the artist

_____, *Timeless*, 1968; oil and tempera on canvas, 34" x 34", collection of H. R. H. Princess Fanda al Saud, Riadh, courtesy of the artist

Paul Laffoley, *Mind Physics: The Burning of Samsara*, 1967, oil and acrylic paint with letters on canvas, 73 1/2" x 73 1/2", courtesy of Kent Gallery, New York

Bernard Maisner, *Moment of Flight*, 1987, 36" x 22", collection of Peter and Helen DuBois

_____, *Spiral*, 1984, 10" x 10", collection of Bernard Maisner

John F. B. Miles, *Dark Rhythms of the Universe*, 1981, acrylic and gouache on unprimed canvas, 43" x 53", courtesy of Robert Beer

_____, *The Room When No One is There,* 1979, *gouache and ink on brown paper,* 59" x 49", courtesy of Robert Beer

Mariko Mori, *Burning Desire*, 1998, color photograph on glass, 10' x 20', courtesy of Deitch Projects, New York

_____, *Enlightenment Capsule*; 1996-1998, plastic, solar transmitting device, and fiber optic cables, 6' x 11' x 9', courtesy of Deitch Projects, New York

Claudia Müller-Ebeling, *Green Tara* and *Rainbow Body Padmasambhava,* photographs. Copyright © 2000 by Claudia Müller-Ebeling

Michael Newhall, *Buddha Field*, 1982, watercolor, 22" x 30", courtesy of the artist

Frank Olinsky, *G Is for Grateful* (from Abecedary), 1991, ink on paper, 8 1/2" x 11", courtesy of the artist

Ed Paschke, *Green Buddha*, 2000, oil on linen, 24" x 36", courtesy of David Floria Gallery

Odilon Redon, *The Buddha*, c. 1905, pastel, collection of Museé d'Orsay, courtesy of Erich Lessing/Art Resource, NY

Randal Roberts, *Divine Messenger of Truth*, 2007, oil on canvas, courtesy of the artist

Ethel Le Rossignol, *Consummation*, c. 1920, courtesy of the College of Psychic Studies, London

Mark Rothko, Rothko Chapel interior with original skylight grid, photograph, 1971, courtesy of the Rothko Chapel

Amanda Sage, *Regeneration*; 2012, acrylic, casein & oil on canvas, 24" x 36", courtesy of the artist

Ang Tsherin Sherpa, *Things that POP in My Head,* 2009, gouache, acrylic and gold leaf on paper, 30" x 40", courtesy of the artist

Carey Thompson, *Tetragrammaton*, 2011, digital art, courtesy of the artist

Fred Tomaselli; *Black Diamond #1*, 2000, photo collage, leaves, pills, acrylic, mushrooms, and resin on wood panel, 30" x 24", courtesy of the James Cohan Gallery

_____, *Datronic*, 1998, photo collage, leaves, acrylic, and resin on wood panel, 60" x 60", courtesy of the James Cohan Gallery

Robert Venosa, *The Enlightenment*, 1977, oil on Masonite, 47 1/4" x 35 3/8, collection of Miguel Bose, Madrid, courtesy of the artist

GLOSSARY

Amrita - (Sanskrit) "immortality," known as "nectar," consumed during religious observances. See *Soma*.

Avidya - (Sanskrit) "ignorance," or "delusion," a misunderstanding of the nature of self and reality.

Ayahuasca - (Spanish) or *Yagé*, tropical vine, native to the Amazon region, noted for its hallucinogenic properties.

Bardo - (Tibetan) "intermediate state" referring to states of existence between death and rebirth, or any other transitional state between planes of existence.

Bodhisattva - (Sanskrit) a being of boundless compassion who delays attaining nibbāna in order to help liberate other suffering beings.

Buddha - (Sanskrit) "awakened" or "enlightened one;" often refers to the historical Buddha of this era (Siddhartha Gautama).

Buddhadharma - (Sanskrit) "path of the awakened one." Teachings of Siddhartha Gautama Buddha that begin with the Four Noble Truths and the Eightfold Path. It denotes both the teachings and the direct experience of nibbāna, the quality at which those teachings are aimed.

Cannabis - (Greek) or marijuana, a tall plant with a stiff upright stem, divided serrated leaves, and glandular hairs; used to produce hemp fiber and as a psychotropic drug.

Cannabidiol - (CBD), one of at least 85 active cannabinoids found in cannabis. Unlike THC, it is not psychoactive. Recent studies indicate CBD's potential to treat a wide range of medical conditions, including epilepsy arthritis, diabetes, alcoholism, MS, chronic pain, schizophrenia, PTSD, Alzheimer's disease, antibiotic-resistant infections and neurological disorders. CBD has demonstrated neuroprotective and neurogenic effects, and its modulation of steps in tumorigenesis in several kinds of cancer is currently being researched.

Chakra - (Sanskrit) "wheel" or "turning," refers to centers of energy in the subtle body, seven of which are typically considered to be of primary importance.

Curandero/a - (Spanish) "folk healer" or "shaman," that uses herbs, plants, magic and spiritualism to treat illness, induce visions and impart traditional wisdom.

Darshan - (Sanskrit) "auspicious sight" refers to the opportunity to receive a blessing from the presence a holy person or deity.

Dharmakaya - (Sanskrit) "body of the great law [phenomenon, order]." In the Mahayana tradition, it is the true nature of all Buddhas, identical with reality, i.e., the essential laws of the universe, symbolizing the fundamental truth of emptiness from which all mental formations arise; also used as the "truth body" in context of the Three Kayas [bodies] of the Buddha: Sambhogakaya and Nirmanakaya being the "enjoyment" and "emanation" bodies, respectively.

DMT - (N,N-dimethyltryptamine), psychedelic compound that when ingested crosses the blood-brain-barrier, acting as a powerful hallucinogen that affects human consciousness.

Dharma - (Sanskrit) "natural law," describing the principle of order in the universe; also used to refer to teachings of Buddha and the path of Buddhist practice.

Ecstasy - (MDMA), an amphetamine-based synthetic drug with euphoric and hallucinatory effects, originally promoted as an adjunct to psychotherapy.

Entheogen - (Greek) "generating divine within," plant or chemical ingested to produce a state of enhanced consciousness for spiritual or religious purposes; coined in 1971 to replace psychedelic or hallucinogen.

Jnana - (Sanskrit) "knowledge," pure awareness that is free of concepts.

Kensho - (Japanese) "seeing nature;" refers to an initial insight or awakening, not full Buddhahood. See Satori.

Koan - (Japanese) "ko" or public. A paradoxical statement intensely meditated upon by Zen practitioners, to train them in abandoning dependence upon analytical reason, in order to be able to obtain sudden, intuitive enlightenment.

Kriya - (Sanskrit) "action, deed, effort." Yogic practice of breath and exercise techniques to purify the channels of the body's energies.

Maya - (Sanskrit) "illusion," the veil of ignorance that leads to belief in a separate existence.

Mescaline - (German), naturally occurring psychedelic with a long history of human use; best known as the primary active chemical in the peyote cactus.

Metta - (Pali) "loving-kindness" or wishing for happiness to extend to all beings, free from discrimination or attachment.

Nadi - (Sanskrit) refers to the channels along which energy flows in the subtle body.

Nibbāna (Pali) or **Nirvana** - (Sanskrit) "to extinguish." His Holiness the Dalai Lama called it a "state of freedom from cyclic existence."

Nirmanakaya – (Sanskrit) see Dharmakaya.

Phenethylamine - the name of a class of chemicals with many members well-known for their psychoactive and stimulant effects.

Prajna - (Sanskrit) "wisdom" or "insight" of the true nature of reality through the understanding of the emptiness of all things.

Psilocybin - (Greek) naturally occurring psychedelic compound produced by more than 200 species of mushrooms, collectively known as psilocybin mushrooms.

Psychedelic - (Greek) denoting drugs, synthetic or plant based, that produce hallucinations and apparent expansion of consciousness. Derived from the ancient Greek words *psychē* and *dēloun* "to make visible, to reveal," translating to "mind-manifesting."

Sadhana - (Sanskrit) spiritual practice or discipline undertaken to achieve liberation, also refers to written texts.

Samadhi - (Sanskrit) "concentration," state where the mind is focused one pointedly.

Sambhogakaya - (Sanskrit) see Dharmakaya.

Samsara - (Sanskrit) "passing through." Endless round of birth and death since beginningless time, transcended only by attainment of Nirvana.

Sangha - (Sanskrit) "assembly" or "community;" including Buddhist monks and nuns, enlightened beings as well as lay practitioners dedicated to the path of Dharma.

Satori - (Japanese) a state of sudden enlightenment, or the direct experience of realizing the nature of existence. See *Kensho*.

Sesshin - (Japanese) "collecting the heart-mind," a period of intensive meditation, typically in a Zen monastery.

Siddha - (Sanskrit) "accomplished." One who has attained perfection and bliss, manifesting spiritual power.

Sila - (Sanskrit) "morality" or a commitment to wholesome actions comprising Right Speech, Right Action and Right Livelihood.

Soma - (Sanskrit) Vedic ritual drink which produces immortality. See *Amrita*.

Sunyata - (Sanskrit) "emptiness," the teaching that nothing has intrinsic existence but exists only in relation to others.

Sutta - (Pali) or Sutra (Sanskrit) literally, "thread," a discourse or sermon by the Buddha or his contemporary disciples. After the Buddha's death, the suttas were passed down in the Pali language according to a well-established oral tradition, and were finally committed to written form in Sri Lanka around 100 BCE.

Upaya - (Sanskrit) "skillful means" or "method," any activity or practice leading to the realization of enlightenment.

Vipassana - (Sanskrit) "special insight" meditation on the nature of reality as distinct from *Samatha* (calm abiding) meditation.

Yidam – (Tibetan) "samaya of mind," [keeping the precepts], i.e., the state of abiding in the inherently pure and liberated nature of mind associated with Vajrayana methods, in which the practitioner identifies with a tutelary deity (such as one of the great bodhisattvas) for purposes of transforming ordinary consciousness into liberated awareness.

BIBLIOGRAPHY

Baudelaire, Charles. *Les Paradis artificlels*, quoted in Robert S. De Ropp, *Drugs and the Mind*. New York: Grove, 1967.

Bourguignon, Erika. *Religion, Altered States of Consciousness*, and *Social Change*. Columbus: Ohio University Press, 1973.

Bucke, Richard Maurice. *Cosmic Consciousness: A Study in the Evolution of the Human Mind*. Bedford: Applewood Books, 2001.

Buddhism & Psychedelics, *Tricycle* magazine: Fall 1996 (The Buddhist Review, Vol. 6, No. 1, New York.

Dalai Lama, from a speech at the Interfaith Celebration of Religious Freedom, Episcopal National Cathedral, Washington, DC, April 14, 1997.

Dass, Ram and Ralph Metzner. *Birth of a Psychedelic Culture: Conversations about Leary, the Harvard Experiments, Millbrook and the Sixties*. Santa Fe, New Mexico: Synergetic Press, 2010

Dass, Ram. *Miracle of Love: Stories About Neem Karoli Baba*. New York: E. P. Dutton, 1979.

Doblin, Rick. "Pahnke's 'Good Friday Experiment': A Long-Term Follow-up and Methodological Critique." *The Journal of Transpersonal Psychology*, volume 23, no. 1, 1991.

Eliade, Mircea. *Yoga: Immortality and Freedom*. New York: Pantheon Books, 1958.

Essen, Gerd Wolfgang, and Tashi Thingo. *Die Götter des Himalaya: Buddhistische Kunst Tibets, Die Sammlung Gerd-Wolfgang Essen*. Munich: Prestel, 1989.

Goldsmith, Neal M. *Psychedelic Healing: The Promise of Entheogens for Psychotherapy and Spiritual Development*. Rochester, Vermont: Healing Arts Press, 2010.

Grob, Charles, S. *Hallucinogens: A Reader (New Consciousness Reader)*. New York/London: Tarcher/Penguin, 2002.

Grof, Stanislav. *LSD Psychotherapy*. Alameda: Hunter House, 1980.

Hagenbach, Dieter and Lucius Werthmüller. *Mystic Chemist: The Life of Albert Hofmann and His Discovery of LSD*. Santa Fe, New Mexico: Synergetic Press, 2013.

Hajicek-Dobberstein, Scott. "Soma Siddhas and Alchemical Enlightenment: Psychedelic Mushrooms in Buddhist Tradition." *Journal of Ethnopharmacology*, volume 48, no. 2, 1995.

Hofstadter, Douglas R. and Daniel Dennett. *The Mind's I: Fantasies and Reflections on Self and Soul*. New York: Basic Books, 1982.

Jung, C. G. *Collected Works*. New Jersey, Princeton: The Bollingen Foundation for the Princeton University Press, 1954.

Kornfield, Jack. *Bringing Home the Dharma: Awakening Right Where You Are*. Boston: Shambhala, 2012.

Kossak, Steven M. and Jane Casey Singer. *Sacred Visions, Early Paintings from Central Tibet*. New Haven: Yale University Press, 1998.

Kripal, Jeffrey J. *Esalen: America and the Religion of No Religion*. University of Chicago Press, 2007.

Leary, Timothy. *Flashbacks*. Los Angeles: J. P. Tarcher, 1983.

Maharshi, Ramana. *Who Am I?* Arunachala: Sri Ramanasramam, 1955.

Pahnke, Walter. "Drugs and Mysticism: An Analysis of the Relationship between Psychedelic Drugs and the Mystical Consciousness." *The International Journal of Parapsychology*, volume VIII, no. 2, Spring 1966.

Smith, Huston. "Do Drugs Have Religious Import?" *The American Journal of Philosophy*, volume LXI, no. 18, September 17, 1964.

Smith Huston. *Forgotten Truth: The Primordial Tradition*. New York: Harper & Row, 1977.

Stolaroff, Myron. "Using Drugs Wisely." *Gnosis*, no. 26, Winter 1993.

Strassman, Rick. *DMT and the Soul of Prophecy: A New Science of Spiritual Revelation in the Hebrew Bible*. South Paris, Maine: Park Street Press, 2014.

Tart, Charles. "On Being Stoned: A Psychological Study of Marijuana Intoxication." *The Journal of the American Society for Psychical Research*, volume 87, 1993.

Walsh, Robert. "Psychedelics and Psychological Well-being." *Journal of Humanistic Psychology*, volume 22, no. 3, 1982.

Weil, Andrew. *The Natural Mind*. Boston: Houghton Mifflin, 1972.

White, David Gordon. *The Alchemical Body*. Chicago: University of Chicago Press, 1996.

ALSO FROM SYNERGETIC PRESS

MYSTIC CHEMIST
The Life of Albert Hofmann and His Discovery of LSD
by Dieter Hagenbach and Lucius Werthmüller
Foreword by Stanislav Grof

BIRTH OF A PSYCHEDELIC CULTURE
Conversations about Leary, the Harvard Experiments, Millbrook and the Sixties
by Ram Dass and Ralph Metzner with Gary Bravo
Foreword by John Perry Barlow

AYAHUASCA READER
Encounters with the Amazon's Sacred Vine
Edited by Luis Eduardo Luna & Steven F. White

VINE OF THE SOUL
Medicine Men, Their Plants and Rituals in the Colombian Amazonia
by Richard Evans Schultes and Robert F. Raffauf
Foreword by Sir Ghillean T. Prance
Preface by Wade Davis

THE RENAISSANCE OF TIBETAN CIVILIZATION
Foreword by the Dalai Lama
by Christoph von Fürer-Haimendorf

Synergetic Press is pleased to print this book with Friesens, a member of the Green Press Initiative (GPI), a non-profit program working with publishers, printers, paper manufacturers and others in the book industry to minimize social and environmental impacts, including on endangered forests, climate change, and communities where paper fiber is sourced. www.greenpressinitiative.org. This book is printed on paper certified by the Forest Stewardship Council®.

SYNERGETIC
PRESS